BOOKS IN HOME ECONOMICS

ELEMENTARY COSTUME DESIGN. By *Marion Featherstone* and *Dorothy Howerton Maack.*

FUNDAMENTALS OF NUTRITION, A WORKBOOK. By *Alberta Dent.*

FEEDING BABIES AND THEIR FAMILIES. By *Helen Monsch* and *Marguerite K. Harper.*

FOOD FOR PEOPLE. By *Margaret G. Reid.*

THE ARTS OF COSTUME AND PERSONAL APPEARANCE. By *the late Grace M. Morton.*

MANAGEMENT IN FAMILY LIVING. By *Paulena Nickell* and *Jean Muir Dorsey.*

HOUSEHOLD EQUIPMENT. Second Edition. By *Louise Jenison Peet* and *Lenore E. Sater.*

A FUNCTIONING PROGRAM OF HOME ECONOMICS. By *Ivol Spafford.*

A GUIDE TO TEXTILES. By *Mary Evans* and *Ellen Beers McGowan.*

ADULT EDUCATION IN HOMEMAKING. By *L. Belle Pollard.*

THE CONSUMER-BUYER AND THE MARKET. By *Jessie V. Coles.*

FOOD SERVICE IN INSTITUTIONS. Second Edition. By *Bessie Brooks West* and *LeVelle Wood.*

FUNDAMENTALS OF TEXTILES, A WORKBOOK. Second Edition. By *Eda A. Jacobsen* and *Helen E. McCullough.*

FOOD FOR FIFTY. Second Edition. By *Sina Faye Fowler* and *Bessie Brooks West.*

FUNDAMENTALS IN TEACHING HOME ECONOMICS. Second Edition. By *Ivol Spafford.*

HOME FURNISHING. By *Anna H. Rutt.*

ECONOMICS OF HOUSEHOLD PRODUCTION. By *Margaret G. Reid.*

FOOD SELECTION AND PREPARATION. Third Edition. By *Marion Deyoe Sweetman.*

MANUAL FOR FOOD PREPARATION STUDY. Second Edition. By *Florance B. King* and *Mary E. Kirkpatrick.*

EXPERIMENTAL COOKERY FROM THE CHEMICAL AND PHYSICAL STANDPOINT. Third Edition. By *Belle Lowe.*

FOOD PREPARATION STUDIES. Second Edition. By *the late Alice M. Child* and *Kathryn Bele Niles.*

FOOD PREPARATION RECIPES. Second Edition. By *the late Alice M. Child* and *Kathryn Bele Niles.*

FOOD FOR FIFTY

FOOD FOR FIFTY

Compiled by:

SINA FAYE FOWLER, M.S.
Medical Department Dietitian
United States Army

and

BESSIE BROOKS WEST, M.A.
Professor of Institutional Management
and Head of Department
Kansas State College

Second Edition
Sixth Printing

NEW YORK
JOHN WILEY & SONS, Inc.
London: CHAPMAN & HALL, Limited

IN THE REPRINTING OF THIS BOOK, THE RECOMMEN-
DATIONS OF THE WAR PRODUCTION BOARD HAVE
BEEN OBSERVED FOR THE CONSERVATION OF PAPER
AND OTHER IMPORTANT WAR MATERIALS. THE
CONTENT REMAINS COMPLETE AND UNABRIDGED.

SECOND EDITION
Sixth printing, September, 1945

Printed in the U. S. A.

FOREWORD TO THE SECOND EDITION

During the four years since the initial publication of "Food for Fifty," it has been widely accepted as an aid to instruction in large-quantity cookery classes. Its services have also been in demand by home economics teachers called upon to assume the responsibility of special community meals and school lunches; by dietitians in hospitals, residence halls and related food services; by those in charge of fraternity and sorority dining rooms; and by managers of commercial food services.

In this revision the purpose of the book, as stated in the original foreword, remains unchanged; namely, "to provide a limited number of carefully tested institutional formulae for use in food services and in institutional cookery classes." The organization of subject matter likewise remains unchanged. However, under this organization amplification of subject matter and recipes has been made, adding to the value and effectiveness of the book.

Indebtedness incurred in the initial preparation of the manuscript was duly acknowledged in the first edition. At this time, we wish to express appreciation of the continued generous and able assistance of staffs of the Departments of Food Economics and Nutrition and Institutional Management, Kansas State College, which has facilitated greatly the preparation of this revision.

Sina Faye Fowler
Bessie Brooks West

Manhattan, Kansas
April, 1941

24990

v

FOREWORD TO THE FIRST EDITION

Every director of an institutional food service, regardless of how large or how small, has felt the need for an adequate manual in institutional cookery. The problems involved in institutional food service and the quantities in which food must be prepared make the familiar and reliable household recipes of little value. The pressure of duties often, if not usually, prevents the food director from undertaking that experimentation necessary to the translation of such recipes into institutional formulae, thus limiting variety in the menus to those dishes for which quantity recipes are at hand. If instruction in quantity food preparation is also her responsibility, the problem is doubly complicated inasmuch as the time of both teacher and student is too valuable to be wasted in dictating or copying recipes or in searching for those distributed in an impermanent form. The only satisfactory basis for laboratory instruction in this field seems to the authors to be the provision of institutional formulae in permanent form.

It is the purpose of this book to provide a limited number of carefully tested institutional formulae for use in food services and in institutional cookery classes. The book is planned primarily to supplement the textbook, "Food Service in Institutions," to be published by John Wiley and Sons, Inc. However, the authors hope that it may also meet the needs of those actively engaged in food services other than in colleges.

These recipes have been carefully tested under usual institutional conditions, having been used with satisfaction in such food services as residence halls for men and women students, high-school cafeterias, college cafeterias, and state institutions.

In addition to the food formulae, suggestions are given concerning meal planning and services, including special occasions. There is also given in detail a table of equivalent weights and measures of common foods and a list of amounts of various foods to serve fifty persons.

Acknowledgment is made of our indebtedness to all those whose work and publications have facilitated indirectly the preparation of this manuscript. Their names are too numerous to cite. Special acknowledgment is due the Committee on Foreign Foods of the Social Club of Kansas State College for their assistance in the collection of foreign recipes.

It is a pleasure to express our thanks to Dean Margaret Justin, to our colleagues, to both students and graduates at Kansas State College who have been generous in their interest and help, and to co-workers in the institutional field who have given liberally from the wealth of their experience both information and courage for the task. To these our efforts are dedicated.

Permission has been obtained from Simon and Schuster, Inc., Publishers, to quote from "The Clean Platter" by Ogden Nash; from Harcourt, Brace and Co., to quote from "Food and Drink" by Louis Untermeyer; from Covici-Friede, Publishers, to quote from the "Cheerful Cherub" by Rebecca McCann; and from the Macmillan Co., to quote from "Borderlands and Thorofares" by W. W. Gibson.

                                              Sina Faye Fowler
Manhattan, Kansas   Bessie Brooks West
May, 1937

CONTENTS

Food for Fifty

PART I

TABLE OF WEIGHTS, MEASURES, AND THEIR ABBREVIATIONS

Abbreviations		Equivalent		
f.g.	Few Grains			
t.	Teaspoon	3 t.	equals	1 T.
T.	Tablespoon	16 T.	"	1 c.
c.	Cup	2 c.	"	1 pt.
pt.	Pint	2 pt.	"	1 qt.
qt.	Quart	4 qt.	"	1 gal.
pk.	Peck			
bu.	Bushel	4 pk.	"	1 bu.
gm.	Gram			
oz.	Ounce	28.35 gm.	"	1 oz.
lb.	Pound	16 oz.	"	1 lb. or 453.6 gm.
kg.	Kilogram	2.2 lb.	"	1 kg.

CONTENT OF COMMON SIZES OF CANS USED FOR FOOD PRODUCTS

Cans	Average Net Weight	Average Cupfuls
8 Z......................	8 oz.	1
Picnic (No. 1 Eastern).....	11 oz.	1⅓
No. 1 Tall.............	16 oz.	2
No. 300	15 oz.	1¾
No. 2	20 oz.	2½
No. 2½...............	28 oz.	3½
No. 3	33 oz.	4
No. 10	6 lb. 10 oz.	13

Note: Many products are now marketed in cans not of a common size, their content being determined by weight only. The weight of the same food in cans of equal size will vary with the pack in different canneries.

1

APPROXIMATE EQUIVALENTS

THICKENING AGENTS:

1 oz. flour is equivalent to 3½ whole eggs.
1 oz. flour is equivalent to 7 egg yolks.
1 oz. flour is equivalent to 1⅓ oz. minute tapioca.
1 oz. flour is equivalent to ¾ oz. bread crumbs.

SHORTENING AGENTS:

1 lb. butter is equivalent to 1 lb. margarine.
1 lb. butter is equivalent to 4/5 lb. hydrogenated shortening.
1 lb. butter is equivalent to 4/5 lb. lard.
1 lb. butter is equivalent to 4/5 lb. oils.
1 lb. butter is equivalent to 7/8 lb. chicken fat.
1 c. butter is equivalent to 2½ c. 40% cream.
1 c. butter is equivalent to 5 c. 20% cream.

LEAVENING AGENTS:

½ t. soda is equivalent to 2 t. baking powder.
½ t. baking powder is equivalent to 1 egg white.

MILK AND CREAM:

1 c. milk is equivalent to 7/8 c. water.
1 c. milk is equivalent to ¼ c. dried whole milk + 1 c. water.
1 c. milk is equivalent to ½ c. evaporated milk + ½ c. water.
1 c. coffee cream is equivalent to 4/5 c. milk + 1/5 c. fat.
1 c. heavy cream is equivalent to 3/5 c. milk + 2/5 c. fat.

CHOCOLATE AND COCOA:

1 oz. chocolate is equivalent to 3 T. cocoa + 1 T. fat.

NOTE: If sweet milk is substituted for sour (no chocolate or molasses in recipe), multiply amount of soda called for in recipe by 4 and add this amount of baking powder to the baking powder in original recipe. Omit soda.

PROPORTIONS

BEVERAGES:

1 lb. coffee to 2½ to 3 gal. water
3 oz. tea to 2½ to 3 gal. water
8 to 10 oz. cocoa to 2½ to 3 gal. liquid

SEASONINGS:

1 to 2 t. salt to 1 lb. flour
1¼ t. salt to 1 lb. meat
2 t. salt to 1 qt. water (cereal)

LEAVENING AGENTS:

2 to 2⅔ T. tartrate or phosphate (quick-acting baking powder) to 1 lb. flour
1½ to 2 T. slow-acting (S. A. S. or combination) to 1 lb. flour
2 t. soda to 1 qt. sour milk or molasses
½ to 1 compressed yeast cake to 1 lb. flour (varies with ingredients and time allowed)

THICKENING AGENTS:

Egg

4 to 6 eggs to 1 qt. milk
8 to 12 egg yolks to 1 qt. milk
8 to 12 egg whites to 1 qt. milk

Flour

1 oz. flour to 1 qt. liquid—very thin sauce (cream soups, starchy vegetables)
2 oz. flour to 1 qt. liquid—thin sauce (cream soups, non-starchy vegetables)
2⅔ oz. flour to 1 qt. liquid—medium sauce (creamed dishes, gravy)
3 oz. flour to 1 qt. liquid—thick sauce (soufflés)
4 to 5 oz. flour to 1 qt. liquid—very thick sauce (croquettes)
1 lb. flour to 1 qt. liquid—pour batter (popovers)
2 lb. flour to 1 qt. liquid—drop batter (cake, muffins)
3 lb. flour to 1 qt. liquid—soft dough (biscuit, rolls)
4 lb. flour to 1 qt. liquid—stiff dough (pastry, cookies, noodles)

Gelatin

2 T. to 1 qt. liquid—plain jellies (gelatin and fruit juices)
2 T. to 1 qt. liquid—whips (gelatin and fruit juices whipped)
3 T. to 1 qt. liquid—fruit jellies (gelatin, fruit juices, and chopped fruit)
3 T. to 1 qt. liquid—vegetable jellies (gelatin and liquid and chopped vegetables)
3 T. to 1 qt. liquid—sponges (gelatin and fruit juices and beaten egg whites)
4 T. to 1 qt. liquid—Bavarian Cream (gelatin and fruit juice and fruit pulp and whipped cream)

VOLUMETRIC MILK CONVERSION TABLE*

Skim Milk

To Replace	Use
1 gal. liquid skim milk	{ ¾ lb. dry skim milk 7¾ pt. water
1 lb. liquid skim milk	{ 1½ oz. dry skim milk 14½ oz. water
1 lb. evaporated skim milk, unsweetened condensed (Government Standard)	{ 3¼ oz. dry skim milk 12¾ oz. water
1 lb. sweetened condensed skim milk (Government Standard)	{ 4 oz. dry skim milk 7 oz. sugar 5 oz. water

Whole Milk

To Replace	Use
1 gal. liquid whole milk	{ 1 lb. dry whole milk 7½ pt. water
1 lb. liquid whole milk	{ 2 oz. dry whole milk 14 oz. water
1 lb. sweetened condensed whole milk (Government Standard)	{ 4½ oz. dry whole milk 6½ oz. sugar 5 oz. water

* Courtesy of Borden's.

TABLE OF EQUIVALENTS
BUYER'S GUIDE AND COOKING TIME

Product	Description	Size	Birdseye Cooking Time		Fresh Equivalents	Number Portions*
			Regular	Pressure Steam		
Vegetables:						
Asp. Tips	5″ Select—Av. 155 tips	40 oz.	14 min.	10 min.	3 bunches	16–20
Asp. Tips	5″ Medium—Av. 100 tips	40 oz.	14 min.	10 min.	3 bunches	16–20
Asp. Tips	5″ Jumbo—Av. 60 tips	40 oz.	14 min.	10 min.	3 bunches	16–20
Asp. Cuts	All green	40 oz.	14 min.	10 min.	....	....*
Asp. Cuts	All green	5 oz.	...	...	....	....*
Broccoli	Tender green	40 oz.	18 min.	20 min.	3 bunches	16–20
Broccoli	Tender green (B.C.)	40 oz.	18 min.	20 min.	3 bunches	16–20
Brus. Sprouts	Close trimmed	40 oz.	8 min.	10 min.	3½ qt.	16–20
Cauliflower	Trimmed florets only	40 oz.	10 min.	12 min.	4 heads	16–20
Corn-on-Cob	Full ears—Golden Bantam	2 ears	3 min.	3 min.	3 ears	2
Cut Corn	Whole kernel—G. Bantam	40 oz.	5 min.	11 min.	20 ears	20–24
Cut Corn	Whole kernel—C. Gent.	40 oz.	5 min.	11 min.	20 ears	20–24
Green Beans	1½″-2″ cut	40 oz.	16 min.	18 min.	3 lb.	20–24
Green Beans	1½″-2″ cut	5 lb.	...	...	6 lb.	40–48
Green Beans	French style cut	40 oz.	16 min.	18 min.	3 lb.	20–24
Green Beans	Asparagus style (whole)	40 oz.	16 min.	18 min.	3 lb.	20–24
Green Beans	1″ cut	5 lb.	...	...	6 lb.	40–48
Wax Beans	1½″-2″ cut	40 oz.	16 min.	18 min.	3 lb.	20–24
Lima Beans	Baby green	40 oz.	20 min.	25 min.	⅓ bu.	20–24
Lima Beans	Baby green	5 lb.	...	...	⅔ bu.	40–48
Lima Beans	Garden run	40 oz.	20 min.	25 min.	⅓ bu.	20–24
Lima Beans	Garden run	5 lb.	...	...	⅔ bu.	40–48
Lima Beans	Fordhook	40 oz.	...	...	....	20–24
Lima Beans	White	5 lb.	...	...	⅔ bu.	40–48
Peas	Shelled green	40 oz.	12 min.	25 min.	⅓ bu.	20–24
Peas	Shelled green	5 lb.	...	...	⅔ bu.	40–48
Peas	Shelled green (B.C.)	5 lb.	...	...	⅔ bu.	40–48
Peas and Carrots	Carrots diced	5 lb.	...	...	....	40–48
Spinach	No sand or stalks	40 oz.	12 min.	20 min.	⅓ bu.	16–20
Squash	Cooked or puréed	40 oz.	7 min.	10 min.	....	5
Fruits and Berries:						
Blueberries	Fancy, selected	40 oz.	...	...	....	20–24
Peaches	Sliced, sugared	40 oz.	...	...	....	16–20
Peaches	Sliced, sugared	10 lb.	...	...	....	64–80
Raspberries	Full ripe—whole—no sugar	40 oz.	...	...	....	16–20
Rhubarb	1″ cut—strawberry variety	40 oz.	...	...	....	16–20
Strawberries	Sliced, sugared	40 oz.	...	...	....	20–24
Strawberries	Sliced, sugared	10 lb.	...	...	....	80–96
Strawberries	Selected—whole—no sugar	10 oz.	...	...	....	For toppings

Courtesy Frosted Foods Sales Corporation.

* Servings vary depending upon use of product.

RECONSTRUCTED DRIED SKIM MILK

Amount	Ingredient	Method
1 gal. 12 oz.	Dried skim milk powder Water	Put water in bowl of electric mixer. Turn to low speed, sprinkle milk powder slowly on water, and continue to mix at low speed until milk powder is completely mixed.

Note: Use as skim milk.

DRIED AND FROZEN EGGS
TABLE OF WEIGHTS AND THEIR EQUIVALENTS IN MEASURE

Dried Eggs			Frozen Eggs	
Number of Eggs	Weight of Fresh Eggs	Dried Weight	Number of Eggs Fresh or Frozen	Liquid
	pound	pound		pound or pint
39 (whole)............	3⅛	1	9 to 11 (whole)	1
70 (whites)..........	7	1	17 to 20 (whites)	1
48 (yolks)...........	2	1	19 to 22 (yolks)	1

APPROXIMATE OR AVERAGE WEIGHTS OF VARIOUS COMMODITIES*

Commodity	Unit	Net Weight in Pounds
Apples, fresh........	Bu.	48
Apples, fresh........	Box	44
Apples, fresh........	Barrel	140
Apricots, fresh......	Bu.	48
Apricots, western....	Crate (4½x16x16⅛ in.)	22
Artichokes, Globe...	Box	40
Artichokes, Jerusalem	Bu.	50
Asparagus, western..	Crate	24
Beans, dry Lima.....	Bu.	56
Beans, other dry.....	Bu.	60
Beans, other dry.....	Sack	100
Beans, Lima, unshelled	Bu.	32
Beans, snap.........	Bu.	30
Beets, table.........	Bu.	52
Blackberries.........	24-qt. Crate	36
Cabbage............	1½-bu. Hamper	50
Cabbage............	Crate	80
Cantaloupes.........	Std.-45 Crate	60
Carrots.............	Bu.	50
Cauliflower.........	Crate	39
Celery.............	⅔ (New York) Crate	90
Cherries, stemmed...	Bu.	64
Cherries, unstemmed.	Bu.	56
Cherries, western....	Lug box	15
Cornmeal...........	Bu.	50
Cranberries.........	Barrel	100
Cranberries.........	½ Barrel box	50
Cucumbers..........	Bu.	48
Dewberries..........	24-qt. Crate	36
Eggplant...........	Bu.	33
Grapefruit, California	Box	60
Grapefruit, Florida...	Box	80
Grapes.............	Bu.	48
Grapes, eastern......	12-qt. Basket	18
Grapes, western.....	Lug box	26
Grapes, western.....	Keg, grapes	32 ⎫
	sawdust	13 ⎭
Hickory nuts........	Bu.	50
Kale...............	Bu.	18

APPROXIMATE OR AVERAGE WEIGHTS OF VARIOUS COMMODITIES (continued)

COMMODITY	UNIT	NET WEIGHT IN POUNDS
Lard................	Tierce	375
Lemons, California...	Box	76
Lentils.............	Bu.	60
Lettuce, western.....	Crate	75
Onions, dry.........	Bu.	54
Oranges, California...	Box	70
Oranges, Florida.....	Box	90
Parsnips............	Bu.	50
Peaches, fresh.......	Bu.	48
Peaches, western.....	Box	20
Peanuts, unshelled...	Bu.	22 to 30
Pears, fresh.........	Bu.	50
Pears, western.......	Box	46
Pears, western.......	Crate (4½x16x16⅛ in.)	22
Peas, dry...........	Bu.	60
Peas, fresh, unshelled.	Bu.	30
Peppers.............	Bu.	25
Pineapples..........	Crate	70
Plums, fresh........	Bu.	56
Plums, N. W. suitcase	Box	16
Plums, western......	Box	20
Potatoes, Irish......	Bu.	60
Prunes, fresh........	Bu.	56
Prunes, N. W. suitcase	Box	16
Prunes, western......	Box	20
Quinces.............	Bu.	48
Raspberries.........	24-qt. Crate	36
Rutabagas..........	Bu.	56
Soy beans...........	Bu.	60
Spinach.............	Bu.	18
Strawberries........	24-qt. Crate	36
Sweet potatoes.......	Bu. (usual wt. when harvested)	55
Tangerines, Florida..	½ Strap	40
Tomatoes...........	Bu.	53
Tomatoes...........	Lug box	31
Turnips.............	Bu.	54

* Adapted from: "Approximate or Average Weights of Various Commodities," U. S. Dept. Agr., Bureau of Agr. Econ., Jan. 1935, revised list.

MENU TERMS[1]

À la, À le (ah lah, ah luh) Fr. To the, with, in the mode or fashion of, or in. À la Crême, "with cream"; À la Newburg, "Newburg fashion"; À la Moutarde, "in mustard."

À la Carte. On the bill-of-fare; prepared as ordered.

A la King. Served in cream sauce containing green pepper, pimiento, and mushrooms.

A la Mode. In America when applied to desserts means with ice cream.

Allemande (al-mângd) Fr. Ger. A smooth yellow sauce consisting of white sauce with the addition of butter, egg yolk, catsup, etc.

Anglaise (âng-glayz) Fr. Eng. À la Anglaise, "in English style."

Antipasti (än-tēē-päs' tēē) It. Appetizer; a course consisting of relishes.

Au (o) Fr. Contraction of à le or à la, "to the."

Bardé (bar-day) Fr. Larded. Covered with salt pork or with slices of bacon. Un Poulet Bardé de Lard, "a pullet larded with bacon."

Bar-Le-Duc (bar-luh-dük) Fr. A preserve originally made of selected whole white currants seeded by hand with the aid of knitting needles. Now gooseberries, strawberries, etc., may be used. It frequently forms a part of the cheese course.

Bavarian. A gelatin dish into which whipped cream is folded as it begins to stiffen.

Bavarois (bav-ar-wâz) Fr. Bavarian.

Béchamel (bay-sham-ayl) Fr. Refers to a sauce supposed to have originated with the Marquis de Béchamel, Maître d'hôtel of Louis XIV. A cream sauce made of chicken stock, cream, or milk and usually seasoned with onion. Sometimes applied to all sauces having a white sauce foundation.

Beef à la Mode (bēf ah lah mōd) Eng. Fr. A well-larded piece of beef cooked slowly in water with vegetables. Similar to braised beef.

Bellevue (bel-vü) Fr. A pleasing sight; in aspic. À la Bellevue, "a food enclosed in aspic through which it can be plainly seen."

Bénédictine (bay-nay-dik-tang) Fr. A religious sect; a liqueur made principally at the Abbey of Fécamp in Europe. Eggs à la Bénédictine, "poached eggs served on broiled ham placed on split toasted muffins and garnished with Hollandaise sauce."

Beurre (buhr) Fr. Butter. Au Beurre Noir, "with butter sauce browned in a pan"; Beurre Fondue, "melted butter."

Beurré (buhr-ay) Fr. Buttered.

Biscotte (bis-kot) Fr. Rusk; biscuit.

Bisque (bisk) Fr. A thick soup usually made from fish or shell fish. Also a frozen dessert. Sometimes defined as ice cream to which finely chopped nuts are added.

Blanquette (blâng-ket) Fr. A meat stew with white sauce.

Bleu (bluh) Fr. Blue. Au Bleu, "plain boiled"; used with reference to fresh-water fish.

Boeuf (buhf) Fr. Beef. Boeuf à la Jardinière, "braised beef with vegetables"; Boeuf Rôti, "roast beef."

Bombe (bongh) Fr. Also called bombe glacée. A frozen dessert made of a combination of two or more frozen mixtures packed in a round or melon-shaped mold.

Bonne Femme (bong fam) Fr. Good wife; in simple home style. Applied to soups, stews, etc.

Bordelaise (bord-lĕz) Fr. Of Bordeaux. Sauce Bordelaise, "a sauce with Bordeaux wine as its foundation, with various seasonings added."

---

[1] Adapted from Department of Food Economics and Nutrition: "A Dictionary of Culinary and Related Terms," Kansas State College, 1933.

Borsch (bōrsh) Rus. Also spelled bortsch. A Russian or Polish soup made with beets. Often sour cream or citric acid is added to give an acid taste.

Bouillabaisse (bool-yab-ays) Fr. A national soup of France. The word comes from the verbs "bouiller," "to boil," and "abaisser," "to go down." A highly seasoned fish soup made especially at Marseilles. Served in plates with dry toast.

Bourgeoise (boor-zhwâz) Fr. Citizen style; with family simplicity. À la Bourgeoise usually means "served with vegetables."

Brioche (bre-yosh) Fr. A slightly sweetened rich bread of French origin.

Broche (brosh) Fr. Skewer; spit for roasting. À la Broche, "cooked on a skewer."

Café (kaf-ay) Fr. Coffee; coffee house; restaurant. Café au Lait, "coffee with hot milk"; Café Noir, "black coffee, after-dinner coffee."

Canapé (kan-ap-ay) Fr. Originally couch, sofa, or divan. Now, an individual appetizer served either hot or cold. Usually fried or toasted bread spread with or supporting a wide variety of highly seasoned foods. Generally used as the first course of a meal as an hors d'œuvre and is eaten with the fingers unless accompanied by a sauce or otherwise made impossible to eat this way. Often served on a doily.

Carte (kart) Fr. Card; bill of fare. À la Carte, "according to the bill of fare"; Carte au Jour, "bill of fare or menu for the day."

Chantilly (shâng-tē-yē) Fr. A castle north of Paris. Name originally given to savoy cakes, scooped out, filled with preserved fruit, and garnished with whipped cream. Now may be applied to anything served with sweetened and flavored whipped cream. Chantilly Cream, "sweetened and flavored whipped cream."

Chartreuse (shar-truhz) Fr. Named from a monastery in the Alps which required of its members absolute abstinence from meat. The name is given to dishes which hold a hidden stuffing, as meat molded in rice, suggesting that meat may have been thus disguised and eaten by the monks. Or it may be a mold of aspic containing vegetables, meat, or fruit filling in the center of the mold. Also the name of a famous liquor.

Chaud (shô) Fr. Hot.

Chemise (sh-mēz) Fr. Shirt. En Chemise, "with their skins on"; generally applied to potatoes.

Chiffonade (shēf-fōn-ăd) Fr. Rags; minced or shredded vegetables or meats. Used on soups or salads.

Cloche (klosh) Fr. Bell; dish cover. Sous Cloche, "under cover."

Confit (kong-fee) Fr. Also called confiture. Preserves or jam made from fruit.

Consommé (kon-so-may) Fr. A clear soup usually made from 2 or 3 kinds of meat, as fowl, veal, and beef. It is highly seasoned.

Creole (krē' ōl) Fr. Relating or peculiar to the Creoles. The term is applied to soups, garnishes, sauces, etc. Tomatoes, peppers, onions, and other seasons are usually characteristic of these dishes.

Crêpe (krayp) Fr. Pancake. The French product is very thin and crisp and may be served for tea.

Croissant (krwâ-sâng) Fr. Crescent. Applied to rolls, and confectionery of crescent shape.

Curry (kŭr' ĭ) Eng. An East-Indian dish originally meaning a stew, characterized by a pungent flavor of curry powder. The finishing or seasoning of the dish is frequently done at the table, and many army and navy officers from western countries pride themselves upon their combinations of seasonings.

De jour. Fr. Ready to serve.

Dejeuner (day-zhuh-nay) Fr. Breakfast; lunch.

Demi-tasse (dŭh-mee-tâss) Fr. A half-cup. Name applied in this country to black coffee served in after-dinner coffee cups. In France, called café noir.

Dîner (de-nay) Fr. Dinner; to dine.

Duglère (doog-lâr) Fr. A French restauranteur who popularized tomatoes. Usually signifies the use of tomatoes.

Écarlate (ay-kar-lat) Fr. Scarlet; a red sauce; one containing lobster roe, red tongue, etc.

Entre Côte (ângtr'kôt) Fr. Between ribs. Name given to a steak cut from between the ribs. Supposed to be second in quality only to the fillet or tenderloin.

Entrée (âng-tray) Fr. A subordinate dish served between the main courses at a dinner. Usually a "made" dish of unusual food or of food prepared in an unusual manner. It is garnished and may be accompanied by a sauce. It should be easy to eat and pleasing to the appetite but not satisfying.

Entremet (âng-truh-may) Fr. From the verb "to place between." A side dish; light "made" dish served after the roast and before the dessert. In French cookery it may be either a sweet or a vegetable course. Entremet de Douceur, "sweet dish"; Entremet de Légume, "vegetable course."

Espagnole (ays-pah-nyol) Fr. Spanish; brown sauce.

Fanchonette (fâng-sho-net) Fr. A small pie or tart with a meringue.

Farci (far-see) Fr. Stuffed.

Fermière (fayr-myayr) Fr. Farmer's wife; in plain country style.

Fines Herbes (fang ayrb) Fr. Fine herbs.

Foie (fwâ) Fr. Liver. Foie Gras, "fat liver." Applied especially to the liver of fat geese. Foie Gras au Naturel, "plain cooked, whole foie gras"; Pâté de Foie Gras, "the most popular form of foie gras. First used in Strasbourg toward the end of the eighteenth century by the chef of the governor of Alsace. The cooked livers are seasoned with truffles, wine, and aromatics."

Fondu (fong-dü) Fr. Melted or blended.

Four (foor) Fr. Oven. Petit Four, "small French pastry used at teas"; Pâte de Petit Four, "pastry of the little oven."

Franconia (frän-kō-nĭ-ă) Eng. An ancient German duchy; in the culinary sense, browned. Franconia Potatoes, "whole potatoes browned with the roast."

Frappé (frap-pay) Fr. Beaten, iced. Applied to a water ice frozen to a mush while stirring. Usually drunk rather than eaten with a spoon or fork.

Glacé (glah-say) Fr. Iced; frozen; glassy; glazed; frosted; candied; crystallized. Glacé fruit, "fruit dipped in a hot sirup which has been cooked to a hard-crack stage."

Gratin (grat-ang) Fr. Crumbs. Au Gratin, "the French term for scalloped." Cheese is much used in au gratin dishes and to many this term implies its use.

Gumbo (gŭmbō) Eng. Okra; also a rich, thick Creole soup containing okra.

Haché (hah-shay) Fr. Minced; chopped.

Hors d'oeuvre (or-duh-vr') Fr. Beyond the works; side dish or relish served at the beginning of the meal. Used for luncheons but not for dinners in France. Usually served cold and made of salty, tart, or crisp materials, as canapés, radishes, olives, pickles, fish, sausages, etc.

Italienne (e-tal-yang) Fr. Italian.

Jardinière (zhar-de-nyayr) Fr. The gardener's wife; a dish of mixed vegetables.

Julienne (zhü-lyayn) Fr. Vegetables cut into fine strips or shreds. Named from the famous chef, Jean Julienne, who invented clear vegetable soup with the vegetables cut into match-like strips.

Jus (zhüs) Fr. Juice or gravy. Au Jus, "served in the natural juice or gravy."

Kippered (kĭp′ẽrd) Eng. "Kipper" is a Scotch term originally applied to salmon. Now a method of preserving fish, especially herring and salmon. The fish are split, then lightly salted and smoked.

Kosher (kō′shẽr) Eng. A term applied to food prepared with special precautions. Kosher meat, "Meat from a strictly healthy animal that has been slaughtered and prepared in accordance with the Jewish requirements."

Kuchen (kōō-ckhen) Ger. Cake, not necessarily sweet.

Lait (lay) Fr. Milk.

Laitue (lay-tü) Fr. Lettuce.

Lebkuchen (lāp′kōō-ckhen) Ger. Also known as sweet cakes or honey cakes. A group of famous German cakes.

Lyonnaise (lyo-nayz) Fr. Word comes from Lyons. Seasoned with onions and parsley, as "Lyonnaise potatoes."

Macédoine (mah-say-dooan) Fr. A mixture or medley; usually applied to cut vegetables but also to fruit.

Maître d'Hôtel (maytr′ dotayl) Fr. Steward. In the culinary sense implies the use of minced parsley. Maître d'Hôtel Sauce or Parsley Butter, "a well-seasoned mixture of creamed butter, chopped parsley, and lemon juice. Served on broiled meats, broiled or boiled fish, and on some vegetables, as potatoes."

Marinade (mar-e-nad) Fr. Usually a French dressing in which salad foods, as cooked vegetables and meats, are allowed to stand to render them more palatable. It is also used for uncooked meat to soften tough fibers and to keep meat fresh. In the latter case the marinade may be nothing more than a brine or pickle solution.

Marinate (măr′ĭ-nāt) Eng. To treat with a marinade.

Milanaise (me-lan-ayz) Fr. From Milan. Implies the use of macaroni and Parmesan cheese with a suitable sauce, often Béchamel.

Minestrone (mēē-nāys-trō′nĕ) It. A famous Italian thick vegetable soup.

Mulligatawny (mul′ĭ-gȧ-tŏ′nĭ) Eng. Derived from two East Indian words signifying "pepper water." A highly seasoned, thick soup characterized chiefly by curry powder. Meats, vegetables, mango chutney, cocoanut flesh, rice, cayenne, etc., are used to suit the taste of the cook.

Neapolitan (nē′ȧ-pŏl′ĭtăn) Eng. Also called harlequin and panachée. The term is applied to a molded dessert of from 2 to 4 kinds of ice cream or water ice arranged in lengthwise layers. The mixture is sliced across for serving. The name is also applied to a gelatin dish arranged in layers of different colors.

Nesselrode (nĕs′ĕl-rôd) Eng. Containing chestnuts. Named after a Russian statesman of the early 19th century. Nesselrode Pudding "a frozen dessert with a custard foundation to which chestnut purée, fruit, and cream have been added. It has been termed the 'most perfect' of frozen puddings."

Newburg (nū′bûrg) Eng. A form of creamed dish with egg yolks added. Originally flavored with lime or sherry. Most often applied to lobster but may be used with other foods.

Nivernaise (nē-vĕr-nĕz) Fr. A garnish of julienne vegetables added to sauce Allemande.

Noir (nooâr) Fr. Black.

Noisette (nooâ-zet) Fr. Literally hazel-nut; nut-brown color. May imply nut-shaped. A small piece of lean meat. Generally a chop minus the bone (fillet). Potatoes Noisette, "potatoes cut into the shape and size of hazel-nuts and browned in fat."

Normande (nor-mând) Fr. From Normandy. À la Normande, "a delicate, smooth mixture often containing whipped cream."

O'Brien. Cubed potatoes cooked in a small amount of fat with chopped onion and pimiento.

Pané (pan-ay) Fr. Covered with bread crumbs or breaded.

Parfait (par-fay) Fr. Perfect; a mixture containing egg and sirup. Frozen without stirring. May be molded but is more commonly served in parfait glasses.

Parmentière (par-mang-tyayr) Fr. Potato. Named after Baron Augustine Parmentier, who introduced potatoes into France, and originated many methods of preparing them. À la Parmentière, "with or of potatoes."

Pâte (pât) Fr. Paste; dough.

Pâté (pâ-tay) Fr. Pie; patty; pastry. Also a meat preparation packed in earthenware jars and small tins, prepared largely in Germany and France, but also of domestic manufacture. The name came from the fact that it was originally sold in pies of "pâté" form. Pâté de Foie Gras, "paste of fat livers."

Persillade (payr-se-yad) Fr. Served with or containing parsley.

Petit (puh-tee) Fr. Small, new. Petits Pois, "little peas, a fine grade of small canned peas with delicate flavor but of low food value."

Petits Fours (puh-tee fōōr) Fr. Small fancy cakes.

Piquant (pe-kâng) Fr. Sharp, highly seasoned. Applied to sauces, etc. Sauce Piquante, "a highly seasoned brown sauce containing lemon juice or vinegar, capers, pickles, etc."

Plank (plånk) Eng. A board made of hard wood designed for use in cooking and serving of broiled meat or fish. Thought to give to the meat a superior flavor. Planked steak, "a broiled steak served on a plank attractively garnished with a border of suitable vegetables or fruits."

Plat (plah) Fr. Dish. Plat au Jour, "as used on menu cards, the food of the day."

Pois (pooâ) Fr. Peas. Petits Pois, "very small peas."

Polenta (po-lěn'ta) It. A popular Italian dish originally of chestnut meal but now often made of farina or cornmeal. Cheese is usually added before serving.

Polonaise (po-lo-nay) Fr. Polish. With beets or cabbage.

Pomme (pom) Fr. Apple. Pomme de Terre, "apple of the earth, potato," Pomme d' amour, "apple of love, tomato"; Pommes de Terre à la Lyonnaise, "Lyonnaise potatoes."

Purée (pü-ray) Fr. Foods rubbed through a sieve; also a nutritious vegetable soup in which milk or cream is seldom used.

Ragout (rag-oo) Fr. Stew. Originally meant "something to restore the taste and tempt the appetite." Generally a thick, well-seasoned stew containing meat.

Ramekin (răm'e-kin) Eng. A small, individual baking dish or a pastry shell; also a cheese-cake.

Ravigote (rav-e-got) Fr. A sauce seasoned with tarragon vinegar, chives, shallots, etc.

Ravioli (rä'vē-ō'lē) It. A term applied to little shapes of Italian or noodle paste which are rolled thin, one-half spread with a filling of minced meat or vegetables and moistened with a sauce if necessary; then folded over and poached in stock.

Rémoulade (ray-moo-lad) Fr. A pungent sauce. Made of hard-cooked eggs, mustard, oil, vinegar, and seasonings. Served with cold dishes.

Rissoler (re-so-lay) Fr. To roast until the food is a golden brown; to brown. **Rissolé:** browned.

Rouelle (roo-ayl) Fr. A round slice or fillet.

Roulade (roo-lad) Fr. Rolled. Applied to rolled meat.

Roux (roo) Fr. The term is often applied to the browned flour and fat used for thickening sauces, stews, etc.

Scallion (skăl′yŭn) Eng. Any onion which has not developed a bulb.

Shallot (shă-lŏt′) Eng. A form of onion, with stronger but more mellow flavor than the common variety.

Sorbet (sor-bay) Fr. A sherbet made of several kinds of fruits.

Soubise (sōō-bēz) Fr. A white sauce containing onion and sometimes parsley.

Springerle (spring′er-le) Ger. A popular cake. The dough is rolled into a sheet and pressed with a springerle mold before baking.

Table d'Hôte (tabl′ dôt) Fr. Table of the host or innkeeper. Service Table d'Hôte, "a meal planned by the establishment and served for a set price. Considerable choice may be permitted."

Terrine (tay-reen) Fr. An earthenware pot resembling a casserole. Chicken en Terrine, "chicken cooked and served in a terrine."

Torte (tôr′ te) Ger. A rich cake made from crumbs, eggs, nuts, etc.

Tortoni (tôr-tōn′ēē) It. Originally "Tortonois," meaning "from the Italian city Tortona." Tortoni Biscuit, "a frozen mixture containing dried, ground macaroons and chopped, blanched almonds."

Tournedos (tōōr-nāy-dōz) Sp. Small round fillets of beef.

Truffle (trŭf′l) Eng. A species of fungi similar to mushrooms, found chiefly in France, growing in clusters some inches below the surface of the ground under oak trees. They are rooted out by pigs trained for the purpose. They are black in color and are used chiefly for garnish and flavor.

Velouté (vuh-loo-tay) Fr. Velvety; a rich white sauce usually made of chicken or veal broth. Considered the principal white sauce just as Espagnole is the chief brown sauce, although some confusion exists in the use of the terms.

Volaille (vo-lah-yuh) Fr. Poultry.

Vol-au-vent (vol-o-vâng) Fr. Flying at the mercy of the wind; large patties of puff paste made without a mold and filled with meat, preserves, etc.

Yorkshire Pudding (yôrk′shĭr pŏŏdĭng) Eng. An English dish usually served with roast beef. It consists of a popover-like mixture which may be baked with the meat or separately with some of the drippings from the roast.

Zwieback or Zwiebach (tsvē′bäk) Ger. A German bread which is twice-baked. Now used largely in feeding small children.

COOKERY TERMS

(Processes and Methods)

Baking is cooking by dry heat, usually in an oven but occasionally on heated metals. This term is used interchangeably with roasting when applied to meat cookery.

Basting is moistening meat or other food while cooking to add flavor and to prevent drying of the surface. Melted fat, meat drippings, water, or water and fat may be used for basting.

Beating is a regular motion that lifts a mixture over and over and thereby introduces air or makes the mixture smooth.

Blanching is pouring boiling water over a food, such as rice, macaroni and other pastes, draining and rinsing it in cold water. Nuts and fruits are blanched by leaving them in boiling water until the skins slip; draining, and rinsing with cold water.

Blending is thoroughly mixing two or more ingredients.

Boiling is cooking in water or a liquid, mostly water, in which the bubbles are breaking on the surface and steam is given off. The boiling temperature of water at sea level is 100°C. (212°F.) but will be approximately 1°C. less for every 1,000 feet elevation. The boiling point will be increased by the solution of solids in the water.

Braising is browning meat or vegetables in a small amount of fat, covering, and cooking slowly in a small amount of liquid. Meat stock or juice, water, milk, or cream may be used for the liquid.

Breading is dipping a food into an egg-milk mixture and then into fine dry crumbs.

Broiling is cooking by direct heat. This may be done by placing the food under or over a clear flame.

Candying is cooking in sugar or sirup.

Carmelizing is heating sugar, or food containing a high percentage of sugar, until a brown color and characteristic flavor develop.

Chopping is cutting food into fairly fine pieces with a knife or other sharp tool.

Creaming is the working of one or more foods until soft and creamy. This term is ordinarily applied to the mixing of fat and sugar.

Cutting is the combination of a solid fat with dry ingredients by a horizontal motion with knives. A fat is thus combined with dry ingredients with the least amount of blending.

Cutting and Folding is combining by the use of two motions—cutting vertically through the mixture, and turning over and over by sliding the implement across the bottom of the mixture with each turn.

Dicing is cutting into cubes.

Dredging is dipping a food into flour or other fine substance so that it is entirely covered.

Egging and Crumbing is dredging a food with fine crumbs, then dipping into dilute slightly beaten egg, and dredging again with crumbs. This treatment is used for dried foods to prevent soaking of the food with fat, or to form a surface easily browned.

Fricasseeing is cooking by browning in a small amount of fat, then stewing or steaming. This method is most often applied to fowl or veal.

Frizzling is cooking in a small amount of fat to produce a food that is crisp and brown with curled edges.

Frying is cooking in hot fat. The food may be cooked in a small amount of fat (formerly called sautéing), or cooked in a deep layer of fat (also called deep-fat frying).

Glacéing is coating with a sugar sirup cooked to the crack stage. It may also refer to a less concentrated mixture, containing thickening, and used for coating certain types of rolls or pastries.

Grilling—*See* Broiling.

Grinding is changing a food to small particles.

Kneading is manipulation with a pressing motion accompanied by folding and stretching. This process may be used to add flour to doughs that are too stiff to stir or beat.

Larding is the insertion of small strips of fat (lardoons) into or on top of uncooked lean meat or fish, to give flavor or prevent dryness.

Marinating is placing a food into a marinade (usually a salad dressing) for a short length of time.

Melting is liquefying by the application of heat.

Mincing is to cut or chop a food into very small pieces, not so fine and regular as grinding, yet finer than those produced by chopping.

Mixing is uniting two or more ingredients.

Pan-broiling is cooking uncovered on a hot metal. The fat is removed as it accumulates. Liquid is never added.

Pan-frying is cooking in a small amount of fat. (*See* Frying.)

Parboiling is partially cooking a food by boiling, the cooking being completed by another method.

Parching is browning by the application of dry heat.

Paring is removing the outside covering usually by a knife.

Peeling is removing the outside covering usually by the aid of heat or mechanical device.

Planking is cooking or serving a food, usually fish or steak, on a hot wooden board or plank made especially for the purpose.

Poaching is cooking in a hot liquid, the original shape of the food being retained.

Roasting is the same as baking. The term is commonly applied to meats.

Sautéing is cooking in a small amount of fat. (*See* Frying.)

Scalloping is baking food, usually cut into pieces and covered with a liquid, or sauce and crumbs. Escalloped is a synonymous term.

Searing is browning the surface of meat by the application of intense heat for a short time. This process usually develops flavor and improves appearance.

Simmering is cooking in a liquid in which bubbles form slowly and break just below the surface. The temperatures range from 85°C. (185°F.) to a temperature just below the boiling point.

Steaming is cooking in steam with or without pressure. Steam may be applied directly to the food, as in a steamer, or to the vessel, as in a double boiler.

Steeping is a process of extracting flavors, colors, or other qualities by adding boiling water and allowing the mixture to stand. The mixture is always just below the boiling point.

Stewing is simmering or boiling in a small amount of liquid.

Stirring is mixing food materials with a circular motion. Food materials are blended or made into a uniform consistency by this process.

Toasting is the application of direct heat until the surface of the food is browned.

Whipping is rapid beating to increase volume by the incorporation of air.

COOKING TEMPERATURES*

OVEN TEMPERATURES

Terms Commonly Used to Describe Oven Temperatures

TERM	TEMPERATURE	
	degrees F.	degrees C.
Slow............................	250 to 300	121 to 149
Very moderate....................	300 to 325	149 to 163
Moderate........................	325 to 375	163 to 191
Moderately hot..................	375 to 400	191 to 204
Hot.............................	400 to 450	204 to 232
Very hot........................	450 to 500	232 to 260

* Adapted from "Terminology Used in Food Preparation," p. 19, American Home Economics Association, Mills Building, Washington, D. C., 1935.

TEMPERATURES USED IN BAKING

Type of Product	Approximate Time Required for Baking	Oven Temperature	
	minutes	degrees F.	degrees C.
Breads			
Biscuits	12 to 15	425	218
• Cornbread	30 to 35	400	204
Muffins	20 to 25	400	204
Popovers	45	450 for 30 min., then 350 for 15 min.	232 for 30 min., then 177 for 15 min.
Yeast bread	50 to 60	375 for 15 min., then 350 for 35 to 45 min.	191 for 15 min., then 177 for 35 to 45 min.
Yeast rolls	20 to 25	425	218
Cakes, with fat			
Plain			
Cup	15 to 20	375	191
Layer	15 to 25	365	185
Loaf	40 to 45	325 to 350	163 to 177
White or chocolate			
Layer	20 to 25	350	177
Loaf	50 to 55	325 to 350	163 to 177
Cakes, without fat			
Sponge and Angel	55 to 60	325 to 350	163
Cookies			
Drop	10 to 15	400	204
Drop (to spread)	10 to 12	350	177
Rolled	8 to 10	375	191
Egg, meat, milk, cheese dishes			
Cheese soufflé	60	325	163
Custard, plain, corn, etc.	50 to 60	350	177
Macaroni and cheese	25 to 30	350	177
Meat loaf	75	350	177
Meat pie	25 to 30	400	204
Rice pudding (raw rice)	120 to 180	250 to 275	121 to 135
Scalloped potatoes	60	350	177
Pastry			
One-crust (custard type)	20	450 for 10 min., then 350 to finish	232 for 10 min., then 177 to finish
Shells	8 to 10	400	204
Two-crust pies	30 to 35	450 for 10 min., then 350 to finish	232 for 10 min., then 177 to finish

* It may be necessary to modify these temperatures for decreased atmospheric pressure.

DEEP-FAT FRYING TEMPERATURES

Type of Product	Amount to Serve 50	Preparation	Method	Temperature degrees F.	Temperature degrees C.	Time minutes
Asparagus (cooked)	12 lb.	Skin and scrape. Cut in pieces 2 in. long.	I	375	191	1 to 3
Bananas	9 lb.	Sprinkle with powdered sugar and lemon juice. Let stand 30 min.	I	375	191	1 to 3
Cauliflower	9, 12-oz. heads	Cold, cooked cauliflower	I	375	191	1 to 3
Cheese Balls	....	See p. 85	.....	350	177	2 to 3
Chicken	25, 2½ to 3 lb. broilers	See p. 169	I	350 to 375	177 to 191	8 to 10
Croquettes (all previously cooked foods)	....	....	.....	375 to 390	191 to 199	2 to 5
Cucumbers	16, 9-in. long	Wash, pare, and cut lengthwise in ⅓-in. slices.	III	390	199	3 to 5
Cutlets	....	See p. 110	.....	360 to 400	182 to 204	5 to 8
Doughnuts	....	....	.....	375	191	3 to 5
Eggplant	8 lb., 1 slice 4 x ½-in.	Pare, cut in ½-in. slices, soak in salt water 2 hr.	I	370	188	5 to 8
Fish Fillets	13 lb., 4 oz. serving	....	III	370	188	4 to 6
Fritters	....	....	.....	370 to 380	188 to 193	2 to 5

Frog Legs	100 large	Trim and clean.	III	375 to 380	191 to 193	6
Onions	8 lb.	Peel, cut in 3/16-in. slices, separate into rings. Soak in milk 1 hr.	I	370	188	1 to 3
Oysters	3 qt.	See p. 115	III	375	191	1 to 3
Perch or Smelts	18 lb., 6-oz. serving	See p. 113 & 114 (Fried Fish II)	III	370	188	3 to 5
Scallops	12 lb. (approx. 20 per lb.) 5 to 6 per serving	Wash and dry.	III	360	182	5
Shrimp	13 lb., 4-oz. serving	See p. 115	I	350 to 365	177 to 185	3 to 5
Summer Squash	12 lb.	Wash and cut in 1/2-in. slices.	III	375	191	3 to 5
Timbale Cases	....	See p. 61		380 to 390	193 to 199	1 to 1 1/2
Potatoes						
French Fried	15 lb. E.P.	Peel. Cut into eighths lengthwise.	....	365 to 375	185 to 191	5 to 12
Shoestring	12 lb. E.P.	Peel. Cut into 1/8-in. strips.	....	325 to 335	163 to 168	3 to 10
Lattice	12 lb. E.P.	Peel. Cut, using lattice slicer.	....	350 to 375	177 to 191	3 to 10
Chips	8 lb. E.P.	Peel. Slice very thin.	....	325	163	3 to 6

Method I
Dip in mixture of:
1 c. Flour
1/2 t. Salt } Mix.
f.g. Pepper
Add
2/3 c. Milk
2 Eggs, beaten.

Method II
Dip in milk.
Drain. Dip in flour.

Method III
Sprinkle with salt and pepper.
Dip in crumbs, egg, and crumbs again.

TEMPERATURES AND TESTS FOR SIRUP AND CANDIES*

Product	Temperature of Sirup at Sea Level (Indicating Concentration Desired)		Stage of Concentration Desired	Behavior at Stage Desired
	degrees F.	degrees C.		
Sirup.........	230 to 235	110 to 112	Thread	The sirup spins a two-inch thread when dropped from fork or spoon.
Fondant........ Fudge......... Penuchi........	235 to 240	112 to 116	Soft ball	The sirup when dropped into very cold water forms a soft ball which flattens on removal.
Caramels.......	244 to 248	118 to 120	Firm ball	The sirup when dropped into very cold water forms a firm ball which does not flatten on removal.
Divinity........ Marshmallows.. Nougat........ Popcorn balls... Salt-water taffy..	250 to 265	121 to 129	Hard ball	The sirup when dropped into very cold water forms a ball which is hard enough to hold its shape, yet plastic.
Butterscotch Taffies........	270 to 290	132 to 143	Soft crack	The sirup when dropped into very cold water separates into threads which are hard but not brittle.
Brittle Glacé....	300 to 310	149 to 154	Hard crack	The sirup when dropped into very cold water separates into threads which are hard and brittle.
Barley sugar....	320	160	Clear liquid	The sugar liquefies.
Caramel........	338	170	Brown liquid	The liquid becomes brown.

* It may be necessary to modify these temperatures for decreased atmospheric pressure.

TABLE OF WEIGHTS AND THEIR APPROXIMATE EQUIVALENTS IN MEASURE

Food	Weight	Approximate Measure
Almonds, blanched...........	1 lb.	4 c.
Almonds in shell.............	1 lb.	3 c.
Almonds, A. P...............	1 lb.	2 c. E. P.
Apples, A. P...............	1 lb.	2½ to 3 medium
Apples, A. P...............	1½ lb.	1 qt. sliced
Apples, diced, ½-inch cubes....	1 lb.	4½ c.
Applesauce.................	1 lb.	2 c.
Apples, canned, pie pack......	1½ lb.	1 qt.
Apricots, dried, A. P.........	1 lb.	3 c.
Apricots, dried, cooked, no juice	1 lb.	2½ lb. or about 5 c.
Apricots, fresh..............	1 lb.	8 apricots
Apricots, canned, halves, without juice........	1 lb.	2 c. or 21 halves
Apricots, pie pack...........	1 lb.	1¾ c.
Asparagus, fresh.............	1 lb.	20 stalks
Asparagus, canned tips, drained.	1 lb.	19 stalks
Asparagus, canned, cuts, drained	1 lb.	2½ c.
Avocado...................	1 lb.	2 medium
Bacon, raw.................	1 lb.	15 to 25 slices
Bacon, cooked..............	1 lb.	85 to 95 slices
Baking Powder..............	1 oz.	2½ T.
Bananas...................	1 lb.	3 medium
Bananas, diced..............	1 lb.	2½ c.
Barley, flour................	1 lb.	4 c.
Barley, pearl...............	1 lb.	2 c.
Beans, baked...............	2 lb.	1 qt.
Beans, dried, Lima, small, A. P.	1 lb.	2⅓ c.
Beans, dried, Lima, 1 lb. A. P., after cooking........	2 lb. 9 oz.	6 c.
Beans, Lima, fresh or canned...	1½ lb.	1 qt.
Beans, kidney, A. P..........	1 lb.	2⅔ c.
Beans, kidney, 1 lb., after cooking.................	2 lb. 6 oz.	7 c.

TABLE OF WEIGHTS AND THEIR APPROXIMATE EQUIVALENTS IN MEASURE (continued)

Food	Weight	Approximate Measure
Beans, navy, A. P.	1 lb.	2⅓ c.
Beans, navy, 1 lb. A. P., after cooking	2 lb. 3 oz.	6 c.
Beans, string, cut, cooked, without juice	1 lb.	3½ c.
Beef, dried, solid pack	1 lb.	1 qt.
Beef, ground, raw	1 lb.	2 c.
Beef, cooked, diced	1 lb.	3 c.
Beets, medium	1 lb.	2 to 3
Beets, cooked, diced	1 lb.	2¼ c.
Beets, cooked, sliced	1½ lb.	1 qt.
Beets, young, A. P.	6 lb. (net)	1 doz.
Blackberries, fresh	3 lb.	1 qt.
Blackberries, pie pack	1 lb.	3 c.
Bran, unwashed	1 lb.	4 qt.
Bran, all bran	8 oz.	1 qt.
Bran, flakes	1 lb.	3 qt.
Bread, loaf	2 lb.	24 slices, ½ in. each
Bread, sandwich	1 loaf	36 to 40 ¼-in. slices
Bread, soft, broken	1 lb.	9 c.
Bread, stale, broken	1 lb.	9 c.
Bread, crumbs, dry	12 oz.	4 c.
Bread, crumbs, soft	8 oz.	4 c.
Brussels Sprouts, A. P.	1 lb.	1 qt.
Butter	1 lb.	2 c.
Cabbage, shredded, E. P.	12 oz.	1 qt.
Cabbage, A. P., shredded, cooked	1 lb.	1½ c.
Cantaloupe	18 oz.	1 melon, 4½ in. diameter
Carrots, diced (A. P. topped)	1 lb.	3¼ c.
Carrots, ground, raw, E. P.	1 lb.	3¼ c.
Carrots, diced, cooked	1 lb.	3 c.
Carrots	1 lb.	6 small

TABLE OF WEIGHTS AND THEIR APPROXIMATE EQUIVALENTS IN MEASURE (continued)

Food	Weight	Approximate Measure
Cake, crumbs, not dry........	10 oz.	1 qt.
Cauliflower, E. P., 1 crate.....	12½ lb.	10 qt.
Cauliflower, head............	12 oz.	1 small
Celery, diced, E. P...........	1¼ lb.	1 qt.
Celery, diced (depending on size)	1 to 2 bunches	1 qt.
Cheese, cottage..............	1 lb.	2¼ c.
Cheese, grated or ground......	1 lb.	1 qt.
Cheese, cubed................	17 oz.	1 qt.
Cheese, Philadelphia cream....	3 oz.	⅓ c.
Cherries, red, pie pack, without juice..............	1 lb.	3 c. (scant)
Cherries, glacé..............	1 lb.	96 cherries
Cherries, Royal Anne, drained..	1 lb.	2¼ c.
Chicken, dressed.............	5 lb.	1 qt. cooked, diced
Chicken, cooked, cubed.......	1 lb.	3 c.
Chili Powder.................	1 oz.	6 T.
Chili Sauce..................	14 oz.	1¼ c.
Chocolate...................	1 lb.	16 squares
Chocolate, grated............	1 lb.	4 c. (plus)
Chocolate, melted...........	1 lb.	2 c. (scant)
Cinnamon, ground............	1 lb.	4 c.
Cinnamon, stick..............	¾ oz.	4 sticks, 5 in. long
Citron, dried, chopped........	3 oz.	1 c.
Cloves, ground..............	1 lb.	3¾ c.
Cloves, whole...............	3 oz.	1 c.
Cocoa......................	1 lb.	4½ c.
Cocoanut, prepared..........	1 lb.	6 to 7 c.
Coffee, ground coarse........	1 lb.	5 to 5½ c.
Coffee, pulverized............	1 lb.	5 c.

TABLE OF WEIGHTS AND THEIR APPROXIMATE
EQUIVALENTS IN MEASURE (continued)

Food	Weight	Approximate Measure
Corn, canned..................	1 lb.	1¾ c.
Cornflakes....................	1 lb.	4 qt.
Cornmeal.....................	1 lb.	3 c.
Corn sirup....................	12 oz.	1 c.
Cornstarch...................	1 lb.	3¼ c.
Crab Meat, flaked............	½ lb.	3 c.
Crackers, graham.............	1 lb.	58 crackers
Crackers, 2⅝ in. sq...........	12 oz.	50 crackers
Crackers, 2 x 2 in............	1 lb.	108 crackers
Cracker, crumbs, medium fine...	10 oz.	1 qt.
Cranberries, raw..............	1 lb.	4 c.
Cranberries, cooked..........	1 lb.	1 qt.
Cranberries, sauce, jellied......	1 lb.	2 c.
Cream of Tartar..............	1 oz.	3 T.
Cream of Wheat, raw..........	1 lb.	2⅔ c.
Cucumbers...................	20 oz.	2, 9 in. long
Cucumbers, diced, E. P........	1 lb.	3 c.
Currants, dried..............	1 lb.	3 c.
Curry Powder................	1 oz.	4 T.
Dates, A. P..................	1 lb.	2½ c.
Dates, pitted................	1 lb.	3 c.
Eggplant....................	1 lb.	8 slices 4 x ½ in.
Eggs, whole, A. P.............	1 lb.	8
Eggs, whole*.................	1 lb.	2 c. (9 to 11 eggs)
Eggs, whites.................	1 lb.	2 c. (17 to 20 eggs)
Eggs, yolks..................	1 lb.	2 c. (19 to 22 eggs)
Eggs, hard cooked, chopped...	1½ lb.	1 qt.

* One case (30 doz.) eggs weighs approx. 41 to 43 lb. and yields approx. 35 lb. of liquid whole eggs.

TABLE OF WEIGHTS AND THEIR APPROXIMATE EQUIVALENTS IN MEASURE (continued)

Food	Weight	Approximate Measure
Rice, puffed..................	1 oz.	1⅔ c.
Rutabagas, raw, cubed, E. P....	1 lb.	3⅓ c.
Salad Dressing, cooked........	1 lb.	2 c.
Salmon, canned..............	1 lb.	2 c.
Salt........................	1 oz.	1½ T.
Sardines, canned.............	1 lb.	48, 3 in. long
Sausage, link, small..........	1 lb.	16 to 17
Sauerkraut...................	1 lb.	3 c. packed
Shrimp......................	1 lb.	3¼ c.
Soda........................	1 lb.	2 c.
Spaghetti....................	1 lb.	4 c. (plus)
Spaghetti, 1 lb. A. P., cooked..	3 lb. 14 oz.	2⅓ qt.
Spinach, raw.................	1 lb.	5 qt. (not packed)
Spinach, 1 lb. raw, cooked.....	13 oz.	2¾ c.
Spinach, canned..............	1 lb.	2 c.
Squash, summer, A. P.........	2 lb.	1 squash, 5 in. diameter
Squash, Hubbard, cooked......	1 lb.	2⅛ c.
Strawberries, A. P............	1 lb.	2¼ c.
Sugar, brown................	1 lb.	3 c.
Sugar, cubes.................	1 lb.	96 cubes
Sugar, granulated............	1 lb.	2⅛ c.
Sugar, powdered, sifted.......	1 lb.	3½ c.
Sweetbreads, 5 lb. A. P.......		1¾ qt. cooked
Tapioca, minute..............	1 lb.	2½ c.
Tapioca, pearl...............	1 lb.	2¾ c.

TABLE OF WEIGHTS AND THEIR APPROXIMATE
EQUIVALENTS IN MEASURE (continued)

Food	Weight	Approximate Measure
Tapioca, 1 lb. after cooking....		7½ c.
Tea.........................	1 lb.	6 c.
Tomatoes, canned............	1 lb.	2 c.
Tomatoes, fresh..............	1 lb.	3 to 4 medium
Tomatoes, fresh, diced........	1 lb.	2¼ c.
Turnips, A. P.................	1 lb.	2 to 3
Tuna Fish...................	1 lb.	2 c.
Vanilla.....................	½ oz.	1 T.
Walnuts, English, in shell.....	1 lb.	55 small nuts, or 1½ qt.
Walnuts, English, 1 lb. A. P., after shelling......		2 c.
Watercress..................	1 lb.	5 bunches
Watermelon.................	1 lb.	1-in. slice, 6 in. diameter
Wheat, puffed...............	1 lb.	32 c.
Wheat, shredded.............	1 lb.	15 to 16 biscuits
White Sauce, medium........	9 oz.	1 c.
Yeast.......................	1 lb.	32 cakes

APPROXIMATE AMOUNTS OF FOODS AS PURCHASED TO SERVE FIFTY

Food	Serving Unit	Order
I. Bakery Products		
Pullman Loaf, 30 oz.....	1 to 2 slices	2 to 4 loaves
Pan Rolls..............	1½ to 2	6 to 8 doz.
II. Beverages		
Coffee.................	1 c.	1 to 1¼ lb.
Cocoa.................	1 c.	8 oz.
Cider.................	½ c.	6½ qt.
Grape Juice.............	½ c.	6½ qt.
Lemons, for lemonade....	1 glass	3 doz.
Oranges, for juice.......	⅓ c.	6 doz. medium
Tea (Amount will vary with quality and blend)		
Hot...................	1 c.	2½ oz.
Iced..................	1 glass	3 oz.
Tomato Juice..........	½ c.	2 No. 10 cans (6½ qt.)
Tomato Juice..........	⅓ c.	5 qt.
III. Cereals and Cereal Products		
Cereal to be cooked, p. 35		
All Bran, 16-oz. pkg.....	½ c. (scant)	3 pkg.
Bran Flakes, 10-oz. pkg..	¾ c.	5 pkg.
Crackers, graham.......	2 crackers	2 lb.
Crackers, 2 x 2 in.......	2 crackers	1 lb.
Cornflakes, 8-oz. pkg.....	⅘ c.	5 pkg.
Krumbles, 8-oz. pkg.....	1 c. (scant)	6 pkg.
Grapenuts, 12-oz. pkg....	¼ c. (scant)	4 pkg.
Puffed Wheat, 3½-oz. pkg.	1 c.	6 pkg.
Puffed Rice, 4-oz. pkg....	1 c.	6 pkg.
Rice Krispies, 6-oz. pkg..	⅔ c.	6 pkg.
Whole Wheat Flakes, 10-oz. pkg..............	⅔ c.	5 pkg.
Shredded Wheat, 12-oz. pkg.................	2 biscuits	7 pkg.
Wheat Krispies, 10½-oz. pkg.................	⅔ c.	4 pkg.
IV. Dairy Products		
Butter for table (allow more if serving hot bread)..............	1 to 1½ pats	1 to 1½ lb.
Butter for vegetables....	————	½ to ¾ lb.
Cream, 20 per cent......	2 T.	1½ qt.
Cream, 40 per cent for garnish..............	1 T.	¾ to 1 qt.

Food	Serving Unit	Order
Cheese, Cottage.........	⅓ c.	8½ lb.
Cheese, Longhorn.......	1½ oz.	4¾ lb.
Ice Cream, bulk........	No. 12 dipper	2 gal.
Ice Cream, brick........	———	7 to 8 bricks
Ice or Sherbet, with meal.	No. 16 dipper	1½ gal.
Milk..................	1 glass	2½ gal.
V. Fruits		
Canned Fruits*		
Dried Fruits		
Apricots.............	3 oz.	4½ lb.
Dates................	5 to 6 each	4½ lb.
Figs, uncooked.......	2 each	2¼ lb.
Peaches.............	3 oz.	4½ lb.
Prunes..............	3 oz.	5½ lb.
Raisins.............	2⅓ oz.	4 lb.
Fresh Fruits		
Apples for sauce......	3 oz.	15 lb.
Apples, for 8-in. pie...	6 to 7 cuts per pie	15 lb.
Bananas, to serve whole, small size	1 each	16 lb.
Bananas, for 8-in. pie..	6 to 7 cuts per pie	5 lb.
Blackberries, for 8-in. pie	6 to 7 cuts per pie	6 to 8 qt.
Blackberries, for short-cake..............	½ c.	6 to 8 qt.
Cherries, red, for 8-in. pie...............	6 to 7 cuts per pie	8 to 10 qt.
Cranberries, for sauce..	¼ c.	3 lb.
Pineapple, (each 2 lb.).	½ c. diced	5 pineapples
VI. Sweets		
Candies, small...........	———	1 lb.
Honey..................	2 T.	5 lb.
Jam....................	2 T.	3 lb.
Jelly..................	2 T.	3 lb.
Sirup..................	¼ c.	2½ qt.
Sugar, loaf.............	1½ cubes	1½ lb.
Sugar, granulated........	1½ t.	¾ lb.
VII. Meats		
Beef		
Chuck Roast..........	2½ oz.	18 to 20 lb.
Country Fried Steak (Round), ½ in. thick..	3 oz.	12½ lb.
Creamed Beef, ground meat	3 oz.	9 lb.
Ground Meat, patties....	3 oz.	12½ lb.

* Canned Fruits and Vegetables.

The number of servings that can be secured from a can of fruit or vegetables will depend upon the grade, pack, size of servings, and size of the can.

A No. 10 can of a standard grade of fruit will yield 30 to 35 servings. A No. 2½ can, 8 to 9 servings.

A No. 10 can of vegetables will yield approximately 25 to 30 servings. A No. 2½ can, 6 to 8 servings.

APPROXIMATE AMOUNTS OF PREPARED FOODS
TO SERVE FIFTY (continued)

Food	Serving Unit	Quantity
VIII. Salads		
Bulky vegetable combination, as cabbage or mixed vegetables......	½ c.	6 qt.
Compact mixture, as potato salad............	½ c.	6¼ qt.
Combination fruit.......	½ c.	6¼ qt.
Fish or meat...........	⅔ c.	8 qt.
Gelatin, liquid.........	⅓ c.	4 qt.
IX. Soups		
Soup..................	1 c.	3 gal.

APPROXIMATE DIPPER EQUIVALENTS

Dipper No.	Approximate Equivalent	Use
30	2 T. plus	Drop cookies
24	2⅔ T. plus	Cream puffs
20	3 T. plus	Muffins, cup cakes
16	4 T. (¼ c.)	Croquettes, desserts
12	5 T. plus	Vegetables, desserts
10	6 T. plus	Desserts
8	8 T. (½ c.)	Luncheon dishes

PART II

RECIPES

A poet, I guess, is more or less
Preoccupied with gender,
Yet I, though custom call me crude,
Prefer to sing in praise of food.
—OGDEN NASH.

The formulae presented provide servings for fifty people unless otherwise stated. It is recognized that many factors affect the probable yield of any formula. For example, a formula that might serve adequate portions to 50 women may yield only 35 portions of the size deemed adequate in a men's commons.

Attention is called to the fact that in all formulae quantities of ingredients other than liquid weighing over an ounce are given by weight and all liquid ingredients are indicated by measure. This is done as a means of facilitating the production of standardized products. The limitations of time and space lead to the inclusion in this book of formulae only those that are basic to the everyday meals in the average food service. Whenever possible variations of a basic formula are given rather than the presentation of numerous recipes. It is hoped by this means attention may be focused on the essentials rather than dispersed among details.

Sodium aluminum sulphate baking powder was used in testing these recipes.

Eggs weighing approximately 2 oz. each were used in the preparation of recipes.

All steamed foods were steamed under approximately 5-lb. pressure.

The weights given are for food as purchased (A.P.) unless otherwise stated.

The cooking time given in each recipe is based on the size of the pan and the amount of the product in the pan. If a larger or smaller pan is used, the cooking time will need to be corrected accordingly.

Food to be held on the steam table for some time will need to be more moist than food to be served at once, for example, macaroni and cheese.

Should the user wish to increase or decrease the recipe, the amounts of each ingredient may be inserted in the left-hand column provided in each recipe for this purpose.

APPETIZERS

When work seems
    rather dull to me
And life is not so
    sweet
One thing at least can
    bring me joy—
I simply love
    to eat!

        —REBECCA McCANN.

Appetizers are often served at the beginning of a meal to stimulate the appetite. They should always be attractive in appearance, spicy, and pleasing in flavor. They include canapés, cocktails, hors d'oeuvres, and soups.

Canapés and Hors d'Oeuvres

Canapés are made by cutting thin slices of bread into rounds, squares, diamonds, crescents, strips, or other desired shapes. The bread may be toasted, sautéd in butter on one side, or fried in deep fat. The bread is then covered with a well seasoned mixture of eggs, cheese, fish, or meat and garnished with a bit of some bright or interesting food.

Hors d'oeuvres are relishes served at the beginning of the meal. They may be canapés, olives, stuffed celery, deviled eggs, pickles, radishes, fish, sausages, or a combination of these. Hors d'oeuvres may be arranged on individual plates when the guests are seated or a platter containing a variety of these may be passed, so that each guest may make his own selection.

Canapés may be served as hors d'oeuvres as the first course of a meal, or an assortment of these may be arranged on a large tray and served at afternoon teas or buffet suppers with cocktails or clear soup.

LEMONADE

Amount	Ingredient	Method
1¼ qt.	Lemon juice (approx. 30 lemons)	} Mix.
2 lb. 8 oz.	Sugar	
	Add	
9 qt.	Water, cold	} Stir until dissolved.
	Chill	
		Yield approx. 2½ gal.

SPICED CIDER (hot)

Amount	Ingredient	Method
2½ gal.	Cider	
	Add	
4 lb.	Sugar, brown	
	Add	
10	Cinnamon sticks, 2 in.	
2½ T.	Cloves, whole	
2½ T.	Allspice	} Tied loosely in a bag.
½ t.	Mace	
1 t.	Salt	
f. g.	Cayenne	
	Bring slowly to the boiling point. Boil 15 min. Remove spices. Serve hot.	
		Yield approx. 2½ gal.

SPICED CIDER (cold)

Amount	Ingredient	Method
2 gal.	Cider	Heat slowly, stirring often.
2 T.	Cloves, whole	} Strain.
2 T.	Allspice berries	Chill.
8	Cinnamon sticks, 2 in.	
	Add orange juice and lemon juice to taste.	
		Yield approx. 2 gal.

HOT SPICED TOMATO JUICE

Amount	Ingredient	Method
3 qt.	Tomato juice	Boil together 5 min. Strain.
8 oz.	Onions	
3	Bay leaves	
12	Cloves	
1 T.	Mustard	
6	Celery stalks	
1½ oz.	Salt	
	Add	
3 qt.	Consommé	
	Serve hot.	
		Yield 50 servings (½ c.).

TOMATO JUICE I

Amount	Ingredient	Method
6 qt.	Tomato juice	Combine. Heat to boiling point. Boil 10 min. Strain. Chill.
2 T.	Salt	
12	Bay leaves	
1 oz.	Cloves	
		Yield approx. 6 qt.

TOMATO JUICE II

Amount	Ingredient	Method
6 qt.	Tomato juice	Mix ingredients. Chill.
½ c.	Lemon juice	
2 T.	Worcestershire sauce	
½ t.	Tabasco sauce	
2 T.	Celery salt	
		Yield approx. 6 qt.

Note: For variety:
1. Omit the seasonings; use 4 qt. tomato juice and 2 qt. sauerkraut juice.
2. Substitute yellow tomato juice for the regular tomato juice.

CRANBERRY JUICE

Amount			Ingredient	Method
4	lb.	8 oz.	Cranberries	
4½ qt.			Water	} Cook and strain.
		1 T.	Cloves, whole	
			Add	
1	lb.	8 oz.	Sugar	} Stir until dissolved. Chill.
		½ c.	Just before serving, add Lemon juice	
				Yield approx. 1 gal.

NOTE: For variety add an equal quantity of orange juice and serve hot.

FRUIT PUNCH

Amount	Ingredient	Method
18 (size 150)	Oranges	
12	Lemons	} Extract juice.
4 (size 80)	Grapefruit	
	Add	
4 lb.	Sugar	} Stir until dissolved.
	Add	
	Ice water—To make 2¾ gal. of liquid	

GINGER ALE FRUIT PUNCH

Amount	Ingredient	Method
1½ qt.	Lemon juice	
1½ qt.	Orange juice	
6 qt.	Water	
4 lb.	Sugar	
1 qt.	Pineapple juice	
	When ready to serve, add	
2 qt.	Ginger ale	
		Yield 3 gal.

NOTE: Lime ice may be added to the punch just before serving.

GRAPE PUNCH

Amount		Ingredient	Method
4 qt.		Grape juice	
1 qt.		Lemon juice	
	1 pt.	Orange juice	
		Add	
2 lb.		Sugar	} Stirred until sugar is dissolved.
6½ qt.		Water	
			Yield 3 gal.

PUNCH (with tea base)

Amount		Ingredient	Method
1 lb.	12 oz.	Sugar	
	1 c.	Lemon juice	
	1 c.	Orange juice	
	1 pt.	Grape juice	
	1 pt.	Tea infusion (1 T. tea to 1 pt. water. Let stand 4 min.)	
7 qt.		Water	
1 lb.		Pineapple, shredded	
1 lb.		Cherries	
			Yield approx. 2½ gal.

RHUBARB PUNCH

Amount		Ingredient	Method
8 lb.		Rhubarb, tender	Cook below boiling point and strain. (There should be 1 gal. of juice.) Chill.
4 lb.		Sugar	
3 qt.		Water	
		Just before serving, add	
	1 pt.	Pineapple juice	
1 qt.		Ginger ale	
			Yield approx. 5½ qt.

Note: The cocktail should be a delicate pink color.

SWEDISH TIMBALE CASE BATTER

Amount	Ingredient	Method
3 1½ c. 1½ t.	Eggs, beaten Milk Oil or melted fat	} Mix.
	Add	
6 oz. 1 t. 1½ t.	Flour Salt Sugar	} Mixed.

Stir until smooth. Pour into a cup and let stand until the air bubbles have come to the top. Fry with a timbale iron in deep fat.

Fry 380° to 390°F. until brown.

NOTE: This recipe may be used to make either rosettes or timbales. Serve timbales filled with creamed chicken or peas. Serve rosettes sprinkled with powdered sugar; heaped with fresh, or preserved, fruits and garnished with whipped or ice cream; or may be used the same as timbales.

WAFFLES

Amount	Ingredient	Method
3 lb. 6 T. 2 T. 4 oz.	Flour, sifted Baking powder Salt Sugar	} Sift together.
	Add	
18 2¼ qt.	Egg yolks, beaten Milk	} Combined.
	Add	
1 lb.	Fat, melted	
	Fold in	
18	Egg whites, beaten stiffly	

Bake on a hot waffle iron.   Yield 1½ gal. batter.

NOTE: Serve immediately with sirup and butter or with creamed chicken.

For variety add:
1. Chopped pecans 6 oz.
2. All bran 4 oz.
3. One lb. chopped bacon, slightly broiled, and substitute its fat for the fat of waffles.

Or substitute:
1. 12 oz. fine cornmeal for 8 oz. flour.

PLAIN ROLLS

Amount	Ingredient	Method
1½ qt.	Milk	} Scald.
	Pour over	
4 oz.	Sugar	
2½ T.	Salt	} Let cool until lukewarm.
12 oz.	Fat	
	Add	
3 oz.	Yeast (6 cakes)	} Stir.
	Add	
4 lb. 12 oz.	Flour	} Mix thoroughly.

1. Turn into greased pan and let rise until double in bulk.
2. Knead and let rise again.
3. Knead, shape, and let rise.
4. Bake.

Bake 15 to 20 min. 425°F.　　　　　　　　Yield 100 rolls.

NOTE: It will require about 4 to 5 hr. for mixing and rising.

VARIATIONS OF PLAIN ROLLS

Kind	Changes in Plain Recipe
Butterhorn......	When dough has doubled in bulk, roll to ¼-in. thickness. Cut 3-in. triangles of dough, brush with melted butter. Roll each triangle to the center, starting with wide side. Brush again with melted butter.
Parkerhouse.....	When dough has doubled in bulk, roll to ⅛-in. thickness. Cut rounds 2 to 2½ in. in diameter. Crease middle of each round with dull edge of knife. Brush half of each round with melted butter, fold over, press together with palm of hand.
Cloverleaf.......	Shape small bits of dough mixture into balls. Fit into oiled muffin pans allowing 3 balls for each roll.
Cinnamon.......	Roll dough ⅛ in. thick, spread with melted butter and 3 T. cinnamon mixed with 4 c. brown or white sugar and 1 c. raisins. Roll dough as for jelly roll, cut in slices ¾ in. thick. Place (cut surface down) in well greased pans or muffin tins. When removed from oven spread over top 1 c. powdered sugar mixed with ½ c. milk.
Orange.........	To make orange rolls, spread with orange sirup. (See Orange Bread recipe p. 54.) Proceed as for Cinnamon Rolls.
Hot Cross Buns..	Cut rounds ½ in. thick, 3 in. in diameter. Brush top with beaten egg. Score top of bun to make cross before baking or after baking make a cross on top with frosting.

VARIATIONS OF PLAIN ROLLS (continued)

Kind	Changes in Plain Recipe
Crescents	Roll 1/8 in. thick. Cut into 4-in. squares. Cut these into 2 triangles, brush top with melted fat. Begin at base, roll each triangle keeping point in middle of roll and bringing ends toward each other to form a crescent shape. Place on oiled baking sheet some distance apart.
Pecan Rolls	Shape as for cloverleaf or cinnamon rolls. In the bottom of each muffin pan place a portion of melted fat, brown sugar, and pecans mixed. Use 2½ lb. sugar, 12 oz. pecans, 8 oz. fat. Invert pan as soon as removed from oven.
Twists	Roll dough 1/3 in. thick, spread with melted butter, sugar, and cinnamon. Cut into strips 1/3 in. x 8 in., bring the two ends together and twist dough.
Poppy Seed	(1) Proceed as for Twists. Substitute poppy seeds for sugar and cinnamon. (2) Proceed as for Cinnamon Rolls. Substitute poppy seed for sugar, cinnamon, and raisins.
Sesame	Proceed as for Twin Rolls. Brush top with melted fat and sprinkle with sesame seeds.
Bow Knot	Roll dough 1/3 in. thick. Spread with melted butter. Cut into strips ½ in. x 9 in. Tie loosely into a single knot.
Twin	Roll dough 5/8 in. thick. Cut rounds 1 in. in diameter. Place in well oiled muffin pans allowing 2 rounds for each roll.
Half and Half	Proceed as for Twin Rolls. Use 1 round of plain dough and 1 round of whole wheat dough for each roll.
Ribbon	Roll dough ¼ in. thick. Spread with melted butter. Place on top of this a layer of whole wheat dough rolled to the same thickness. Repeat, using the contrasting dough until five layers thick. Cut with a 1½-in. cutter. Place in oiled muffin pans with cut surface down.
Cheese	Proceed as for Cinnamon Rolls. Use grated well ripened cheese in place of cinnamon, sugar, and raisins.
Whole Wheat	Substitute 2 lb. and 6 oz. of whole wheat flour for 2 lb. and 6 oz. of white flour. Proceed as for plain rolls.
Rosettes	Follow directions for Bow Knots. After tying, bring one end through center and the other over the side.
Braids	Roll dough out ¼ in. thick and cut in strips 6 in. long and ½ in. wide. Cross 3 strips in the middle and braid from center to end. Press ends together and fold under.
Fan Tan	Roll out rectangular sheet very thin. Brush with melted butter. Cut in strips about 1 in. wide. Pile 6 or 7 strips together. Cut 1½-in. pieces and place on end in oiled muffin pans.
Butterscotch	Proceed as for Pecan Rolls, omitting pecans, or proceed as for Cinnamon Rolls, using only brown sugar.

ICE BOX ROLLS

Amount	Ingredient	Method
1½ qt.	Milk	
1½ c.	Potatoes, mashed	Place in a pan and bring to the
12 oz.	Sugar	boiling point.
12 oz.	Fat	Let cool until lukewarm.
2 oz.	Salt	
	Add	
½ T.	Soda	
1½ oz.	Yeast (3 cakes, compressed.)	
1 T.	Baking powder	
4 lb.	Flour—Add only enough to make a stiff batter.	
	Let rise 15 min.	

Add flour to make a stiff dough. Knead and put in ice box for 24 hr. Before using,
remove from ice box, mold, and let rise 1 to 1½ hr.

Bake 15 to 20 min. 425°F.   Yield 6 doz.

BRAN ROLLS

Amount	Ingredient	Method
1 lb.	Fat	
1 pt.	Water, boiling	Mix. Stir until fat is melted.
12 oz.	Sugar	Let stand until mixture is
1 T.	Salt	lukewarm.
4 oz.	All Bran	
	Add	
2 oz. (4 cakes)	Yeast, compressed	Dissolved.
1 pt.	Water, lukewarm	
	Add	
4	Eggs, beaten	
	Add	
3 lb.	Flour (more if necessary) } Beat thoroughly.	

Cover and place in refrigerator over night or until ready to use. Remove from
refrigerator, form balls of dough to half fill muffin tins. Let rise 2 hr.

Bake 15 min. 425°F.   Yield 6 doz.

CHOCOLATE ROLL

Amount	Ingredient	Method
24	Eggs yolk, beaten	
	Add	
2 lb. 4 oz.	Sugar	} Mix.
	Add	
12 oz.	Chocolate, melted	
2 T.	Vanilla	
	Add	
9 oz.	Flour, cake	
1 T.	Baking powder	} Mixed.
1½ t.	Salt	
	Fold in	
24	Egg whites, beaten	
	Pour into four 12- x 20-in. pans lined with waxed paper.	

Bake 20 min. 325°F.   Yield 48 servings.
Note: Trim edges; turn onto cloth; remove waxed paper. Cover with custard filling, fluffy icing, or quick icing flavored with peppermint. Roll as jelly roll while hot.

JELLY ROLL

Amount	Ingredient	Method
15	Eggs, whole	} Beat well.
	Add	
1 lb. 8 oz.	Sugar	} Mix well.
	Fold in	
12 oz.	Flour	
1 T.	Cream of tartar	} Sifted together.
2 T.	Baking powder	
	Add	
¾ t.	Lemon extract	
	Pour into three 12- x 20-in. pans lined with waxed paper.	

Bake 12 min. 425°F.   Yield 48 servings.
Note: Trim edges; turn onto cloth; remove waxed paper. Cover with custard filling, fruit jam or jelly. Roll while hot.

FRUIT CAKE

Amount	Ingredient	Method
8 oz. 1 lb.	Butter Sugar	} Cream.
	Add	
4	Eggs, beaten	} Mix well.
	Add	
8 oz.	Jelly	
2 t.	Cinnamon	
2 t.	Cloves	
2 t.	Soda dissolved in	
1½ c.	cold coffee infusion	} Partially mix.
2 lb.	Raisins	
1 lb.	Currants	
1 lb.	Dates	
8 oz.	Nutmeats	
	Add	
1 lb. 4 oz.	Flour	
	Pour into 4 pans (3½ in. x 9 in.) that have been lined with a double thickness of waxed paper.	

Bake 2 hr. and 15 min. 250°F.   Yield approx. 8 lb.

GINGERBREAD

Amount	Ingredient	Method
1 lb. 1 lb.	Fat Sugar	} Cream.
	Add	
1 qt.	Sorghum	
	Add alternately flour mixture and water.	
2 lb. 8 oz.	Flour	
4 t.	Cinnamon	
4 t.	Cloves	} Mixed.
4 t.	Ginger	
1 qt.	Water, hot	} Combined.
1½ oz.	Soda	
	Add	
8	Eggs, beaten	
	Pour into 12-in. x 20-in. oiled baking pan.	

Bake 45 to 50 min. 325°F.   Yield approx. 60 servings.

NOTE: For Almond Meringue Gingerbread, cover baked gingerbread with meringue, sprinkle with almonds, and brown in a moderate oven.

ORANGE CUP CAKES

Amount			Ingredient	Method
	10	oz.	Fat	} Cream.
1 lb.	1	oz.	Sugar	
			Add	
	1	T.	Vanilla	} Mix until smooth.
	5		Eggs, beaten	
			Add	
	7	oz.	Raisins, ground	
	3		Orange rinds, grated	
			Add alternately	
	1¾	c.	Milk, sour	
			and	
1 lb.	8	oz.	Flour, pastry	
	¾	T.	Soda	} Mixed.
	1½	oz.	Baking powder	
	¾	t.	Salt	
			Mix only until smooth. Use a No. 30 dipper to fill muffin tins.	

Bake 25 min. 375°F.   Yield 50 cakes.

SUGAR COOKIES

Amount			Ingredient	Method
1 lb.			Sugar	} Cream.
	8	oz.	Fat	
			Add	
	4		Egg yolks, beaten	} Mix.
			Add	
	8	oz.	Flour	
	¾	t.	Salt	
	2	t.	Cream of tartar	} Mixed.
	1	t.	Soda	
			Mix thoroughly, add	
	4		Egg whites, beaten	
	1	t.	Vanilla	
			Add	
	8	oz.	Flour, or enough to make a soft dough	
			Roll dough on floured board to ⅛-in. thickness. Cut into desired shapes.	

Bake approx. 10 min. 400°F.   Yield approx. 100 cookies.

VARIATIONS OF SUGAR COOKIES

Kind	Changes in Plain Recipe
Autumn........	Cut rolled dough with leaf cutters. Sprinkle lightly with yellow, orange, or red sugar.
Cocoanut.......	Cut rolled dough with a round cookie cutter. Brush each cookie with melted fat and sprinkle with shredded cocoanut.
Confetti Strips..	Cut rolled dough into strips 3½ inches long and 1 inch wide with a pastry wheel. Brush with melted fat and sprinkle with tiny multicolored candies.
Filled..........	Cut dough with a round cutter. Put fig, date, or mincemeat filling on ½ of cookies. Brush edges with milk, cover with the remaining cookies. Press edges together with tines of a fork.
Peanut..........	Cut rolled dough with crescent cutter, brush with milk, and sprinkle with chopped nuts.
Pinwheel.......	Use ½ of sugar cookie recipe. Divide dough into two portions. Add 1 square of melted chocolate to one portion. Roll each into ⅛-inch sheets the same size. Place the chocolate dough over the white dough and press together. Roll as for jelly roll. Chill thoroughly. Cut into thin slices.
Ribbon.........	Cut chocolate and plain dough into long strips 1¾ inches wide. Arrange alternately the chocolate and plain strips, until 1¼ inches high. Press together. Chill thoroughly. Cut into thin slices.
Special Cookies..	Cut rolled dough with heart shaped cutter for Valentine's Day; hatchet cutter for Washington's birthday. Sprinkle with sugar. Scalloped and diamond cutters also make interesting variations.
Wreath.........	Cut rolled dough with a doughnut cutter. Brush with beaten egg and sprinkle with chopped nuts. For Christmas cookies decorate with candied cherry rings and pieces of citron arranged to represent holly.

BUTTER TEA COOKIES

Amount	Ingredient	Method
8 oz. 4½ oz.	Butter Sugar	} Cream.
3	Add Egg yolks	} Cream.
10 oz. ½ t.	Add Flour Vanilla Shape with a cookie press.	

Bake 10 to 12 min. 400°F.　　　　　Yield 50 to 75 cookies.
Note: Dough should be cold when shaped.

CHOCOLATE TEA COOKIES

Amount	Ingredient	Method
8 oz.	Butter, creamed	
6 oz.	Add gradually Sugar	
1	Add Egg, unbeaten	
½ t. ⅛ t. 9 oz. 2 T.	Add gradually Baking powder Salt Flour, sifted Cocoa	} Mixed.
2 t.	Add Vanilla Chill and shape with a cooky press.	

Bake 6 to 10 min. 375°F.　　　　　Yield 50 to 75 cookies.

BUTTERSCOTCH DROP COOKIES

Amount		Ingredient	Method
8	oz.	Butter	⎫ Cream.
12	oz.	Sugar, brown	⎭
		Add	
2		Eggs, beaten	
		Add in order given	
1 lb.		Flour	⎫
1	t.	Cream of tartar	⎬ Mixed.
⅛ t.		Salt	⎭
1	t.	Soda, dissolved in 4 T. hot water.	
1	t.	Vanilla	
6	oz.	Pecans, chopped	
		Measure with a No. 30 dipper and drop on oiled baking sheet.	

Bake approx. 15 min. 375°F.   Yield 8 doz. cookies.

CHOCOLATE-CRUNCH COOKIES

Amount		Ingredient	Method
6	oz.	Fat	⎫
6	oz.	Sugar	⎬ Cream.
4	oz.	Sugar, brown	⎭
		Add	
2		Eggs, beaten	⎬ Mix well.
		Add	
10	oz.	Flour	⎫
1	t.	Salt	⎬ Mixed.
1	t.	Soda	⎭
		Add	
1	t.	Vanilla	
1	c.	Nuts, chopped	
14	oz.	Chocolate, sweet, chopped	
		Drop from teaspoon on oiled baking sheet.	

Bake 10 to 12 min. 375°F.   Yield 8·doz.

RUSSIAN ROCKS

Amount		Ingredient	Method
9	oz.	Sugar, brown	} Cream.
8	oz.	Butter	
		Add, one at a time	
3		Eggs	} Beat after each addition.
		Add	
12	oz.	Flour	
1	t.	Soda	
1/4	t.	Cloves	
1/4	t.	Nutmeg	} Mixed.
1	t.	Cinnamon	
6	oz.	Raisins, cooked	
4	oz.	Nut meats, chopped	
		Measure with a No. 30 dipper and drop on an oiled baking sheet.	

Bake approx. 15 min. 400°F.   Yield 50 cookies.

ROLLED OATS DROP COOKIES

Amount		Ingredient	Method
8	oz.	Sugar, brown	} Cream.
6	oz.	Butter	
		Add	
2		Eggs, beaten	
		Add	
7	oz.	Rolled Oats	
		Add alternately	
8	oz.	Flour	
2	t.	Baking powder	
		and	
5	T.	Milk	
1/2	t.	Soda dissolved in 1 T. water	
		Add	
6	oz.	Raisins, cooked, chopped	
1	t.	Vanilla	
		Drop from teaspoon on oiled baking sheet.	

Bake approx. 12 min. 350°F.   Yield 50–60 cookies.

MINCEMEAT FILLED COOKIES

Amount		Ingredient	Method
1 lb.		Fat	⎫ Cream.
	12 oz.	Sugar, brown	⎭
		Add	
4		Eggs	} Mix.
		Add	
	14 oz.	Rolled Oats	
	14 oz.	Flour	
	2 t.	Soda	

Cut cookies with a 2¼-in. cutter. Bake. Put 2 cookies together with mincemeat.

Bake 10 min. 350°F. Yield approx. 7 doz. filled cookies.

OATMEAL BARS

Amount		Ingredient	Method
	9 oz.	Butter	⎫
	4 oz.	Shortening	⎬ Cream in mixer for 20 min.
1 lb.	6 oz.	Sugar, brown	⎭
		Add	
1 lb.		Flour	⎫
	12 oz.	Oatmeal	⎬ Mixed.
	4 t.	Soda	⎭

Oil a pan 12 in. x 20 in. and spread with ⅔ of dough. Pat down by hand. Add date filling and spread evenly over entire surface. Cover with remainder of dough and pat down. Bake. Cut into bars.
Bake 45 min. 325°F.

DATE BARS

Amount		Ingredient	Method
12		Egg whites	} Beat until stiff.
		Fold in (in order given)	
12		Egg yolks, beaten	
2 lb.		Sugar	
1 lb.		Nuts, chopped	
4 lb.		Dates	
1 lb.		Flour	⎫
	1½ T.	Baking powder	⎬ Mixed.

Bake 30 min. 325°F. Yield 48 servings 1 in. thick.
Note: Cut and roll in powdered sugar or serve with a rich custard sauce.

CRISP GINGER COOKIES

Amount		Ingredient	Method
1	c.	Molasses	} Boil together 1 min.
8	oz.	Sugar	} Cool.
		Add (in order given)	
4	oz.	Butter	
4	oz.	Fat	} Mix well.
2		Eggs, beaten	
		Add	
½	t.	Salt	
1	t.	Soda	
2	t.	Ginger	} Mixed.
1 lb. 12	oz.	Flour (or more)	
		Form into a roll, chill, and slice.	

Bake 8 to 10 min. 375°F.   Yield approx. 90 (2¼-in.) cookies.
NOTE: Dough may be rolled as any cookie dough and cut into fancy shapes.

PEANUT BUTTER COOKIES

Amount		Ingredient	Method
8	oz.	Sugar	
5⅓	oz.	Sugar, brown	} Cream together.
4	oz.	Fat	
4	oz.	Butter	
		Add	
2		Eggs, beaten	
1	c.	Peanut butter	
		Add	
8	oz.	Flour	
1	t.	Soda	} Mixed and sifted.
½	t.	Salt	
		Add	
1	t.	Vanilla	
		Form into balls and flatten with fork.	

Bake 8 min. 375°F.   Yield approx. 200 small cookies.

CORNFLAKE KISSES

Amount	Ingredient	Method
4	Egg whites, beaten	
1 lb.	Add gradually Sugar, sifted	
	Fold in	
4 oz.	Cornflakes	
8 oz.	Nuts, chopped	
3 oz.	Cocoanut, shredded	
1 t.	Vanilla	
	Drop from teaspoon on oiled baking sheet.	

Bake 15 min. 325°F.

COCOANUT DROP COOKIES

Amount	Ingredient	Method
1½ c.	Milk, condensed, sweetened	
1 lb.	Cocoanut, shredded	Mix.
1 T.	Vanilla	
8 oz.	Filberts	
	Drop from teaspoon on oiled baking sheet.	

Bake 12 min. 325°F.   Yield 50 small cookies.

KRISPIE MARSHMALLOW SQUARES

Amount	Ingredient	Method
5½ oz.	Butter	Melt.
1 lb.	Marshmallows	
	Add	
1 t.	Vanilla	
	Pour above mixture over	
11 oz.	Rice Krispies	Mix well.
	Press into buttered pans to ½ in. thickness. Cool and cut.	

Yield 4 doz.

COCOANUT MACAROONS

Amount	Ingredient	Method
8	Egg whites, beaten	
	Add gradually	
12 oz.	Sugar, granulated	
12 oz.	Sugar, powdered	
2 t.	Vanilla	
⅛ t.	Salt	
	Fold in	
1 lb. 8 oz.	Cocoanut, shredded	
	Drop from teaspoon on oiled baking sheet.	

Bake 15 min. 325°F.
Note: Do not enlarge this recipe.

BROWNIES

Amount	Ingredient	Method
1 lb.	Butter, melted	
2 lb.	Sugar	} Cream.
12	Eggs, beaten	
	Add	
12 oz.	Flour	
8 oz.	Cocoa	} Mixed.
4 t.	Baking powder	
2 t.	Salt	
	Add	
12 oz.	Nuts, chopped	
2 lb.	Dates, chopped	
4 T.	Vanilla	

Bake 30 min. 325°F.   Yield 100 bars 1 in. x 4 in.
Note: The mixture should be ½ in. thick in pan before baking. May use 3 squares chocolate in place of cocoa. Dates may be omitted.

BROKAW ICE BOX COOKIES

Amount	Ingredient	Method
12 oz.	Sugar	} Cream.
8 oz.	Shortening	
	Add	
3	Eggs	} Beat 5 min.
	Add	
1 lb. 2 oz.	Flour	
1 t.	Soda	
1 t.	Cloves	
1 t.	Nutmeg	} Mixed.
½ t.	Salt	
6 oz.	Raisins, ground (or dates)	
	Form into a roll, chill, and slice.	

Bake 10 min. 400°F.   Yield 60 to 70 (2½-in.) cookies.

BUTTERSCOTCH ICE BOX COOKIES

Amount	Ingredient	Method
8 oz.	Butter	
8 oz.	Fat	} Cream 5 min.
1 lb.	Sugar, brown	(second speed).
12 oz.	Sugar, white	
	Add	
4	Eggs, beaten	} Cream 5 min.
2 t.	Vanilla	
	Add	
2 t.	Cream of tartar	
8 oz.	Nuts, chopped	
2 t.	Soda	} Mixed.
8 oz.	Dates, chopped	
2 lb.	Flour	

Place dough on waxed paper, form into rolls. Wrap. Let stand over night, or longer in a cool place. Cut into slices ⅛ in. thick.
Bake 8 to 10 min. 400°F. Yield approx. 100 (2 in. x 3 in.) cookies.

CHEESE AND EGG DISHES

Since what we love has always found
Expression in enduring sound,
Music and verse should be competing
To match the transient joy of eating.
—Louis Untermeyer

CHEESE BALLS

Amount		Ingredient	Method
4 lb.	8 oz.	Cheese, grated	
	4 oz.	Flour	Mix.
	1 T.	Salt	
	f.g.	Cayenne	
		Fold in	
24		Egg whites beaten stiff	
		Shape into balls 1–1¼-in. diam. Crumb(Method III, p. 19)	

Fry in deep fat 2–3 min. 350°F.   Yield 150 balls.
Note: For serving as first course accompaniment, shape into balls ½–¾-in. diam.
Yield approx. 300 balls.

CHEESE CROQUETTES

Amount		Ingredient	Method
1 lb.		Fat, melted	
	8 oz.	Flour	Make a white sauce.
2 qt.		Milk	
		Add	
32		Egg yolks, beaten	Stir until cheese is melted.
2 lb.		Cheese, diced	Measure with a No. 16
	1 oz.	Salt	dipper. Cool. Shape.
	4 t.	Paprika	
		Chill several hours.	
		Bread each croquette using	
16		Egg whites and 8 T. water, beaten	
1 lb.		Crumbs	
		Place in a wire basket and fry in deep fat.	

Fry approx. 3 to 4 min. 375° to 390°F.

CHEESE FONDUE

Amount	Ingredient	Method
4½ qt.	Milk, scalded	
4 oz.	Fat, melted	
1½ t.	Mustard	Mix together.
1 T.	Salt	
f. g.	Cayenne	
	Pour over	
3 lb. 8 oz.	Bread cubes, soft, stale	
	Cool slightly and add	
4 lb. 8 oz.	Cheese, ground	
	Add	
24	Egg yolks, beaten	Beat mixture until thoroughly blended.
	Fold in	
24	Egg whites, stiffly beaten	
	Pour into 2 oiled pans 12 in. x 20 in.	

Bake 40 to 50 min. 300°F. Serving approx. 4 oz.

CHEESE SOUFFLÉ

Amount	Ingredient	Method
2½ qt.	Milk, hot	
	Add	
10 oz.	Tapioca, Minute	Stirring constantly.
1½ oz.	Salt	
	Cook in steamer 15 min. Stir frequently during first 5 min.	
	Add	
3 lb.	Cheese, ground	
24	Egg yolks, beaten	
	Fold in	
24	Egg whites, beaten	
	Pour into 3 oiled pans 9 in. x 14 in.	
	Cook over water in oven.	

Bake 50 min. 300°F. Serving approx. 2 oz.

NOTE: Serve with Spanish Sauce.

Variation: For Mushroom Soufflé, add one No. 1 can of drained, chopped mushrooms, 1 c. chopped green peppers to uncooked mixture. Serve with Béchamel Sauce.

SCALLOPED MACARONI

Amount			Ingredient	Method
1 lb.	8	oz.	Macaroni	Wash. Cook until tender.
6 qt.			Water, boiling	Drain and wash.
	2	oz.	Salt	
			Add	
2 lb.			Cheese, cubed	Mix.
1 lb.	2	oz.	Bread, fresh, cubed	
			Pour into an oiled pan 12 in. x 20 in. Pour over the macaroni.	
	6		Eggs, beaten	
	8	oz.	Fat, melted	Mixed.
	2	oz.	Salt	
3 qt.			Milk	

Bake 45 min. 350°F.   Serving approx. 4 oz.

MACARONI AND CHEESE

Amount		Ingredient	Method
2 lb.		Macaroni	Wash and cook until tender.
8 qt.		Water, boiling	Drain and wash.
	1 oz.	Salt	
		Add	
1 lb.	8 oz.	Cheese, ground	
		Pour macaroni into a pan 12 in. x 20 in.	
		Add	
	4 oz.	Fat	
	4 oz.	Flour	Made into a white sauce.
	1 oz.	Salt	
2 qt.		Milk	
		Sprinkle over the top	
	12 oz.	Bread crumbs	Mixed.
	4 oz.	Fat, melted	

Bake 45 min. 325°F.   Serving approx. 4½ oz.
Note: For variety add:
  1. Fresh tomato and green pepper.
  2. Pimiento.

CORN RAREBIT

Amount	Ingredient	Method
4 oz.	Onions	} Brown onions in fat.
6 oz.	Fat	
	Add	
1 qt.	Milk	} Heat to boiling point.
	Add gradually, stirring constantly	
1 pt.	Milk	} Blended.
6 oz.	Flour	
1½ oz.	Salt	
	Add	
1 lb. 8 oz.	Cheese, ground	} Cook in double boiler until melted.
3 oz.	Green pepper, chopped	
	Add	
1 No. 10 can	Corn (whole grain) hot, drained	

Dip with No. 8 dipper. Serve immediately on toasted buns.

BAKED EGGS WITH CHEESE

Amount	Ingredient	Method
50	Eggs	} Break and drop into oiled muffin tins or custard cups.

On the top of each egg, place, in order given, a portion of the following:

Amount	Ingredient	
4 t.	Salt	
1 lb. 8 oz.	Cheese, grated or ground	
6½ c.	Cream or White Sauce II	
8 oz.	Crumbs, buttered	

Set cups in a pan of hot water.

Bake approx. 25 min. or until firm. 350°F.
Note: A thin slice of raw tomato may be placed in the bottom of each cup.

BAKED EGGS AND BACON RINGS

Amount	Ingredient	Method
50	Eggs	} Place bacon around the inside of 50 baking cups (or muffin tins), with fat side up.
2 lb. 8 oz. (approx.)	Bacon, sliced	

Place in hot oven until fat is clear. Remove from oven. In each cup place 1 egg. Return to oven.
Bake approx. 25 min. or until firm. 350°F.

EGG CUTLETS

Amount	Ingredient	Method
2 qt.	Milk	
12 oz.	Butter	Make a white sauce.
6 oz.	Flour	
2 oz.	Salt	
	Add sauce to	
48	Eggs, hard cooked, coarsely ground	
	Mix well.	

Measure cutlets with a No. 12 dipper. Let cool 3 hours or longer. Shape into cutlets. Bread and fry.
Fry approx. 3 min. 375°F.

EGGS À LA KING

Amount	Ingredient	Method
1 lb.	Mushrooms	
2 T.	Onion	Fry.
12 oz.	Butter	
	Add	
4 qt.	Chicken broth (or milk)	Make a white sauce.
7 oz.	Flour	
	Add	
50	Eggs, hard cooked, cubed	
10 oz.	Green pepper, shredded	
8 oz.	Pimiento, shredded	
2 oz.	Salt	
f. g.	Cayenne	
		Serving approx. 3½ oz.

Note: Reheat, if necessary, after sauce is poured over eggs.

CURRIED EGGS OR CREAMED EGGS

Amount			Ingredient	Method
4 qt.			Milk, hot	
1 lb.			Fat	Make a white sauce.
	8	oz.	Flour	
			Add	
	1	oz.	Salt	
	¼	t.	Pepper	Mixed.
	1	T.	Curry	
			When ready to serve pour over	
75			Eggs, hard cooked, sliced	

Note: Serve with steamed rice. For creamed eggs omit the curry powder. 1 qt. stock may be substituted for 1 qt. milk.

OMELET

Amount			Ingredient	Method
1 lb.			Butter, melted	
	8	oz.	Flour	
3 qt.			Milk, hot	Make a white sauce.
	1½	oz.	Salt	Cool.
	½	t.	Pepper, white	
			Add	
24			Egg yolks, beaten	Mix well.
			Fold in	
24			Egg whites, beaten	
			Pour into 2 oiled pans 12 in. x 20 in.	

Bake approx. 45 min. 325°F.   Serving approx. 3 oz.

Note: Place a pan of water in the bottom of the oven. For Spanish Omelet serve with Spanish Sauce.

CHINESE OMELET

Amount	Ingredient	Method
1 qt.	White Sauce, No. III	
1 lb.	Add Cheese, ground	
24 1 t. 1½ oz. 1 t.	Add Egg yolks, beaten Mustard Salt Paprika	} Mixed.
2 lb.	Add Rice, raw	} Washed and steamed.
24	Fold in Egg whites, beaten Pour into 3 oiled pans.	

Bake 45 min. 325°F. Serving approx. 4 oz.

POTATO OMELET

Amount	Ingredient	Method
50	Bacon slices	Arrange bacon close together in meat pans and bake in oven until crisp. Remove from pans.
9 lb. (E.P.)	Add to bacon fat Potatoes, cooked, diced } Brown slightly. Remove to 2 baking pans 12 in. x 20 in. Pour over the potatoes.	
36 2 oz. 1 t. f. g. 3 qt.	Eggs, beaten Salt Pepper, white Cayenne Milk, hot	} Beaten until light.

Bake 1 hr. 325°F. Serving approx. ½ c.

NOTE: Lay the slices of crisp bacon on top of omelet when removed from oven. Serve at once.

DEVILED EGGS

Amount	Ingredient	Method
50	Eggs, hard cooked	Peel and cut in half lengthwise. Remove yolks and mash thoroughly.
1 c.	Add Milk, hot	} Mix.
1½ c. 1 T. ¾ T. ½ c.	Add Mayonnaise Salt Mustard, dry Vinegar	Mix thoroughly.
	Refill the whites with the mixture. Use approximately 1½ T. filling for each half of egg white.	

Note: 6 oz. of finely chopped celery or pimientos may be added to the yolk mixture.

HOT STUFFED EGGS

Amount	Ingredient	Method
50	Eggs, hard cooked	Cut eggs lengthwise and remove yolks.
3 oz. 2 t. ⅛ t. 1 T. 1 lb.	To the mashed yolks add Butter, melted Salt Cayenne Mustard, prepared Ham, minced	Mix thoroughly and refill the whites. Arrange in baking pans. Heat in steamer or slow oven.
1 gal.	Pour over eggs White Sauce No. III	
¼ c.	Sprinkle over the top Parsley, chopped	

Note: Serve on toast or en casserole. Tuna fish may be substituted for ham.

EGG-RICE CASSEROLE

Amount	Ingredient	Method
2 lb. 8 oz.	Rice	} Wash and cook until tender. Drain and wash.
	Add	
18	Eggs, hard cooked	} Chopped.
1 lb. 2 oz.	Cheese, grated	
1½ t.	Paprika	
2 oz.	Salt	
	Add	
3 oz.	Onion, minced	
6 oz.	Green pepper, minced	} Cooked together.
12 oz.	Oil or butter	
	Add	
3 qt.	Tomato purée	} Mix well.
	Dip with a No. 8 dipper into individual casseroles.	

Bake approx. 30 min. 350°F.   Yield fifty 5-oz. servings.
NOTE: When baked, garnish with grated cheese.

MUSHROOM-EGG CASSEROLE

Amount	Ingredient	Method
24	Eggs, hard cooked, sliced	
5 lb.	Celery, diced, cooked	
4 No. 1 cans (2 lb. fresh)	Mushrooms, chopped	} Mix.
6 oz.	Green pepper, chopped	
4 oz.	Pimiento, chopped	
1 No. 10 can or 5 lb. fresh	Peas	
1 oz.	Salt	
	Add and mix	
1½ qt.	Milk	
6 oz.	Butter	
4 oz.	Flour	} Made into white sauce.
1 T.	Salt	
½ t.	Pepper	
	Dip with a No. 8 dipper into individual casseroles. Serve hot garnished with four 2½-oz. cans fried noodles.	

Bake approx. 30 min. 350°F.   Yield approx. 50 servings (⅔ c.).

CORN PUDDING

Amount	Ingredient	Method
12 oz. 4 oz.	Bacon, chopped Pepper, green	} Fry until lightly browned.
	Add	
6 oz.	Flour	} Blend well.
	Add, while stirring	
2½ qt.	Milk	} Blend well.
	Add	
14 1½ oz. 1 t. 6 No. 2 cans 4 oz.	Eggs, beaten Salt Pepper Corn (cream style) Pimiento	} Mix well.

Measure with a No. 8 dipper into 50 custard cups. Place cups in pans of hot water. Bake 45 min. 325°F.

GOLDENROD TOAST

Amount	Ingredient	Method
3 qt. 1 qt. 1 lb. 8 oz. 1 oz.	Milk, hot Water, hot Butter, melted Flour Salt	} Make into a white sauce.
	Add	
50 35	Egg whites, hard cooked, chopped Egg yolks, hard cooked, chopped Serve on toasted bread and sprinkle the top with	
15	Egg yolks, riced	

PRUNE WHIP

Amount		Ingredient	Method
15		Egg whites, beat until stiff	} Combine.
	8 oz.	Sugar	
		Add	
2 lb.		Prunes	}Cook and pit.
		Add	
	2 T.	Lemon juice	
		Chill.	

Dip with No. 12 dipper. Yield 50 servings.

FROZEN FRUIT DESSERT

Amount			Ingredient	Method
	4		Egg whites, beaten	
1 lb.			Marshmallows, cut	
			Add	
	½ c.		Milk, hot	} Mix.
			Add	
	2		Lemons, juice	} Mix.
	1	t.	Mustard	
			When cold, pour over	
4 lb.	8	oz.	Cherries, Royal Anne, pitted, drained	
2 lb.	4	oz.	Pineapple, diced, drained	
			Fold in	
1 qt.			Cream, whipped	
			Add	
	12	oz.	Almonds, toasted, chopped	
			Pour into molds and freeze.	

Yield approx. 4½ qts.

BISQUE MOUSSE

Amount	Ingredient	Method
4 qt.	Cream, 40 per cent	} Whip until stiff.
	Fold in	
4 lb.	Peanut brittle, ground	
	Pour into 8 cold molds and freeze without stirring.	

Yield 8 qt.

Note: Peanut Brittle Fluff. Serve above mixture, without freezing, on angel food cake.

APRICOT BAVARIAN

Amount	Ingredient	Method
3 oz. 1 pt.	Gelatin Water, cold	} Sprinkle gelatin over water. Soak 5 min.
	Dissolve in	
1½ pt. 1 lb. 8 oz. 2 t.	Apricot juice Sugar Salt	} Heated to boiling point.
	Combine with	
3 pt. 3 T. 2 t.	Apricot juice Lemon juice Vanilla	
	When starting to congeal, whip until it doubles in bulk and fold in	
3 lb. (A.P.) 6 1 pt.	Apricots, dried, cooked, and sieved Egg whites, beaten stiff Cream, whipped	
	Mold or pour into flat pan and place in refrigerator. Serving approx. ½ c.	

PINEAPPLE BAVARIAN CREAM

Amount	Ingredient	Method
3 oz. 1 qt.	Gelatin Water, cold	} Soak 10 min.
	Add	
1 No. 10 can 1 lb. 12 oz.	Pineapple, crushed Sugar	} Heated to boiling point.
	Stir until gelatin is dissolved.	
	Add	
2 oz.	Lemon juice	
	Chill. When mixture begins to congeal, fold in	
1 qt.	Cream, heavy, whipped	
	Pour into 50 individual molds. Serving approx. 4 oz.	

Note: This may be used for pie filling.

ICE BOX CAKE

Amount			Ingredient	Method
3	lb.	8 oz.	Sugar	} Cream.
1	lb.	3 oz.	Butter	
			Add	
18			Egg yolks	} Cream.
			Add	
1½ qt.			Pineapple, crushed	
		1 c.	Cream	
			Cook in double boiler until thick.	
			Add	
		4 oz.	Nuts, chopped	
		3 oz.	Cherries, maraschino, chopped	
3	lb.	8 oz.	Wafers, vanilla	
			Place a thin layer of crushed wafers in the bottom of a pan 12 in. x 20 in., then fill pan with alternate thin layers of above mixture and crushed vanilla wafers. Serving approx. 3 oz.	

NOTE: Let stand in ice box over night. Serve with whipped cream.

VARIATIONS OF ICE BOX CAKE

Kind	Changes in Plain Recipe
Chocolate.......	For the filling use ⅔ of the Chocolate Chiffon Pie recipe in place of the pineapple filling. Lady fingers may be substituted for crushed wafers.
Lemon..........	For the filling use ⅔ of the Lemon Chiffon Pie recipe. Thin slices of Sponge Cake may be substituted for the wafers.
Prune...........	For the filling use the Sour Cream Pie recipe and substitute prunes for the raisins. Graham Crackers may be substituted for the wafers.
Pumpkin........	For the filling use ⅔ of the Pumpkin Chiffon Pie recipe. Ginger Snaps may be substituted for the wafers.
Caramel Nut....	For the filling use ¾ of the Caramel Blanc Mange recipe. 12 oz. of chopped nuts may be substituted for a part of the crushed wafers.

GRAHAM CRACKER CUSTARD

Amount		Ingredient	Method
1 lb.		Sugar	⎫
	⅔ t.	Salt	⎬ Beat until well blended.
12		Egg yolks	
	1 c.	Milk	⎭
		Add	
	1 pt.	Milk, scalded	
		Add	
	3 oz.	Gelatin	
	1½ pt.	Water, cold	
		Cool and add	
12		Egg whites, beaten	
	1½ pt.	Cream, whipped	
		Place a layer of crumb mixture on the bottom of pans, cover with custard, and place crumb mixture on top of custard.	

Crumb Mixture

Amount		Ingredient
	8 oz.	Butter, melted
	6 oz.	Sugar, brown
1 lb.		Graham crackers, crushed
	½ t.	Cinnamon
		Chill in 2 pans 9 x 14 in.

Yield 48 servings (small).

DATE ROLL

Amount		Ingredient	Method
2 lb.	8 oz.	Dates, chopped fine	⎫
2 lb.	8 oz.	Marshmallows, cut	⎬ Combine.
2 lb.	8 oz.	Crackers, graham, ground	
	8 oz.	Nuts, chopped	⎭
		Add	
	1 pt.	Milk	⎬ Mix well. Form into 4 rolls.
		Roll in powdered sugar.	
		Place in ice box for 24 hours.	
			Serving approx. 2½ oz.

Note: Cut in slices and serve with hard sauce or whipped cream.

CHRISTMAS PUDDING

Amount			Ingredient	Method
1 lb.	4	oz.	Carrots, raw grated	
1 lb.	11	oz.	Potatoes, raw grated	
1 lb.	4	oz.	Raisins	
1 lb.	4	oz.	Dates	Mix.
2 lb.			Sugar	
1 lb.			Butter, soft	
	12	oz.	Nuts, chopped	
			Add	
	1⅓ T.		Soda	
	1	T.	Cinnamon	
	1	T.	Cloves	Mixed.
	1	T.	Nutmeg	
	¼ t.		Salt	
1 lb.			Flour	

Measure with a No. 16 dipper. Fill oiled muffin tins.
Cover each filled tin with an empty tin.
Steam for ¾ to 1 hr. under pressure.
NOTE: Serve with vanilla sauce or hard sauce.

STEAMED PUDDING

Amount			Ingredient	Method
	2⅓ oz.		Butter	
1 lb.	3	oz.	Sugar	Cream.
	5		Eggs	
	2⅓ c.		Molasses	
			Add milk and flour mixture alternately.	
	2⅓ c.		Milk, sour	
	4½ oz.		Flour	
	1	T.	Soda	
	1	T.	Cloves	Mixed.
	1½ T.		Cinnamon	
1 lb.	14	oz.	Crumbs, bread	
			Add	
	12	oz.	Raisins	
	8	oz.	Nuts, chopped	
			Measure with a No. 16 dipper.	
			Place in oiled muffin tins. Cover.	

Steam 1 hr. under pressure.   Serving 2½ oz.

FIG. I.—The cheese tray presenting an assortment of both cheese and breads is increasing in popularity as a dessert dish.

FISH

Let us join chiming vowel with vowel
To rhapsodize fish, flesh and fowl.
— Louis Untermeyer.

PREPARATION AND COOKING OF FRESH FISH AND SHELL FISH

Fresh Fish

To Skin: Remove fins, cut off a narrow strip of skin down the full length of back. Cut skin around gills, loosen, and draw it off from one side of fish. To do this, pull gently with one hand and push with back of a knife held in the other hand. Repeat process on the other side of fish.

To Scale: Hold fish by the tail. Use a blunt knife to scrape over fish from tail to head. Wipe fish and knife occasionally to remove loosened scales.

To Dress: Split the underside of scaled or skinned fish and remove internal organs. Remove head. Wash inside and out, drain, and wipe dry.

To Bone: Run a sharp pointed knife close to the back bone beginning at tail and continuing the entire length of one side of fish. Remove flesh carefully from bones with knife and fingers. Repeat on the other side. (Fish that have been boned are usually stuffed and baked.)

Fish may be cooked in many ways but some methods are more suitable for certain varieties than for others. The table on page 116 will show not only the preferred cooking procedure but also the season for the various kinds of fish.

Boiled Fish

Cut fish into thick pieces. Use sufficient water to cover the fish. Add 2 t. salt and 2 T. of vinegar to each gallon of water. These give flavor and keep the flesh white and firm. Place fish in a frying

113

basket, and place in warm water. Bring to the boiling point; then reduce temperature, and simmer until fish separates from the bones. Allow 5 to 8 minutes per pound, according to thickness of fish. Serve boiled fish with a rich sauce.

Broiled Fish

Split fish down back and wipe as dry as possible. Sprinkle with salt and pepper. Place, skin side down, in a well-oiled broiler. Broil, turn skin side up just long enough to crisp and brown.

Fried Fish (I)

Leave small fish whole, cut large ones into servings. Sprinkle with salt and pepper; roll in flour or cornmeal and cook in a small amount of fat.

Fried Fish (II)

Prepare as Fried Fish I. Sprinkle with salt and pepper, then egg and crumb and fry in deep fat.

Shell Fish

Clams if purchased in the shell should be alive. Several hours before using place them in a tub of shallow water to which a small amount of cornmeal has been added to eliminate sand which may be lodged in the bodies of the clam. Wash the shells well and rinse if the clams are to be cooked in the shell. To remove the shells hold them in the palm of the hand and insert a slender strong knife in the muscle and pry open. The skin of the Razor and soft clam should be removed before cooking.

Crabs should be alive at the time they are cooked. In preparing soft-shell crabs, place them face down. The taper points of the shell are turned back about half way and the spongy substance which is found next to the shell is removed. The tail or apron is removed, the crab is thoroughly washed, and is then ready to cook. Soft-shell crabs are usually parboiled and then fried in butter.

In preparing hard-shell crabs, plunge them head first into rapidly boiling water to which salt or soda has been added: 1 T. salt to each gallon of water or 1 oz. soda to each 1½-lb. crab. Crabs are boiled in a covered container from 20 to 30 minutes, depending upon their size. After chilling in cold water the claws and apron of the crab are removed, the shells broken apart, and the spongy material removed from between the halves of the body and next the shell. Any orange-colored material is also discarded. The meat is removed from the back and cracked claws.

Lobsters should be alive when the cooking process begins. If the lobster is to be boiled, the live lobster is plunged head down in boiling salted water and allowed to cook 20 to 30 minutes. Crack the claws and lay the opened fish as flat as possible on the broiler, brush with butter, salt and pepper. The time for broiling varies with the size of the lobster, but the usual time is 20 to 25 minutes with shell side down, and 10 to 15 minutes on opposite side.

Oysters are not ordinarily washed before using. If washing is deemed necessary, care should be taken to remove the oysters from the water quickly so that they may not be soaked or water logged in the fresh water. They should be inspected and any bits of shell removed. Oysters should be cooked only until the edges begin to curl. When making oyster stew, sauté oysters in butter and add to hot milk. Serve at once.

Shrimps should be washed carefully. Cover with water. Simmer until tender in water to which 1 t. of salt to each quart has been added. Drain. Remove shell. Remove dark vein from the center back of each shrimp.

FISH, SHELL FISH, AND AMPHIBIANS

Name of Fish	Type	Methods of Cookery				Seasons Months (incl.)
		Baked	Boiled Steamed	Broiled	Fried	
Barracuda	Fat	Best		Good	Fair	Feb.–June
Bass, Black	Lean	Good		Good	Best	All year
Bass, Sea	Fat	Good		Best	Good	All year
Bluefish	Lean	Best		Good	Fair	May–Oct.
Bonito	Fat	Best		Good	Fair	June–Oct.
Catfish	Lean	Fair			Best	Apr.–Oct.
Clams, Long	Lean	Good	Best		Good	All year
Clams, Razor	Lean	Usually minced and canned				
Cod	Lean	Best	Fair	Good	Good	Best in Oct. and Dec.
Crabs, Blue					Fried in batter after parboiling	May–Oct.
Crabs, Hard Shell			Best			Nov.–June
Flounder	Lean	Good		Good	Best	All year
Frogs	Fat	Good			Best	June–Oct.
Haddock	Lean	Good	Fair	Best	Good	All year
Halibut	Fat	Good	Fair	Best	Good	All year (West)
Herring	Fat	Fair		Best	Good	All year (Alaska) Apr.–Nov. (Atlantic) Dec.–Apr. (Calif.)
Kingfish	Lean	Good	Fair	Best		Jan.–June
Lobster	Lean		Good	Best		All year
Mackerel	Fat	Good	Fair	Best		Apr.–Nov.
Oysters	Lean	Fair	Good		Best	Sept.–Apr.
Pickerel	Lean	Good		Fair	Best	All year
Pike	Lean	Good		Fair	Best	All year
Pompano	Fat	Good		Best	Fair	All year
Salmon	Fat	Best	Fair	Good		May–Nov.
Scallops	Lean			Good	Best	Sept.–Apr.
Shad	Lean		Best		Good	All year
Shrimp	Lean		Best		Good	All year
Smelts	Fat			Good	Best	Sept.–May
Snapper, Red	Lean	Best	Good	Good		All year
Sole	Lean	Fair		Good	Best	All year
Sturgeon	Lean	Best		Good		Mar.–June
Swordfish	Lean	Good		Best		July–Sept.
Trout	Lean	Fair		Good	Best	Apr.–Nov.
Tuna	Fat	Best	Good	Good		Mar.–Dec.
Whitefish	Fat	Best		Good	Fair	Apr.–Dec.
Whiting	Lean		Good	Good	Best	Summer

BAKED HALIBUT

Amount	Ingredient	Method
15 lb.	Halibut	} Cut into 50 steaks.
	Dip each steak in	
1 lb.	Butter, melted	
1 T.	Salt	
1 t.	Pepper, white	} Mixed.
4 oz.	Lemon juice	
1 T.	Onion juice	
	Dredge with	
14 oz.	Flour	
	Place close together in oiled baking pan.	
	Pour over the top 2 oz. of melted butter in ¾ c. milk.	

Bake approx. 20 min. 400°F.

STUFFED HADDOCK

Amount	Ingredient	Method
20 lb.	Haddock	} Dress fish. Leave whole. Wash and dry inside. Sprinkle with salt and pepper, inside and outside.
	Stuff and sew or fasten with skewers. Dredge with flour. Place in baking pan in which has been arranged	
1 lb.	Salt pork, sliced	
8	Bay leaves	
1 T.	Cloves	
	Baste with hot water every 15 min.	

Bake approx. 1½ hr. 350°F.

BAKED SCALLOPS AND MUSHROOMS

Amount	Ingredient	Method
2 lb.	Mushrooms, fresh, sliced	
2 oz.	Brown in Butter	
6 lb.	Add Scallops	} Cooked until tender in their juice and 2 oz. butter.
4 qt.	Divide evenly into 50 casseroles. Fill casseroles with White Sauce No. III Cover with buttered crumbs.	

Bake 30 min. 350°F.
Note: 10 lb. sweetbreads (parboiled and membranes removed) diced may be used in place of scallops.

SALMON AND POTATO CHIP CASSEROLE

Amount	Ingredient	Method
6 1-lb. cans 2 lb.	Salmon, flaked Potato chips, crushed	} Save ½ lb. for topping.
6 10-oz. cans 6 oz. 4 oz.	Add Cream of Mushroom Soup Butter Flour	} Made into a sauce.
	Mix well. Pour into casserole. Cover with crushed potato chips.	

Bake 20 min. 375°F.

CASSEROLE OF RICE AND TUNA

Amount	Ingredient	Method
1 lb. 1 oz.	Rice Salt Drain and wash.	} Wash and cook in 8 qt. of boiling water until tender.
4 qt. 6 13-oz. cans	Add White Sauce No. III Tuna fish, flaked	} Mix carefully.
	Pour into a pan 12 in. x 20 in. Sprinkle over the rice and tuna	
9 oz. 4 oz.	Crumbs Butter	} Mixed.

Bake approx. 45 min. 300°F.   Serving approx. 4 oz.

SCALLOPED OYSTERS

Amount	Ingredient	Method
3 qt.	Cracker crumbs	
1 lb.	Butter, melted	
1 oz.	Salt	Mix.
½ t.	Paprika	
½ t.	Pepper	
6 qt.	Oysters	Drain and remove any bits of shell.

Spread ⅓ of the crumbs over the bottom of an oiled baking pan 12 in. x 20 in. Cover with ½ of the oysters; repeat with crumbs and oysters.

		Pour over the top of oysters
1 qt.	Milk or cream	
1½ pt.	Oyster liquor or water	
	Cover with remaining crumbs.	

Bake 30 min. 350°F.
NOTE: Two cups of finely chopped celery may be added for variety.

DEVILED CRAB

Amount	Ingredient	Method
12 6½-oz. cans	Crab meat, flaked	
	Add	
4 T.	Lemon juice	
1 oz.	Salt	
2 t.	Pepper	
f. g.	Cayenne	Mix.
5	Eggs, beaten	
1 T.	Worcestershire sauce	
	Add	
12 oz.	Butter	
2 qt.	Milk	
6 oz.	Flour	Made into a white sauce.
1½ t.	Mustard, prepared	
	Mix well; fill ramekins and cover with	
1 qt.	Crumbs, buttered	

Bake 15 min. 400°F.

CREOLE SHRIMP WITH RICE

Amount	Ingredient	Method
6 oz.	Onions, chopped	
12 oz.	Celery, chopped	
	Brown in	
3 oz.	Fat	
	Add	
3 T.	Flour	
1 oz.	Salt	} Cook 15 min.
1 pt.	Water	
	Add	
1½ qt.	Tomatoes	
6 T.	Vinegar	
2 T.	Sugar	
3 lb.	Shrimp, fresh	} Keep hot.
4 lb. 8 oz.	Rice, cooked	} Keep hot.
	Serve rice with No. 12 dipper. Place 1 oz. shrimp on rice. Top each serving with sauce.	

SALMON LOAF

Amount	Ingredient	Method
2½ c.	Milk	} Heat to boiling point.
	Add	
12 oz.	Bread cubes, soft	} Mix well.
	Add	
6 1-lb. cans	Salmon	
1 T.	Salt	
½ t.	Paprika	
2	Lemon rinds, grated	} Mix.
½ c.	Lemon juice	
6 oz.	Butter, melted	
12	Egg yolks, beaten	
	Fold in	
12	Egg whites, beaten	
	Form into 4 loaves approx. 4 in. x 9 in.	

Bake 1 hr. 15 min. 325°F. Serving approx. 3½ oz.

CODFISH BALLS

AMOUNT	INGREDIENT	METHOD
5 lb. (A.P.)	Potatoes	} Cook and mash.
	Add	
5 lb.	Codfish, salt	} Cooked until tender and boned.
2½ oz.	Fat	
10	Eggs, beaten	
	Form into balls 1½ in. in diameter. Bread and fry. Serving 2 balls.	

NOTE: If codfish is very salty some soaking may be needed. Serve with White Sauce No. II to which 2 oz. of pimiento has been added.

TUNA FISH AND NOODLES

AMOUNT	INGREDIENT	METHOD
1 lb. 12 oz.	Noodles	} Cook, drain, and wash.
	Add	
6 13-oz. cans	Tuna fish, flaked	
	Add	
2 qt.	Milk	
1 oz.	Salt	} Made into a white sauce.
4 oz.	Flour	
8 oz.	Butter	
	Place in baking pan 12 in. x 20 in. Bake 30 min. Sprinkle over the top	
1 lb.	Cheese, ground (Bake 15 min. longer)	

Baking temp. 300°F.

TUNA FISH RAREBIT

AMOUNT	INGREDIENT	METHOD
5 13-oz. cans	Tuna fish, flaked	
	Mix with	
9 oz.	Butter	
6 oz.	Flour	
3 qt.	Milk	} Make a white sauce.
1 T.	Salt	
f. g.	Cayenne	
	Add	
1 lb. 8 oz.	Cheese, ground	} Cook over hot water until cheese is melted.
	Serve with No. 12 dipper on toasted bun.	

CREAMED TUNA FISH

Amount		Ingredient	Method
12 oz.		Butter, melted	Make a white sauce.
7 oz.		Flour	
3¾ qt.		Milk	
		When thickened, add	
6 T.		Worcestershire Sauce (may omit)	
¼ t.		Cayenne	
1 T.		Salt	
		Add	
9		Eggs, hard cooked, chopped	
6 oz.		Green pepper, chopped	
6 oz.		Pimiento, chopped	
		When ready to serve pour over	
6 13-oz. cans		Tuna fish, flaked, hot	
			Serving approx. 4 oz.

Note: Serve on toast.
Other cooked fish may be substituted for tuna.

LOBSTER À LA NEWBURG

Amount		Ingredient	Method
12 oz.		Butter, hot	
		Add	
12 6½-oz. cans		Lobster meat, diced	Cook slowly 10 min.
		Add	
3 oz.		Flour	Mix well.
2 t.		Salt	
		Add	
1½ qt.		Cream, 20 per cent, hot	Stir constantly. Cook until sauce thickens.
		Add	
1¾ c.		Egg yolks, beaten	Cook 1 min. but do not boil.
		Serve at once.	

FROSTINGS AND FILLINGS

Were it as easy to cook, as to tell how to cook, and a wish
were a dish, we could dine from our book.

—ANON.

BOILED FROSTING

AMOUNT	INGREDIENT	METHOD
4 lb. 2½ c.	Sugar Water, hot	Stir until sugar is dissolved. Boil without stirring to 238°F. or soft ball stage.
8	While beating, pour gradually over Egg whites, beaten Continue beating until frosting is of consistency to spread.	
2 T.	Add Vanilla Spread on cake at once. Yield approx. 4½ qt.	

FLUFFY FROSTING

AMOUNT	INGREDIENT	METHOD
2 lb. 8 oz. 1½ c. 5 T. ¼ t.	Sugar Water Corn sirup Salt	Boil together until mixture reaches the soft ball stage (238°F.).
10	Add ½ of the mixture to Egg whites, beaten	Stirring constantly.
	Add Remainder of sirup mixture	Cooked until it forms a hard ball (250°F.).
	Beat until it holds its shape.	
1 T.	Add Vanilla Yield 4¼ qt.	

PLAIN POWDERED SUGAR FROSTING

Amount	Ingredient	Method
2 lb.	Sugar, powdered, sifted	
	Gradually add	
¾ c.	Water, boiling	} Beat until right consistency to spread.
	Add	
2 t.	Vanilla	
		Yield approx. 4 c.

COCOA-MOCHA FROSTING

Amount	Ingredient	Method
1 c.	Coffee infusion	} Mix together and bring to the
2 oz.	Butter	boiling point.
	Add	
3 oz.	Cocoa	} Mix well.
	Add	
½ t.	Salt	
2 lb.	Sugar, powdered	} Mix until smooth.
½ t.	Vanilla	
		Yield approx. 4 c.

Note: Add more sugar if necessary to make frosting hold its shape.

QUICK FROSTING

Amount	Ingredient	Method
6	Egg whites, unbeaten	
1½ c.	Corn sirup	
2 t.	Vanilla	

Mix and beat with electric beater until mixture will hold its shape, approx. 15 min. on second speed.

Yield approx. 7 c.

ICE CREAM FROSTING

Amount		Ingredient	Method
18		Egg whites, beaten	⎱ Combine. Beat until the con-
	6 oz.	Sugar, powdered	⎰ sistency of meringue.
		Add slowly	
3 lb.		Sugar, granulated	⎱ Combine and boil until it spins
1 pt.		Water, hot	⎰ a 3-in. thread (238°F.).
		Beat until mixture is thick and creamy.	
		Add	
	13 oz.	Sugar, powdered, sifted	
	2 T.	Vanilla	
			Yield approx. 2 gal.

NOTE: Add more powdered sugar if necessary to make frosting hold its shape when spread. Can be kept several days in ice box.

ORANGE FROSTING

Amount		Ingredient	Method
1 lb.	12 oz.	Sugar, powdered, sifted ⎱	
	2 T.	Orange peel, grated	
	3 oz.	Orange juice	⎰ Beat together.
	1 oz.	Lemon juice	
	4	Egg yolks ⎰	
			Yield approx. 1 qt.

NOTE: If necessary add more sugar for the proper consistency.

CARAMEL FROSTING

Amount		Ingredient	Method
2 lb.	4 oz.	Sugar, light brown	⎱ Place over low flame and stir constantly until sugar is dissolved and mixture boils.
	1¼ c.	Water, hot	Continue cooking until mixture forms a medium ball (240°F.).
	6	Pour sirup in fine stream over Egg whites, beaten Continue beating until cold and stiff enough to spread on cake.	
		Add	
	1 t.	Vanilla	
			Yield 2½ qt.

BUTTER CREAM

Amount	Ingredient	Method
1 lb. 5	Sugar, powdered Eggs	} Mix. Place on stove. Cook and beat until lukewarm.
1 lb.	Remove from stove and add Butter, unsalted, creamed Mix well.	
		Yield approx. 1 qt.

Note: Make several hours before using. May be used as frosting for petits fours.

CHOCOLATE BUTTER CREAM

Amount		Ingredient	Method
2 lb. 1 lb.		Butter, unsalted Fat	} Cream until light and fluffy.
	9 oz.	Add Milk, condensed	} Mix well.
2 lb.	8 oz.	Add Sugar, powdered	} Mix well.
	8 oz. 1 t.	Add Chocolate, unsweetened, melted Vanilla	
		Yield: Frosting for 48 cakes 2½ in. x 4 in.	

Note: Keep in a cool place.

LADY BALTIMORE FILLING

Amount		Ingredient	Method
	1 t. 1½ T. 7 oz. 4½ oz. 5 oz.	Orange juice Lemon juice Cherries, candied Macaroon crumbs Almonds, chopped	} Combine.
1¾ qt.		Add Boiled Frosting, Blend and spread between layers for cake.	
		Yield 1⅞ qt.	

CUSTARD FILLING

Amount		Ingredient	Method
	6 oz.	Cornstarch	
1 lb.		Sugar	} Mix.
	½ t.	Salt	
		Add	
	1 pt.	Milk, cold	} Stir until smooth.
		Add	
	2½ qt.	Milk, hot	} Stirring constantly.
		Cook over water until thick.	
		Add	
	6	Eggs, beaten	} Mix thoroughly. Cook 7 min.
		Remove from fire, add	
	2 t.	Vanilla	
			Yield approx. 3 qt.

NOTE: Use as a filling for cream puffs or Washington Cream Pie.

DATE FILLING

Amount		Ingredient	Method
2 lb.	(A.P.)	Dates or figs, chopped	
	2¼ c.	Water	} Cook until mixture is thick.
	12 oz.	Sugar	

NOTE: Cool and spread on cookies, or use as a cake filling. ½ c. jelly or ¼ c. orange juice may be added to filling.

PRUNE FILLING

Amount		Ingredient	Method
1 lb.		Sugar	
	4	Eggs, well beaten	
	1 c.	Sour cream	
	½ t.	Salt	
	2 oz.	Butter	
	1 oz.	Flour	
1 pt.		Prunes, cooked, chopped	
		Mix and cook in a double boiler.	
			Yield approx. 1 qt.

MEAT

The turnpike road to people's hearts I find
Lies through their mouths or I mistake mankind.
　　　　　　　　　　—DE WOLCOTT.

The following material is a report[1] of methods of cookery regarded by investigators in the field as suited to the various retail and wholesale cuts of meat.

BEEF*

	Retail Cut	Whole-sale Cut	Cooking	
			1st Method	2nd Method
I. Hindquarter				
1. *Round*.....	Hind shank	Round	Simmer	Stew
	Heel of round	"	Braise	Simmer
	Round steak	"	"	Fry
	Top round (steak)	"	"	Broil
	Bottom round	"	"	Fry
	Eye of round	"	"	Braise
	Sirloin tips steak	"	"	Broil
	Rump roast	"	"	Roast
	Rump roast (boned)	"	"	"
	Dried beef sets	"	Creamed chipped beef	
2. *Loin*..:.....	Butt end sirloin	Loin	Broil	Panbroil
	Wedgebone sirloin	"	"	"
	Round bone sirloin	"	"	"
	Double bone sirloin	"	"	"
	Hip bone sirloin	"	"	"
	Sirloin roast	"	Roast	Braise
	Sirloin butt	"	"	"
	Porterhouse or T-bone	"	Broil	Panbroil
	Tenderloin steak	"	"	"
	Club steak	"	"	"
3. *Flank*.....	Flank steak	Flank	Braise	Stew
	Flank steak fillet	"	"	Fry
	Flank, cubed	"	"	Stew

[1] Unpublished material, Home Economics laboratory manual. Courtesy D. L. Mackintosh, Dept. Animal Husbandry, K. S. C.

BEEF (continued)

Retail Cut	Whole-sale Cut	Cooking 1st Method	Cooking 2nd Method
II. Forequarter			
1. *Ribs* ...... Rib roast—1st cut (11–12 rib)	Rib	Roast	Roast
Rib roast—2nd cut (8–9–10 rib)	"	"	"
Rib roast—3rd cut (6–7 rib) or blade roast	"	"	"
Rib steak	"	Broil	Panbroil
2. *Chuck* ...... Chuck rib	Chuck	Braise	Roast
Cross arm or shoulder arm	"	"	Braise
Chuck rib steak	"	"	Fry
Cross arm steak	"	"	Braise
Top chuck	"	"	Simmer
Knuckle	"	Simmer	"
Neck	"	"	Stew
Inside roll	"	Roast	Braise
Outside roll	"	Braise	Roast
Ground beef (hamburger)	"	Panbroil	Fry
3. *Plate* ...... Rolled plate	Plate	Braise	Braise
Plate pot roast	"	"	Simmer
Skirt fillets	"	"	Fry
Short ribs	"	"	Simmer
4. *Brisket* ..... Fresh brisket	Brisket	Simmer	Braise
Boned brisket	"	"	"
Corned brisket	"	"	Simmer
5. *Shank* ..... Fore shank	Shank	"	"
Specialties .... Kidney†	Special-ties	Braise (stew)	Broil
Brains†	"	Fry	Braise
Heart	"	Braise	Simmer
Liver	"	Fry	Braise
Tongue	"	Simmer	Simmer
Plain tripe†	"	"	"
Honeycomb tripe†	"	"	"
Sweetbreads†	"		
Pancreas	"	Fry	Braise
Thymus	"	"	"

* Cooking methods are suggested for meat grading good or higher (U. S. Standard).
† Preliminary preparation may be desirable before using the suggested methods of cooking, i.e., sweetbreads are parboiled; kidneys and brains are soaked in salt water. Fancy meats, meat specialties, sundries, and offal products are synonymous terms.

VEAL

	RETAIL CUT	WHOLESALE CUT	COOKING	
			1ST METHOD	2ND METHOD
I. Hind Saddle				
1. *Round*.....	Hind shank	Leg	Simmer	Stew
	Veal cutlets	"	Braise	Fry
	Rump	"	Roast	Braise
	Heel of veal	"	Braise	Simmer
2. *Loin*......	Loin end chop	Loin	"	Fry
	Center loin chop	"	"	"
	Kidney veal chop	"	"	"
	Loin roast	"	Roast	Braise
3. *Flank*.....	Cubed	Flank	Braise	Stew
II. Fore Saddle				
1. *Ribs—Rack*	Rib chop	Rib	Braise	Fry
	Rib roast	"	Roast	Braise
2. *Shoulder*...	Blade shoulder	Shoulder	"	"
	Shoulder arm	"	"	"
	Blade shoulder chop	"	Braise	Fry
	Shoulder arm chop	"	"	"
	Neck	"	Simmer	Braise
3. *Breast*.....	Breast cubed	Breast	Stew	"
	Breast rolled	"	Braise	Roast
4. *Shank*.....	Fore shank	Shank	Simmer	Simmer
	Ground veal (meat loaf)	Shank Trimmings	Bake	Braise
*Meat specialties**..	Kidney	Specialties	Braise (stew)	Broil
	Brains	"	Fry	Braise
	Heart	"	Braise	Simmer
	Liver	"	Broil	Fry
	Tongue	"	Simmer	Simmer
	Tripe	"	"	"
	Sweetbreads	"	Fry	Braise

* See note for beef specialties.

LAMB

	Retail Cut	Wholesale Cut	Cooking	
			1st Method	2nd Method
I. Saddle				
1. *Leg*.......	Leg	Leg	Roast	Roast
	Leg slice	"	Broil	Panbroil
2. *Loin*.......	Loin end roll	Loin	Roast	Roast
	Center loin	"	"	"
	Loin end chop	"	Broil	Panbroil
	Center loin chop	"	"	"
	English loin chop	"	"	"
	English kidney chop	"	"	"
3. *Flank*.....	Rolled flank (with breast)	Flank	Roast	Braise
II. Rack				
1. *Hotel Rack*.	Rib roast	Hotel rack	Roast	Roast
	Crown rib roast	" "	"	"
	Rib chop	" "	Broil	Panbroil
	Frenched lamb chop	" "	"	"
2. *Shoulder* ...	Cushion style shoulder	Shoulder	Roast	Roast
	Rolled shoulder	"	"	"
	Blade chop	"	Broil	Braise
	Shoulder arm chop	"	"	"
	Mock duck	Shoulder & breast	Roast	
	Saratoga roll	Shoulder	"	Roast
	Saratoga chop	"	Broil	Panbroil
	Neck slices	"	Braise	Stew
3. *Breast*.....	Breast, cubed	Breast	Stew	"
	Breast, rolled	"	Roast	Braise
	Lamb shanks	"	Braise	"
	Ground lamb (patties)	Trimmings	Broil	Panbroil
*Meat Specialties**..	Kidney	Specialties	Panbroil	Stew
	Brains	"	Fry	Braise
	Heart	"	Braise	Bake
	Liver	"	"	Fry
	Tongue	"	Simmer	Simmer

* See note for beef specialties.

PORK

RETAIL CUT	WHOLESALE CUT	COOKING	
		1ST METHOD	2ND METHOD
Fresh			
1. *Feet* . . . . Feet	Feet	Simmer	Simmer
2. *Ham* . . . . Ham	Ham	Roast	Roast
Fresh ham hock	"	Simmer	Bake
Center cut	"	Roast	Roast
Ham butt	"	"	"
Center slice	"	Braise	Bake
Ham butt slice	"	"	"
Cured			
Hock	Hock	Simmer	"
Ham	Ham	Roast	Simmer
Center cut ham	"	"	Braise
Ham butt	"	"	Simmer
Center slice	"	Broil	Panbroil
Ham butt slice	"	"	"
Ham shank	"	Simmer	Bake
3. *Loin* . . . . Blade end chop	Loin	Braise	Fry
Rib chop	"	"	"
Center loin chop	"	"	"
Loin end chop	"	"	"
Shoulder end roast	"	Roast	Roast
Rib roast	"	"	"
Center loin roast	"	"	"
Loin end roast	"	"	"
Tenderloin	"	"	Braise
4. *Fresh side* . . . . . Fresh side pork	Side	Panbroil	Fry
Cured bacon	Bacon	Broil	Panbroil
Bacon brisket	"	Panbroil	Broil
Dry salt belly	brisket Belly	"	"
5. *Fat back* . . . . . . Dry salt fat back	Fat back	"	"
6. *Spare ribs* . . . . . Spare ribs	Spare ribs	Braise	Simmer
Spare ribs (cured or smoked)	" "	"	"
7. *Shoulder* . . . . *Fresh*			
Shoulder	Shoulder	Roast	Roast
Picnic	"	"	"
Shoulder slices	"	Braise	Fry
Shoulder roast	"	Roast	Roast
Boston butt	Boston butt	"	"
Boston butt chop	" "	Braise	Fry
Neck bones	Neck bones	Simmer	Braise
Pork shoulder hock	Hock	"	"
Cured			
Picnic	Picnic	Roast	Simmer

PORK (continued)

	RETAIL CUT	WHOLESALE CUT	COOKING	
			1ST METHOD	2ND METHOD
	Picnic slices	Picnic	Braise	Fry
	Cottage roll	Cottage roll	Bake	Simmer
	Smoked pork shoulder hock	Hock	Simmer	"
8. *Clear plate*.....	Clear plate (dry salt)	Clear plate	Panbroil	Broil
9. *Head*.........	Pork cutlets	Cutlet	Braise	Fry
	Bacon square	Bacon sq're	Broil	Panbroil
	Ground pork (sausage)	Trimmings	Fry	"
Meat specialties*..	Kidney	Specialties	Braise	Stew
	Brains	"	Broil	Fry
	Heart	"	Bake	Braise
	Liver	"	Fry	"
	Tongue	"	Simmer	Simmer

* See note for beef specialties.

Meat when delivered should be unwrapped and stored at a temperature of 1° to 2°C. (33° to 36°F.) with a relative humidity of 80 to 90 per cent. Temperature should not fall below freezing, unless frozen meat is being stored.

A low temperature in meat cookery, regardless of the method, is desirable for the greater part of the cooking period, since a high temperature over a long period of time toughens protein and results in large shrinkage losses. The method of cookery is ordinarily determined by the amount of connective tissue in the meat.

INTERNAL TEMPERATURES* FOR VARYING DEGREES OF DONENESS IN ROASTS

Meat	Degree of Doneness	Temperature		Time per Pound (approx.) Minutes
		Degrees C.	Degrees F.	
Beef..............	Rare	54 to 60	130 to 140	16
	Medium done	66 to 71	145 to 155	22
	Well done	77 to 82	160 to 170	30
Veal..............	Well done	74	165 to 175	20 to 25
Lamb..............	Well done	82	180	30 to 35
Pork, fresh........	Well done	85	185	30
Pork, mild cured...	Well done	71	160 to 170	18

* Determined by the use of a meat thermometer.

The methods of cooking meat are classified as (1) those using dry heat, including roasting, broiling, and panbroiling, and (2) those using moist heat, including braising, stewing, and cooking in water. Tender cuts are cooked by dry heat and the less tender are more successfully prepared by the use of moist heat.

Broiled Steak

Steaks, in institutions, are usually broiled in a special broiler or salamander. If a broiling oven is used it should be preheated to a temperature of 177°C. (350°F.) and the steaks placed on a rack 2 to 3 inches from tip of gas flame or from electric unit. A 1-inch steak or chop is placed 2 inches from the heat; a 2-inch steak or chop is placed 3 inches from the heat. Steaks are browned on one side, seasoned, turned and browned on the opposite side and cooked to the desired degree of doneness. For a steak 2 inches thick this will require approximately 9 to 10 minutes' cooking on each side. The meat should be turned only once.

SPANISH MEAT BALLS

Amount			Ingredient	Method
12 lb.			Meat, ground	
12			Eggs, beaten	
	1		Onion, small	Combine. Measure with No. 8
	1½ oz.		Salt	dipper and form into balls.
1 lb.	2	oz.	Rice, partially cooked	Place in covered roaster.
1 lb.			Potatoes, mashed	
	4	oz.	Pepper, green	
			Pour over balls	
3 qt.			Tomato purée	Mixed.
2 qt.			Water	
				Serving approx. 4 oz.

Cook approx. 2½ hr. 300°F.

CREAMED DRIED BEEF

Amount	Ingredient	Method
2 lb.	Beef, dried, chipped, freshened	
	Add	
5 qt.	White Sauce No. III	

Note: Serve on toast or with baked potato.

CREAMED BEEF ON TOAST

Amount	Ingredient	Method
9 lb.	Beef, ground	Cook beef in own fat, in heavy pan.
	Add	
1	Onion, small, chopped. (May omit.)	
	Add	
3 pt.	Stock, hot	
3 pt.	Milk, hot	
6 oz.	Flour	Made as white sauce.
12 oz.	Butter, melted	
2 oz.	Salt	

Note: Serve on toast.

BRAISED TONGUE

Amount	Ingredient	Method
14 lb.	Tongue	Wash tongues. Cook until tender. Remove skin.
	Place in pan, add	
4 oz.	Onions	
5 oz.	Carrots	Diced fine.
4 oz.	Celery	
	Add	
3 qt.	Broth, hot	
10 oz.	Butter, melted	
5 oz.	Flour	Made as white sauce.
2 oz.	Salt	
2 t.	Pepper	
	Let simmer 2 hr., turning meat occasionally. Serving approx. 2 oz.	

NOTE: Cut the tongue into thin slices. Pour the sauce over slices and serve.

BRAISED LIVER

Amount	Ingredient	Method
10 lb.	Liver, sliced, 5/1	
	Dredge with	
8 oz.	Flour	
2 oz.	Salt	Mixed.
2 t.	Pepper	
	Brown liver in	
1 lb. 8 oz.	Fat, hot	
	Place in a roaster, cover with Spanish Sauce, and cook until tender.	

Cook approx. 1½ hr. 300°F.   Serving approx. 3½ oz.

VEAL CHOPS BAKED WITH SOUR CREAM

Amount	Ingredient	Method
50 (approx. 18 lb.)	Veal chops, cut ¾ in. thick	
8 oz.	Pound, then dredge with Flour	
2 oz.	Salt	} Mixed.
1 t.	Pepper	
1 lb. 8 oz.	Brown in Fat, hot Remove to a roaster.	
2 qt.	Add Cream, heavy, sour	} Mixed.
2 qt.	Water	

Bake approx. 2 hr. 250°F.
NOTE: Either sweet or sour cream may be used. Veal steak may be substituted for chops.

BREADED VEAL

Amount	Ingredient	Method
13½ lb.	Veal, round, sliced	} Bone. Trim. Cut into 50 equal servings.
8 oz.	Dredge each piece in Flour	} Mixed.
2 oz.	Salt	
1 c.	Egg and crumb using Milk	
6	Eggs	
1 lb.	Crumbs, fine	
1 lb. 8 oz.	Brown in Fat, hot Place on a rack in a covered roaster.	

Cook 2 hr. 250°F.

MOCK DRUM STICKS

Amount	Ingredient	Method
10 lb. 7 lb. 50	Veal, 1 in. thick Pork, loin, 1 in. thick Skewers	Cut meat into cubes and place on skewers, alternating the veal and pork. 2 pieces pork and 3 of veal on each skewer.
	Dredge in	
8 oz. 2 oz.	Flour Salt	Mixed.
	Egg and crumb using	
1 c. 6 1 lb. 4 oz.	Milk Eggs Crumbs, bread	
	Brown in	
1 lb.	Fat, hot Place on a rack in covered roaster.	

Cook approx. 1½ hr. 300°F.   Serving approx. 5 oz.

NOTE: A fresh mushroom may be placed at each end of skewer before cooking.

VEAL PATTIES

Amount	Ingredient	Method
10 lb. 2 lb. 6 oz. 10 2 oz. 2 t. 1 oz. 1 c.	Veal, ground Salt pork, ground Crumbs, bread Eggs, beaten Salt Pepper Onion, grated Milk	Mix.
	Measure with a No. 10 dipper. Form into patties.	

Bake approx. 30 min. 350°F.

NOTE: Wrap with a strip of bacon and fasten with a toothpick if desired.

For Lamb Patties:

12 lb. ground lamb shoulder meat; 2 oz. salt; 1 t. pepper. Wrap with bacon strips. Broil 18 min.

For stuffed meat cakes:

Place a thin slice of onion and tomato between 2 thin meat patties. Press edges together and fasten with a toothpick. Broil.

VEAL BIRDS

Amount	Ingredient	Method
12½ lb.	Veal, round, ¼ in. thick	Remove bone, trim, cut into 50 oblong pieces.
		(1) Spread one oz. of stuffing on each piece of meat. ¼ recipe, p. 171.
		(2) Roll and skewer each with a round toothpick.
		(3) Roll each piece in
8 oz.	Flour	Mixed.
2 oz.	Salt	
	Brown in	
1 lb. 8 oz.	Fat, hot	
	Add	
1 qt.	Water	
	Place on a rack in a covered roaster.	
	Cook until tender.	

Cook 2½ hr. 300°F.

Note: Pork tenderloin may be substituted for veal.

VEAL SOUFFLÉ

Amount	Ingredient	Method
4 qt.	Milk, scalded	Make a white sauce.
2 oz.	Butter, melted	
4 oz.	Flour	
2 oz.	Salt	
½ t.	Pepper, white	
	Add in order given	
1 lb. 4 oz.	Bread, cubed	
24	Egg yolks, beaten	
6 lb.	Veal, cooked, minced	
	Fold in	
24	Egg whites, stiffly beaten	
	Pour into 3 oiled pans 9 in. x 14 in. Cook over water in oven.	

Bake 45 to 55 min. 325°F.   Serving ½ c.

Note: Serve with Béchamel Sauce or Pimiento White Sauce. Chicken or fish may be used in place of veal.

VEAL FRICASSEE

Amount	Ingredient	Method
15 lb.	Veal, breast or shoulder } Cut into 1-in. cubes.	
8 oz.	Dredge in Flour	
1 lb.	Brown floured veal in Salt Pork	
4 qt. 2 oz.	Add Water Salt	

Let simmer 2 hr. or until meat is tender.

NOTE: Curried veal may be made by adding 1 oz. of curry powder when water
is added.

VEAL STEW WITH VEGETABLES

Amount	Ingredient	Method
10 lb.	Veal } Cut into 1-in. cubes. Place in kettle and add	
3 qt.	Water } Cover and let simmer 1 hr.	
1 lb. 4 oz. 4 oz. 2 oz. 1 t.	Add Carrots Onions Celery Salt Pepper	Let simmer for 1½ hr. or until meat is tender.
5 oz.	Add Flour, made into a paste Cook until gravy is thickened.	

SWEETBREAD CUTLETS

Amount	Ingredient	Method
10 lb. (A. P.)	Sweetbreads	Soak 30 min. in cold water. Boil gently in acidulated water (2 T. vinegar, 1 t. salt to 1½ qt. water).
	Add	
8 oz.	Mushrooms, chopped	
2 oz.	Salt	
1 t.	Pepper	
5 T.	Lemon juice	
½ t.	Nutmeg	
	Add	
2 qt.	White Sauce No. IV	Mix well.
8	Eggs, slightly beaten	
	Dip with a No. 12 dipper. When cool, shape, egg, and crumb. Chill until firm.	

Fry in deep fat 3 to 4 min. 375°F.
Note: Cutlets should be held at room temperature at least 30 min. before frying.
Cutlets may be served on toast points with Hollandaise Sauce.
Cooked chicken may be used in place of sweetbreads.

PORK AND NOODLE CASSEROLE

Amount	Ingredient	Method
8 lb.	Pork shoulder, diced	Brown together.
12 oz.	Onion, chopped	
	Add	
8 qt.	Water	Cook until tender. Add more water if necessary.
2 oz.	Salt	
	Add	
2 lb.	Noodles, cooked	
	Place in casseroles.	

Bake approx. 30 min. 350°F. Serving approx. 4 oz.
Note: Chicken may be substituted for pork.

PORK CHOPS WITH STUFFING

Amount	Ingredient	Method
12½ lb.	Pork chops, 4/1	
8 oz.	Brown chops in Fat, hot	
2 oz.	Arrange chops in roaster. Sprinkle over chops Salt	
3 qt.	Place 2 oz. stuffing on each chop. Pour over them Milk, skim Baste frequently with the milk.	Use ¼ bread stuffing recipe, p. 171.

Bake 1½ hr. 300°F.

NOTE: For Stuffed Pork Chops, cut pork chops ½-in. thick, split. Fill with stuffing. Proceed as for Pork Chops with Stuffing.

DEVILED PORK CHOPS

Amount	Ingredient	Method
8 oz.	Butter, creamed	
1 c.	Add Chili sauce	
1 c.	Tomato catsup	
½ c.	Worcestershire sauce	Mix and brush on chops.
½ c.	Mustard, prepared	
2 oz.	Salt	
¼ t.	Cayenne	
12½ lb.	Pork chops, cut 4/1 Pour remainder of sauce over chops. Add	
1 c.	Water	

Bake approx. 2 hr. 350°F.

CREOLE SPAGHETTI

Amount	Ingredient	Method
5 oz.	Onion	} Fry.
8 oz.	Fat	
	Add	
2 oz.	Flour	} Make as white sauce.
1 No. 10 can	Tomatoes, hot	
	Add	
4 lb.	Meat, chopped or ground, cooked	
	Add	
1 lb.	Spaghetti	} Cooked until tender. Drained
7 qt.	Water, boiling	and washed.
1 oz.	Salt	
	Pour into an oiled pan.	
	Sprinkle over the top	
6 oz.	Cheese, ground	

Bake approx. 45 min. 300°F.   Serving approx. 5 oz.

MEXICAN CHILI

Amount		Ingredient	Method
2 lb.	12 oz.	Beans, kidney	} Cook.
		Add	
1 qt.		Tomato purée	
	8 oz.	Onions, chopped	
9 lb.		Beef, ground, seared	
	3 oz.	Suet	} Mix.
	2¼ oz.	Chili powder	
	2 oz.	Salt	
		Water, to make a total	
		volume of 12 qt.	
		Let simmer about 3 hr.	
		Add	
	5 oz.	Flour	} Made into a paste.
		Heat until flour is cooked.	

Serving approx. 8 oz.

CHOP SUEY

Amount	Ingredient	Method
5 lb. 3 lb.	Veal, ½-in. cubes Pork, ½-in. cubes	} Sear.
	Add	
3 oz. 1 gal.	Salt Water	} Stew until tender.
	Add	
8 oz. 1 pt.	Flour Water	} Smoothed to a paste.
4 oz. 8 oz. 5 lb.	Add Green peppers, cut fine Onions, chopped Celery, diced	} Cook approx. 30 min.
3 lb.　6 oz. 1–1½ c.	Add Bean sprouts Chinese sauce	
3 lb.	Serve on mounds of Rice	} Steamed.
3 (No. 2½) cans	Garnish with Chinese noodles	

NOODLE RING

Amount	Ingredient	Method
1 lb.　12　oz. 6 qt. 1½ oz.	Noodles Water Salt	} Cook until tender. Drain and wash.
8　oz. 4　oz. 2　oz. 3　oz. 2　t. 12 1 qt. 1　t.	Add and mix Bread, soft crumbs Onion Green pepper Pimiento Parsley Eggs, beaten Milk Paprika	} Chopped fine.

Pour into 50 individual oiled ring molds, or 4 large molds. Set in pan of hot water. Bake 30 min. 350°F. Unmold, fill with creamed chicken or ham.

NOTE: For rice ring, substitute 1½ lb. of rice for the noodles. Noodles may be cooked in broth.

PASTRY

Dame, get up and bake your pies,
Bake your pies, bake your pies,
Dame, get up and bake your pies,
On Christmas day in the morning.

—MOTHER GOOSE.

PASTRY I

AMOUNT		INGREDIENT	METHOD
25 lb.		Flour	Mix (low speed) until flour and fat are thoroughly mixed.
18 lb.		Shortening	
		Add	
3¾ qt.		Water, cold	Combined.
	12–14 oz.	Salt	
		Mix until dough will hold together.	
			Yield approx. 50 lb.

NOTE: Use approx. 4 oz. for lower crust and 3 oz. for upper crust. This pastry should be mixed several hours before it is to be used and may be kept, covered, in refrigerator for several days.

PASTRY II

AMOUNT		INGREDIENT	METHOD
1 lb. 6 oz.		Flour, sifted	Mix.
1 lb.		Shortening	
		Add slowly	
	1¼ c.	Water, cold	Combined.
	1 T.	Salt	
		Divide dough into 16 portions.	
		Roll each portion to ⅛-in. thickness.	
		Yield six 8-in. double crust pies.	

NOTE: For the best results this pastry should be used the day that it is made.

WHOLE WHEAT PASTRY

Amount	Ingredient	Method
1 lb. 14 oz. 1 lb. 5 oz.	Flour, white Flour, whole wheat Shortening	Mix together until crumbly.
	Add	
1¾ c. 1 oz.	Water, cold Salt	Combined.

Mix with a lifting and folding motion until all the wet spots have disappeared. Do not overmix. Let stand several hours before using.

Yield eight 8-in. double crust pies.

PIE MERINGUE

Amount	Ingredient	Method
16 ½ t.	Egg whites Salt	Whip past frothy stage approx. 1½ min. (third speed).
	Add gradually, while beating	
14 oz. 2 T.	Sugar, granulated Cornstarch	Mixed.

Beat until stiff enough to hold peaks but not dry. Spread on pie.

Bake approx. 15 min. 350°F. Yield meringue for eight 8-in. pies.

APPLE PIE

Amount	Ingredient	Method
10 lb. 8 oz.	Apples, tart, sliced	Arrange apples in 8 deep pie tins that have been lined with pastry.
	Sprinkle over the apples	
2 lb. 4 oz. 6 oz. 2 t.	Sugar Cornstarch Nutmeg	Mixed.
	Add	
8 oz.	Butter, melted	
	Cover with pastry. Brush top with milk.	

Bake approx. 15 min. 400°F. Lower temperature to 325° and bake 40 min., or until apples are done. Yield eight 8-in. pies.

Note: The amount of cornstarch may vary with juiciness of the apples used.

CANNED FRUIT PIE FILLING

Amount	Ingredient	Method
1 qt.	Juice	} Heat.
	Add, while stirring	
1 pt.	Juice	} Mixed.
6 oz.	Cornstarch	
	Cook until stiff.	
	While still hot, add	
3 lb. 4 oz.	Sugar	} Mix thoroughly and bring to
1 T.	Salt	} boiling point.
	Add	
1½ No. 10 cans	Fruit, water pack, drained	
	Mix carefully.	
	Cool at room temperature before using.	

Bake approx. 30 min. 425°F.   Yield eight 8-in. pies.

NOTE: This recipe may be used for all canned fruit fillings such as apricot, black-berry, cherry, gooseberry, or raspberry.

RAISIN PIE FILLING

Amount	Ingredient	Method
4 lb.	Raisins, washed	} Let simmer until raisins are plump.
4½ qt.	Water, hot	
	Add, while stirring	
2 lb. 4 oz.	Sugar	}
6 oz.	Cornstarch	} Mixed.
2 t.	Salt	}
	Cook until thick.	
	Add	
6 T.	Lemon juice	
3 oz.	Butter	
	Pour into unbaked pie shells.	

Bake 15 min. 425°F. and 15 min. 375°F.   Yield eight 8-in. pies.

NOTE: A superior product is obtained if 3 qt. cream are substituted for 3 qt. water.

DRIED APRICOT PIE FILLING

Amount	Ingredient	Method
5 lb.	Apricots, dried	Wash and drain. Cover with water. Cook slowly without stirring until tender (approx. 45 to 60 min.).
	Add	
4 lb.	Sugar	
2½ oz.	Cornstarch	Mixed.
½ c.	Water	

Continue cooking until juice is clear.
Cool before pouring into unbaked pie shells.

Bake 30 min. 450°F. Yield eight 8-in. pies.
Note: For prune pie filling use 8 lb. prunes (cook and pit), 4 c. prune juice, 2 lb. sugar, 8 oz. butter, ½ c. lemon juice, 4 oz. flour, and 1 t. salt.

CRANBERRY PIE

Amount	Ingredient	Method
2 lb.	Raisins, cooked	
5 lb.	Cranberries	
	Add while stirring	
2½ c.	Orange juice	
8 oz.	Cornstarch	
5 lb.	Sugar	Mixed.
1 T.	Salt	

Cook over low heat until thick.
Cool before pouring into unbaked pie shells.

Cut pastry for upper crust into ⅜-in. strips. Arrange in lattice fashion across top.
Bake 30 min. 425°F. Yield eight 8-in. pies.
Note: If cranberries are tart, more sugar may be needed.

RHUBARB PIE FILLING

Amount	Ingredient	Method
4 lb.	Sugar	
1 t.	Salt	
4	Lemon rinds, grated	Mix.
8 oz.	Flour	
	Add	
12	Eggs, beaten	
7 lb. 8 oz.	Rhubarb, cut fine	Mixed.
	Fill unbaked pie shells.	

Bake approx. 30 min. 350°F. Yield eight 8-in. pies.
Note: A top crust may be made of ⅜-in. pastry strips arranged in lattice fashion.

CREAM PIE FILLING I

Amount	Ingredient	Method
4 qt.	Milk	} Heat until boiling point is reached.
	Add, while stirring. Cook until thick.	
3 lb. 3 oz.	Sugar	
11 oz.	Cornstarch	} Mixed.
2 t.	Salt	
	Add, while stirring	
16	Egg yolks, beaten	} Cook approx. 10 min.
	Add	
4 oz.	Butter	
2 T.	Vanilla	} Beat thoroughly.
	Pour into baked pie shells. Cover with meringue.	

Bake 15 min. 350°F.   Yield eight 8-in. pies.

CREAM PIE FILLING II

Amount	Ingredient	Method
2 qt. + 1 c.	Milk	
1 T.	Salt	} Heat to the boiling point.
1 lb. 8 oz.	Sugar	
	Add slowly, stirring constantly	
6 oz.	Flour	
6 oz.	Cornstarch	
6	Eggs, whole	} Mixed.
6	Egg yolks	
1½ pt.	Milk	
	Stir until thick, cook well. Remove from fire.	
	Add	
1 T.	Vanilla	} Mix well, when butter is melted.
3 oz.	Butter	
	Pour over	
16	Egg whites, beaten	} Mixed.
12 oz.	Sugar	
	Pour into baked pie shells while mixture is hot. Chill.	

Yield eight 8-in. pies.

NOTE: For fruit tarts: Substitute 2 qt. cream for equal quantity of milk. Fill baked individual pastry shells ⅓ full of cream pie filling; add fresh, canned, or frozen fruits (blueberries, peaches, cherries). Cover with whipped cream.

CREAM PIE VARIATIONS

KIND	CHANGES IN CREAM PIE FILLING I
Cocoanut Cream.	Add 12 oz. browned cocoanut to meringue and filling.
Grapenut Cream.	Add ½ package of grapenuts and 2 oz. butter.
Chocolate.......	Add 6 oz. cocoa and 3 oz. sugar. Omit 1 oz. cornstarch.
Banana.........	Slice 1 large banana in each pie shell before adding cream filling.
Nut............	Add ½ c. chopped pecans or other nuts.

BUTTERSCOTCH CREAM FILLING

AMOUNT		INGREDIENT	METHOD
1 lb.		Butter, melted	
		Add	
2 lb.	8 oz.	Sugar, brown	} Mix thoroughly. Stir and cook
	1 oz.	Salt	} over a low flame to 220°F.
		Add slowly, while stirring	
3 qt.		Milk, whole } Stir well.	
		Heat the above mixture to the boiling point.	
		Add while stirring	
	6 oz.	Cornstarch	
	6 oz.	Flour, pastry	
1 qt.		Milk, warm	} Thoroughly blended.
	5	Eggs, whole	
	10	Egg yolks	
		Cook until thick. Remove from fire.	
		Add	
	2 T.	Vanilla	
	4 oz.	Butter, in small pieces.	
		Cool. Fill baked pie shells.	
		Cover with meringue.	

Bake 15 min. 350°F.   Yield eight 8-in. pies.

PUMPKIN PIE

Amount			Ingredient	Method
	14		Eggs, beaten	} Combine.
2 qt.	1	pt.	Pumpkin	
			Add	
1 lb.	12	oz.	Sugar	
	10	oz.	Sugar, brown	
	1	T.	Ginger	} Mixed.
	1½	T.	Cinnamon	
	1	T.	Salt	
			Add	
2 qt.			Milk	
	3	c.	Cream	
			Pour into unbaked pie shells.	

Bake 15 min. 425°F.; lower temp. to 275°F. and bake 45 min.

Yield eight, 8-in. deep pies.

LEMON PIE FILLING

Amount			Ingredient	Method
2 qt.	1	c.	Water	
	2	t.	Salt	} Heat to the boiling point.
	3		Lemon rinds, grated	
			Add slowly, stirring constantly	
	12	oz.	Cornstarch	} Cook until clear and until boil-
	1½	pt.	Water	ing point is reached.
			Add	
3 lb.	8	oz.	Sugar	
			Remove from fire.	
			Add slowly, stirring constantly	
	1½	c.	Whole eggs, or 16 yolks, well beaten	
			Add	
	3	oz.	Butter	
			Add	
	1½	c.	Lemon juice	} Mix well.
			Pour into baked pie shells. Cover with meringue.	

Bake 15 min. 350° F. Yield eight 8-in. pies.

GRAHAM CRACKER PIE

Amount	Ingredient	Method
1 lb. 5 oz.	Graham cracker crumbs	Mix.
1 lb. 12 oz.	Sugar	
1 lb. 12 oz.	Butter, melted	
2 oz.	Flour	

Save 4 c. for topping.
Pat mixture into pie pans.
Place pie pans in cold place and allow to stand for several hours. Fill with cream or caramel pie filling.
Cover with meringue and sprinkle ½ c. crumb mixture over the top of each pie.

Bake approx. 15 min. 350°F.   Yield eight 8-in. pies.

SOUR CREAM RAISIN PIE

Amount	Ingredient	Method
3 lb.	Raisins	Soak in hot water for 1 hr. Wash well and drain.
	Add	
16	Egg yolks, beaten	Mixed well.
4 lb.	Sugar	
2 qt.	Cream, sour, heavy	
	Pour into unbaked pie shells.	

Bake 45 min. 300°F.   Yield eight 8-in. pies.
NOTE: A meringue made of the egg whites may be placed on top after the pie is baked.

SOUR CREAM PIE

Amount	Ingredient	Method
2½ qt.	Cream, sour	Mix and cook until thick.
2 lb. 12 oz.	Sugar	
6 oz.	Flour	
21	Egg yolks, beaten	
3 T.	Cinnamon	
1½ T.	Cloves	
2 T.	Nutmeg	
	Add	
3 lb. 8 oz. A. P.	Raisins, cooked.	
	Pour into baked pie shells.	
	Top with meringue.	

Bake 15 min. 350°F.   Yield eight 8-in. pies.

PECAN PIE

Amount			Ingredient	Method
4 lb.			Sugar	
	4	oz.	Butter	} Cream.
	1	T.	Salt	
			Add	
24			Eggs, beaten	} Mix well.
			Add	
1 qt.			Corn sirup, white	} Mix well.
	2½	T.	Vanilla	
			Add	
1 lb.			Pecans	
			Pour into unbaked pie shells.	

Bake 1 hr. 300°F. Yield eight 8-in. pies.

STRAWBERRY BAVARIAN CREAM PIE

Amount			Ingredient	Method
12			Egg yolks	
1 lb.			Sugar	} Cream.
	¼	t.	Salt	
			Add to	
1 qt.			Cream, hot	} Cook 3 min.
			Add	
	2	T.	Gelatin	} Sprinkle gelatin over water.
	1	c.	Water, cold	Soak 10 min.
			Add	
1½ qt.			Cream, whipped	
	2	t.	Vanilla	

Fill 50 individual baked pie shells. Around edge of filling place strawberries, fresh or frozen, cut lengthwise in halves. Fill center with whipped cream (sweetened) and place a whole strawberry in center.

CHOCOLATE CHIFFON PIE

Amount	Ingredient	Method
1½ oz.	Gelatin	Sprinkle gelatin over water.
1½ c.	Water, cold	Soak 10 min.
	Add, stirring until dissolved	
1½ pt.	Water, boiling	Combined.
8 oz.	Chocolate	
	Add	
24	Egg yolks, slightly beaten	
1 lb. 8 oz.	Sugar	Mixed. Cook until mix-
1½ t.	Salt	ture begins to thicken.
2 T.	Vanilla	
	Cool until gelatin begins to set.	
	Fold in	
24	Egg whites, stiffly beaten	Folded together.
1 lb. 8 oz.	Sugar	
	Pour into baked pie shells and chill. Spread whipped cream over the pies just before serving.	
	Yield eight 8-in. pies.	

LEMON CHIFFON PIE

Amount	Ingredient	Method
21	Egg yolks	
1 lb. 8 oz.	Sugar	Beat well. Cook over boiling
2 t.	Salt	water until the consistency
2½ c.	Lemon juice	of custard.
	Pour over	
1½ oz.	Gelatin	Which has been soaked in 1¾ c. cold water 5 min.
	Stir until dissolved, add	
2 T.	Lemon rind	
	Place in ice box until mixture begins to congeal.	
	Fold in	
21	Egg whites, beaten	Folded together.
1 lb. 2 oz.	Sugar	
	Fill baked pie shells.	
	Yield eight 8-in. pies.	

Note: Just before serving spread 1 c. whipped cream over the top of each pie. Orange juice may be substituted for lemon juice.

LEMON FLUFF PIE

Amount	Ingredient	Method
24	Egg yolks	
1 c.	Lemon juice	
6	Lemon rinds, grated	Mix and cook in a double
2 lb.	Sugar	boiler until thick.
1 t.	Salt	
3 oz.	Butter	
	Fold in	
24	Egg whites, beaten	Folded together.
2 lb.	Sugar	
	Pour into baked pie shells.	

Bake 10 min. 350°F.   Yield eight 8-in. pies.
NOTE: If baked too long, pies will fall.

PUMPKIN CHIFFON PIE

Amount			Ingredient	Method
2 qt.	1	pt.	Pumpkin	
	3	c.	Milk	
	2	t.	Salt	
2 lb.	8	oz.	Sugar, brown	Mix. Heat to the boiling
	1	T.	Ginger	point.
	½	T.	Nutmeg	
	½	T.	Cinnamon	
			Add	
16			Egg yolks, beaten	Cook until mixture thickens (20 to 25 min. if cooked in double boiler).
			Pour over	
	2	oz.	Gelatin	Sprinkle gelatin over water.
	1	pt.	Water, cold	Soak 10 min.
			Add	
	2	oz.	Lemon rind, grated	Cool until mixture begins to
	¼	c.	Lemon juice	congeal.
			Fold in	
24			Egg whites	Beaten together to form me-
	8	oz.	Sugar	ringue.
			Pour into baked pie shells. Chill.	
			Top with whipped cream and chopped nuts.	

Yield eight 8-in. pies.

PREPARATION AND COOKING OF POULTRY*

Stuff it and roast it and baste it with care;
Daintily then the gravy prepare,
While 'round you the savory odors shall tell
What e'er is worth doing is worth doing well.

A fowl is said to be dressed when it has been killed, bled, and plucked. A dressed fowl is not ready to cook until it has been "drawn" and trussed or disjointed. Trussing refers specifically to fastening the wings and legs to the body but is used here in the broader sense, including all the final operations of preparing a roasting fowl for the oven.

The first step in the further preparation of a dressed bird for cooking is to remove the hair or filoplumes by singeing over a fire. The bird should then be thoroughly cleaned with a vegetable brush. Some prefer to wash it also with soap and water.

Preparing a Roaster

1. *Pull tendons and remove shanks.* The tendons which connect the muscles of the leg or drumstick with the toes make that portion of the carcass tough and stringy. These may easily be removed (provided the bird has been chilled 24 hours or longer) by making an incision in the back side of the shank, slipping a nail or hook under one tendon at a time, and giving a steady pull. A patented sinew puller may be used, with which all the tendons may be removed at once. After the tendons have been pulled, the shanks should be cut off at the hock joint.

2. *Remove the head, neck, gullet, and crop.* After the above operation, place the bird on a table covered with clean wrapping-paper, and with a sharp knife make an incision in the skin, down the back of the neck to the point where it joins the body. Then loosen the skin from the neck as well as the gullet, crop, and windpipe, and pull the windpipe from the body. Cut off the head, leaving the gullet, crop, and windpipe attached to the head and the loose neck skin

---

* Adapted from mimeographed material: Department of Poultry Husbandry, Kansas State College.

164

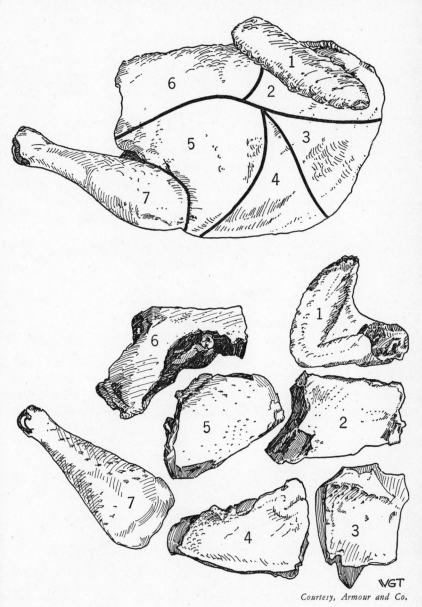

FIG. II.—Cutting seven portions of fowl for fricassee.

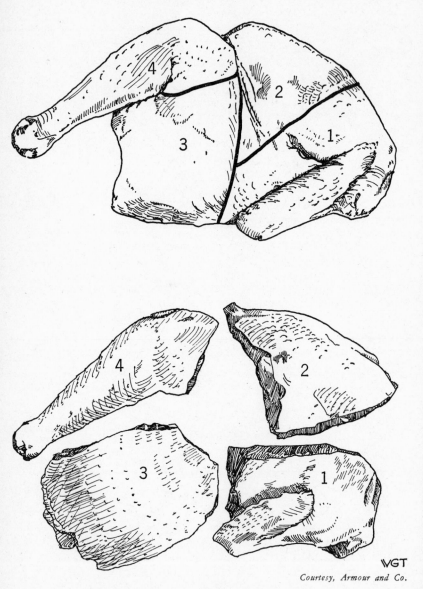

FIG. III.—Cutting four portions of fowl for fricassee.

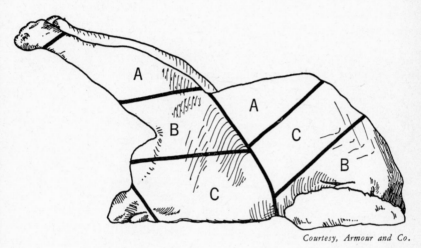

Courtesy, Armour and Co.

Fig. IV.—Carving six portions of roast chicken—dark and light meat equally divided.

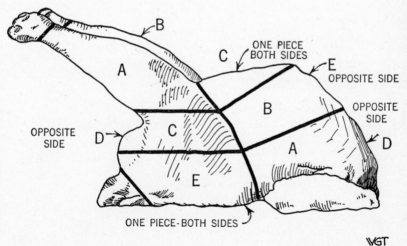

Courtesy, Armour and Co.

Fig. V.—Carving five portions of roast chicken—dark and light meat equally divided.

attached to the carcass. The neck is disjointed from the body at the shoulders. If one wishes to remove the wishbone, it should be done at this time. The bird is placed on its rump, the skin of the neck and crop is folded back, and the flesh is scraped from the wishbone with the back side of the knife blade. The knife is then passed under both sides of the bone, cutting it loose at the shoulders, after which the bone is easily removed.

3. *Drawing*. Removing the internal organs is referred to as drawing. There are several ways by which this may be accomplished, but the method here described has proved very satisfactory.

Place the first finger in the opening at the crop and loosen both lungs. Then insert the knife at the side of the vent and cut completely around it. Wrap vent with paper and push into body cavity. Make a second cut 2 inches long half way between the vent and the end of the keel, perpendicular to the keel. Insert the finger through this last or larger incision, loosen the intestines, and draw them out as carefully as possible. The giblets, which include the heart, liver, and gizzard, are separated from the intestines, cleaned, and washed. The oil sac at the base of the tail should then be removed. The carcass is again washed inside and out and is ready for stuffing and roasting.

Order of Procedure in Preparing a Roaster

1. Preparation:
   (*a*) Singe over a paper, alcohol, or gas flame.
   (*b*) Brush.
   (*c*) Pull tendons and remove shanks at hock joints.
   (*d*) Cut down back of neck.
   (*e*) Remove crop, gullet, windpipe, and head.
   (*f*) Cut neck from body at shoulders.
2. Drawing:
   (*a*) Insert first finger and loosen the lungs.
   (*b*) Remove wishbone, if desired.
   (*c*) Make incision around vent, wrap with paper.
   (*d*) Cut across abdomen.
   (*e*) Insert first and second fingers and draw.
   (*f*) Separate giblets (heart, liver, and gizzard) from intestines.

3. Trussing:
   (*a*) Sever tendons between drumsticks and thighs.
   (*b*) Place end of drumsticks through slit and out vent opening.
   (*c*) Draw neck skin over front opening on to back.
   (*d*) Fold wings in place.
   (*e*) Remove oil sac at base of tail.
4. Stuffing:
   (*a*) Salt inside and outside of roaster.
   (*b*) Stuff with dressing (1 c. per pound of weight).
   (*c*) Rub the bird with flour and butter paste. (Use 4 oz. of flour to 6 oz. of melted butter to make paste.)
5. Roasting:
   (*a*) Place on rack in roasting pan with breast down. Turn bird with breast up when half cooked.
   (*b*) Roast approx. 35 to 40 min. per lb. 325°F. Baste with butter and hot water when necessary (4 oz. butter to 1 qt. hot water).
   NOTE: Roast turkey 25 to 30 min. per lb. 300°F.

Preparing Broilers

After the broiler is singed and brushed or washed, the back is split and the internal organs are removed. The neck is next removed and the broiler is left in one piece. After broiling, it may be served whole, in halves, or in quarters, depending upon the size.

Preparing Fryers and Fowls

1. *Disjointing fryers and fowls.* Young chickens which are too large to broil and fowls that are not desirable for roasters are usually cut up into small pieces and fried, fricasseed, or stewed. The bird to be so treated is handled in the same manner as the bird to be roasted, until the time of drawing. The bird is then cut into 12 pieces as follows: The two wings are removed at the joint next to the body; then the legs are disjointed at the back; each leg is cut into 2 portions at the knee, which gives 2 drumsticks and 2 thighs. An incision is next made through the thin muscle tissue at the rear of the breast or keel bone, and the knife is passed forward and upward to the juncture of the last rib and the back. After this is repeated on the opposite side, the back is broken at that point. The intestines and giblets are removed, and the latter are put to one side to be cleaned later. The breast is separated from the ribs and cut into three pieces. The neck and ribs constitute the two last pieces.

Cooking Fryers and Fowls

Fried Chicken. Cut 2½- to 3½-lb. chicken into desired pieces. Dip into seasoned flour (or flour and cornmeal mixed). Fry slowly for 30 min. in approx. 4 to 6 oz. of neutral fat. May be covered the last few minutes of cooking period.

Chicken à la Maryland. Cut 4- to 5-lb. fowl into desired pieces. Dip into seasoned flour and brown in hot fat. Place in roaster and cover with thin cream. Bake until tender, approx. 2½ to 3 hr. 325°F.

AVERAGE PER CAPITA DRESSED WEIGHT ALLOWANCE FOR VARIOUS KINDS OF POULTRY*

Poultry	Method of Preparation	Class	Average Dressed Weight as Purchased	Per Capita Allowance Dressed Weight
Chicken..........	Roast	Rooster	4 to 7 lb.	¾ to 1 lb.
		Capon	6 to 9 lb.	¾ to 1 lb.
	Broil	Broiler	¾ to 2½ lb.	1 to 1¼ lb.
	Cream or scallop	Fowl or Hen	3½ to 6 lb.	⅜ lb.
	Fricassee or stew	Fowl or Hen	3½ to 6 lb.	⅜ to ½ lb.
	Fry	Fryer	2½ to 3½ lb.	½ to ⅝ lb.
Turkey...........	Roast	Hen or Tom	12 to 16 lb.	¾ to 1 lb.
Duck.............	Roast	....	4½ to 6 lb.	¾ to 1 lb.
Goose............	Roast	....	10 to 12 lb.	¾ to 1 lb.
Guinea...........	Roast	Hen	2 to 3 lb.	¾ to 1 lb.

* Adapted from Bessie Brooks West and LeVelle Wood, "Food Service in Institutions," p. 107. John Wiley & Sons, 1938.

BREAD STUFFING

Amount	Ingredient	Method
6 lb.	Bread, stale, cubed	
1 t.	Pepper	
2 t.	Sage	} Mix.
2 t.	Salt	
2 oz.	Onion, minced	
	Add	
2½ qt.	Water, (or more)	
6 oz.	Butter, melted	} Mix thoroughly and lightly.
3	Eggs, beaten	

NOTE: The amount of water required will depend upon the dryness of the bread. Chicken fat may replace part of the butter, and broth may be used in place of water. For variety add: 3 c. celery, chopped fine; 3 c. chopped apple; 3 c. cooked chestnuts; 3 c. oysters and liquor; or 2 lb. sausage. Do not use whole wheat bread.

VARIATIONS OF PLAIN BREAD STUFFING

Kind	Ingredients*
Rice..............	Combine thoroughly 2 c. cooked rice; heart, liver, and gizzard of bird, cooked and minced; ⅛ t. pepper; 1 t. salt; ½ c. minced celery; 3 T. melted butter; and 1 small onion minced.
Giblet............	Add cooked giblets, chopped, to recipe for Bread Stuffing.
Mushroom........	2 c. mushrooms browned in 4 T. butter. Add 3 c. stale bread, cubed; ½ t. minced onion; 1 t. salt; 1 T. minced parsley; and ½ c. hot water.
Almond...........	1 c. diced celery browned in 2 T. melted butter. Add, and combine lightly, 3 c. stale bread cubed; ½ c. chopped almonds; ½ c. evaporated milk; ½ t. minced onion; 1 t. salt; and ⅛ t. pepper.

* Stuffing for one 4- to 5-lb. chicken.

CHICKEN FRICASSEE

Amount	Ingredient	Method
25 lb. (8 3-lb. fryers)	Chicken	Prepare as for stewed chicken. Season with salt and pepper.
1 oz.	Salt	
½ t.	Pepper	
	Dip each piece in	
12 oz.	Flour	
	Brown chicken in	
8 oz.	Butter, hot	
8 oz.	Fat, hot	

Remove to roasting pan and cover with boiling water. Cook slowly. When tender remove from stock and make gravy in pan where chicken was browned. For gravy use 1¼ c. fat, 1¼ c. flour, and 3 qt. liquid in which chicken was cooked.

CHICKEN TIMBALES

Amount	Ingredient	Method
1 lb.	Butter	}Melt.
	Add	
12 oz.	Bread crumbs	Cook 5 min. stirring con- stantly.
2⅔ qt.	Milk	
5 lb. 6 oz. (4 4½- to 5-lb. fowls)	Add Chicken, chopped	
3 T.	Parsley (may omit)	
32	Eggs, beaten slightly	
1 oz.	Salt	
1 t.	Pepper, white	
	Pour into 50 custard cups and bake as custard in pans of water.	

Bake 30 min. or until firm. 325°F.
Note: Serve with Béchamel Sauce. Garnish with riced egg yolk. May use ham in place of chicken.

CHICKEN PIE

Amount	Ingredient	Method
5 lb. (4 4½- to 5-lb. fowls)	Chicken, cooked, cubed	
3 lb. 8 oz.	Potatoes, partially cooked, cubed	
2 lb.	Peas, fresh or frozen	
	Place in each of fifty 5-oz. baking dishes 5 potato cubes 1 T. peas approx. 1 oz. chicken	
	Add ⅓ c. chicken gravy	
	Cover with	

Batter Crust

Amount	Ingredient	Method
2 lb. 4 oz.	Flour	
1½ oz.	Baking powder	Mix.
1 T.	Salt	
2 oz.	Sugar	
	Add	
2 qt. ½ c.	Milk	
18	Egg yolks, beaten	
4 oz.	Butter, melted	
	Stir only enough to mix.	
	Fold in	
18	Egg whites, beaten	

Bake 12 to 15 min. 450°F.

CREAMED CHICKEN

Amount	Ingredient	Method
1 lb.	Flour	
3½ c.	Chicken fat	Make as white sauce.
3¼ qt.	Chicken stock, hot	
1½ oz.	Salt	
	Add	
2 qt.	Milk, hot	
5 lb. (4 4½-lb. hens)	Chicken, cooked, cubed	
		Serving approx. 6 oz.

CHICKEN À LA KING

Amount	Ingredient	Method
12 oz. 10 oz. 3 qt. 2 qt.	Fat, chicken, melted Cornstarch Stock, chicken, hot Milk, hot	} Make as white sauce.
	When well cooked, add	
5 lb. (4 4½- to 5-lb. fowls)	Chicken, diced	
1½ oz. 5 oz. 6 oz.	Salt Pimientos, shredded Butter	
12	Bring to the boiling point, add Hard cooked sliced eggs.	
		Yield 10 qt.

CHICKEN AND RICE CASSEROLE

Amount	Ingredient	Method
4 lb.	Rice	} When cooked, moisten with chicken broth.
4 oz. 2½ qt. 2 qt. 4 oz.	Butter Milk Broth Flour	} Make as white sauce.
	Add	
5 lb. (4 4½- to 5-lb. fowls)	Chicken, cooked, diced	
1½ oz.	Salt	
	Arrange in layers in buttered casseroles Rice, chicken, and	
1 lb. 12 oz. 8 oz. 4 oz.	Mushrooms Almonds, shredded Pimiento Cover with layer of rice. Sprinkle with buttered crumbs.	

Bake 1 hr. 350°F.   Serving approx. ¾ c.

SCALLOPED CHICKEN

Amount	Ingredient	Method
5 lb. (4 4½- to 5-lb. fowls)	Chicken, cooked, cubed	
2 c. 8 oz. 4 qt. 1 oz.	Fat, chicken, melted Flour Broth, hot Salt	} Combine as white sauce.
12	When thick and smooth add Eggs, well beaten	} Stirring constantly.

Bake 30 to 40 min. 350°F.   Serving approx. 6 oz.

NOTE: The fowl should be cooked and the sauce made the day before using. Put a layer of sage dressing in baking pan 12 in. x 20 in., a layer of sauce, a layer of chicken, then another layer of sauce. Cover with buttered crumbs.

CHICKEN CROQUETTES

Amount	Ingredient	Method
1 lb. 8 oz. 3 qt.	Rice Chicken stock	} Cook rice in broth.
1 T. 2 T. 2 oz. 1 t.	Add Lemon juice Onion juice Salt Celery salt	
6 oz. 1 qt.	Add Flour Chicken stock	} Made into a thick sauce.
5 lb. (4 4½- to 5-lb. fowls)	Add Chicken, cubed	} Mix well.
	Measure with a No. 12 dipper. Let cool. Shape, egg, and crumb using	
8 1 c. 8 oz.	Eggs Milk Bread crumbs, dry Place croquettes in a wire basket.	} Mixed.
3 lb.	Fry in Fat	

Fry in deep fat 3 to 4 min. 375°F.

CHICKEN CUTLETS

Amount			Ingredient	Method
6 lb. (5 4½- to 5-lb. fowls)			Chicken, cooked, cut fine	
			Add	
1 qt.			Broth	
	1	pt.	Milk, whole	
	12	oz.	Butter	Make as white sauce.
	6	oz.	Flour	
	1½	oz.	Salt	
	8		When thickened, add Eggs, beaten	
			Measure with a No. 12 dipper. Shape. Dip in egg and crumbs. Let stand at least 2 hr. before frying.	

Fry in deep fat 3 to 4 min. 375°F.

CHICKEN TURNOVERS

Amount		Ingredient	Method
4 lb. (3 4½- to 5-lb. fowls)		Chicken, cooked, cubed	
		Add	
1 qt.		Chicken broth	
	4 oz.	Flour	
	6 oz.	Butter	Make as white sauce.
	1 T.	Salt	
50 (approx. 5 lb.)		Place a No. 20 dipper of mixture on Pastry rounds, 6 in. in diameter Fold rounds over and seal. Perforate top.	

Bake approx. 20 min. 400°F.
NOTE: Serve with chicken gravy.

JELLIED CHICKEN LOAF

Amount	Ingredient	Method
1½ qt.	Water, cold	
2½ oz.	Add Gelatin	}Let stand 10 min.
4½ qt.	Dissolve in Broth, hot	}Cool.
5 lb. 8 oz. (4 4½- to 5-lb. fowls)	Add Chicken, diced	
1 lb.	Celery, diced	
2 T.	Onion juice	
2 oz.	Pimiento, chopped	
4 oz.	Green pepper, chopped	
1 t.	Pepper, white	
1 t.	Salt	
½ c.	Lemon juice	
	Pour into 6 loaf pans and chill.	

NOTE: Peas and carrots may be substituted for the celery, pimiento, and green peppers. Veal may be substituted for chicken.

SALADS

A Salad

Oh, green and glorious! Oh, herbaceous treat!
'Twould tempt the dying anchorite to eat;
Back to the world he'd turn his fleeting soul,
And plunge his fingers in the salad bowl!
Serenely full, the epicure would say,
Fate cannot harm me, I have dined today!
—SIDNEY SMITH.

PREPARATION AND SERVICE OF SALADS

I. Selection of Ingredients.
  1. The ingredients must be:
    a. Clean.
    b. Fresh.
    c. Tender.
    d. Chilled.
    e. Crisp.
  2. Ingredients must form combinations:
    a. Simple.
    b. Palatable.
    c. Not too strong in flavor.
    d. Harmonizing in flavor with the food it accompanies.
    e. Colorful but not too strong in color.
    f. Harmonizing in color with other salad ingredients and the food it accompanies.
    g. Contrasting in texture with the food it accompanies.
II. Preparation of Ingredients.
  1. Fruit, fresh.
    a. Apples.
    Wash, peel, core, remove bruises and spots.
    (1) Dice.
      Cut into rings and dice with sectional cutter. (If the skins are tender and the color desired, do not peel.) Drop diced pieces into salad dressing, lemon, pineapple, or other acid fruit juice to prevent discoloration. If diced apple is placed in fruit juice, drain before using in a salad.
    (2) Section.
      Cut into uniform pieces, so the widest part of the section is not

more than ½ inch thick. Remove core from each section. If the peeling has not been removed, score it in several places to facilitate cutting when it is served. Use the same method as above to prevent discoloration, only do not use opaque salad dressing.

b. Apricots.

Cut into halves or sections and remove seed. Remove skins if desired.

c. Avocado.

Pare, cut into halves or quarters, and remove seed. Slice, dice, or cut into balls. Dip into French dressing or lemon juice. Pare only a short time before serving.

d. Bananas.

Remove skins. Cut into strips, sections, wedges, or slice. Dip each piece into pineapple, other acid fruit juice, or salad dressing to prevent discoloration.

e. Cantaloupe and other melon.

Peel, dice, cut into balls with a French vegetable cutter, or cut into uniform wedges or strips.

f. Cherries or grapes.

Wash, drain, halve, and remove seeds.

g. Grapefruits.

(1) Sections.

(Select large grapefruits, wash, and dry. Cut off a thick layer of skin from the top and bottom. Place grapefruit on cutting board, start at the top, and cut toward the board. (Always cut with a downward stroke and deeply enough to remove all the white membrane.) Turn grapefruit with the left hand. When paring is completed and pulp is exposed, remove sections by cutting along the membrane of the next section and out to the exterior of the fruit. Turn the knife and force the blade along the membrane of the next section and out to the exterior of the fruit. Repeat for each section.

h. Oranges.

(1) Sections.

Peel and section as grapefruit.

(2) Slice or dice.

Place in boiling water and allow to stand 5 to 10 minutes. Peel, chill, and slice, dice (or section). All the white membrane is not removed by this method.

i. Peaches.

Pare or submerge in boiling water for a few minutes and remove skins. Chill. Cut into halves, wedges, or slices. Remove skins only a short time before using. Drop into acid fruit juice to prevent discoloration.

    j. Pears.

        Pare and remove core and seeds a short time before serving. Cut into halves, wedges, or slices.

    k. Pineapple.

        Cut top from pineapple. Pare and cut out eyes. Cut into 4 sections. Remove hard center and cut sections into 1/4-inch pieces or cut into cubes. Sprinkle with sugar. Let stand over night or at least a few hours before using.

2. Fruit, canned.

    a. Whole fruit.

        Select pieces uniform in size and shape and with a firm appearance. Drain.

    b. Cubed or sections.

        Drain. Cut into pieces uniform in size and shape with well-defined edges. Pieces should not be too small.

3. Fruit, dried.

    a. Prunes.

        (Size 20 to 30). Wash, soak, cook in steam jacketed kettle, or let simmer on top of stove until tender. Remove seeds. Chill before stuffing.

    b. Raisins.

        Soak in warm water, wash, drain, and dry. Add to salad ingredients or dressing.

4. Gelatin salads.

    a. Plain gelatin.

        (1) Place cold liquid in pan and sprinkle granular gelatin over it. Let stand 5 to 10 minutes.

        (2) Add only enough boiling liquid to dissolve the hydrated gelatin. Add cold liquid to make up the total volume required, or place the hydrated gelatin in the steamer until it is dissolved. The required liquid may then be added cold.

        (3) Allow the gelatin solution to reach room temperature if hot liquid has been added, then place in refrigerator.

        (4) When liquid begins to congeal add fruit, vegetable, or other ingredients in desired shapes and quantities.

    b. Flavored gelatin.

        (1) Dissolve prepared powder in a small amount of boiling water or fruit juice. The remainder of the liquid may be added cold.

        (2) Place in refrigerator as soon as room temperature has been reached.

        (3) When liquid begins to congeal add desired ingredients.

5. Meat, fish, eggs, cheese, and nuts.
   a. Eggs.
      Hard-cook eggs by placing in cold water, bringing to the boiling point, and cooking 25 to 30 minutes below the boiling point. As soon as cooked, cool quickly under running cold water. Remove shells. Use whole, halved, sliced, or sectioned. Slice or mince whites. Force yolks through ricer.
   b. Cheese.
      Grate, cut in tiny cubes, put through a ricer or pastry tube.
   c. Nuts.
      Blanch if necessary. Heat in hot oven to freshen if desired. Use whole, shredded, or chopped.

      Blanched almonds.
      (1) Shell almonds.
      (2) Cover with boiling water and let stand until skins will slip.
      (3) Drain. Cover with cold water.
      (4) Rub off skins.
      (5) Place skinned almonds between clean dry towels to remove water.

      Toast blanched nuts or prepare as for salted nuts.
   d. Chicken.
      Remove skin, gristle, and bone. Cut into 1/3-inch cubes. Mix with dressing and other ingredients just before serving.
   e. Fish.
      Cook, remove skin and bones. Flake.
   f. Meat.
      Cut in 1/3-inch cubes. Mix just before serving.
6. Vegetables, fresh.
   If cooked, strive to preserve shape, color, flavor, and crispness.
   a. Asparagus.
      Cook and marinate tips.
   b. Beans, dry.
      Soak, cook, keep whole.
   c. Beans, string.
      Remove strings. Leave whole or cut lengthwise. Wash, cook, and marinate.
   d. Beets.
      Wash, cook, peel, remove any blemishes. Cut into desired shape and marinate. Raw beets may be pared 2 minutes in an electric peeler and then cooked. Cut into desired shapes and marinate.
   e. Cabbage.
      Remove outer leaves. Wash heads; cut into 4 to 6 pieces. Remove the center stalk. Shred the remaining portion as desired, with

a long sharp knife or shredder. Crisp in ice water 15 to 30 minutes if necessary.

f. Carrots.

Pare 2 minutes in electric peeler. Remove remaining skins, eyes, and blemishes by hand. Cut into wedges, rounds, or strips. Grind or shred, or cook, then cut into desired shapes and marinate.

g. Cauliflower.

Remove all leaves and cut away any dark spots. Separate into flowerets with 1 inch of stem left on each. Soak in salt water (1 oz. salt per gal. or ⅓ c. vinegar per gal.). Cauliflower may be cooked and marinated, or it may be marinated and served raw.

h. Celery.

Separate outer stalks from heart of the bunch. (Use outer stalks for soup.) Wash, trim, and remove strings, bruised and blemished parts.

(1) Shred.

Cut lengthwise. Several stalks may be cut at one time. Place them on a board and cut crosswise with a sharp knife.

(2) Celery curls.

(a) Cut celery into 2½-inch lengths.

(b) Make lengthwise cuts ⅛ inch apart and about 1 inch in length on one or both ends of the celery strips.

(c) Place in ice water for at least 2 hr. before serving.

(3) Celery rings.

Cut celery into 2-inch lengths and then into pieces ⅛ inch thick. Place in ice water for several hours. (Each strip of celery will form a ring.)

i. Celery cabbage.

Remove outer leaves. Wash and shred as lettuce.

j. Chives.

Remove roots and any dried or objectionable portions. Wash. Drain. Cut leaves crosswise with a sharp knife or scissors.

k. Chicory.

See endive.

l. Cucumbers.

Wash, pare to remove green skin. Crisp in refrigerator.

(1) Slice.

Score cucumber lengthwise with a fork. Slice in thin slices.

(2) Wedges or strips.

Cut cucumber into 4 pieces lengthwise. Remove any large seeds and spongy pulp. Cut into sections, wedges, or strips.

m. Endive.
  Wash, remove any objectionable portion. Drain, wrap in cloth, and place in ice box.
n. Escarole.
  See endive.
o. Green peppers.
  Wash, remove seeds and stems. Cut into rings, strips; dice or chop.
p. Head lettuce.
  Remove all dirty, ragged, and objectionable leaves from head and discard.
  (1) If to be used for a garnish, cut out stem end or core. Hold the inverted head of lettuce under running cold water until the leaves are loosened.
  (2) Turn heads right side up to drain. Separate the leaves and stack 6 or 7 leaves in a nest.
  (3) Invert the nest and pack in a covered container. Place in refrigerator 2 hr. or more to complete crisping.
q. Leaf lettuce.
  Wash, drain, wrap in cloth, and place in refrigerator.
r. Onions.
  Pour hot water over onions to cover them. Under the water remove wilted leaves, outer layer of the bulb, firm root end, and all bruised or decayed parts. Cut as desired.
s. Peas.
  Remove from shells. (Hot water may be poured over pods to facilitate shelling.) Cook and marinate. Drain before using.
t. Potatoes.
  (1) Pare 2 minutes in electric peeler. Remove remaining skin, eyes, and bruised part. Cut into ½-inch cubes and cook; or wash, cook with skins on, peel, and dice.
  (2) Marinate 2 hours before using.
u. Romaine.
  See lettuce.
v. Spinach.
  (1) Remove tough stems. Examine leaves and discard all dry, yellow, wilted, or slimy leaves.
  (2) Wash in warm water first, then cold water as many times as necessary to remove sand.
  (3) Crisp and use as lettuce.
w. Tomato.
  Wash and remove skins.
  Place tomato on a fork and rotate in a clear gas flame until skin begins to crack and then plunge into cold water. Remove skins.

Or

Place a few tomatoes in a wire basket, and dip in boiling water until the skin begins to loosen. Then dip in cold water and remove skins. Chill.

x. Turnips.

Remove tops, wash, pare by hand. Shred or cut into fine strips.

y. Watercress.

See endive.

III. Making the Salad.

1. Drain and toss ingredients lightly together, if a mixed salad. (Place on individual salad plates or place in salad bowl.)
2. If ingredients are to be marinated, marinate each separately.
3. Drain fruit or any ingredients that are surrounded by liquid.
4. Set up salads as follows:
   a. Arrange cold plates on large trays or in rows on table. Select china, if possible, that will add to the attractiveness of salad.
   b. Place salad green on plates. Place a lettuce cup so the frilly edge is at the back and top of the salad. (The leaf should not extend over the edge of the plate.)
   c. With the salad green as a base, build from the back to the front.
   d. Top salad lightly with some material that will give accent in color or flavor, if desired.
   e. Add salad dressing just before serving, if it is to be used.

IV. Service of Salads.

Salads may be used:

1. As a first course in a dinner menu.
   (Fruit or sea food.)
2. As a main course of a luncheon.
   (Meat, fish, poultry, cheese.)
3. As an accompaniment to the main course of a dinner or luncheon.
   (Salad greens with vegetables, fruit, or combination.)
4. As a second course in a dinner menu.
   (Fruit or vegetable.)
5. As a last course in a dinner menu.
   (Fruit.)

V. Accompaniments for Salads Used as a Separate Course.

1. Breads.
   a. Hot breads, buttered.
      Biscuits (small, various kinds).
      Yeast rolls (various shapes and kinds).
      Muffins (small, various kinds).
   b. Crisp breads.
      Crackers; plain, toasted.
      Wafers; plain and cheese.

Toast; strips, points.
Hard rolls.
c. Sandwiches (small).
Toasted.
Rolled.
Ribbon.
Nut Bread.
Orange Bread.

FIG. VI.—A simple salad, attractively garnished.

Banana bread.
Open.
Bread sticks.
2. Cheese.
Cream cheese balls, plain or rolled in nuts or parsley.
Cottage cheese balls.
American cheese, toasted on crackers.
American cheese balls, cooked or raw.
Cream cheese and Bar-le-Duc.
Cheese sandwiches, fried.
Cheese straws.

3. Miscellaneous crisp materials.
   Celery curls, hearts, or stuffed celery.
   Olives, plain, stuffed, or ripe.
   Pickles: sweet, sour, dill, burr gherkins, fans, rounds.
   Melon strips.
   Potatoes, chips or latticed, shoe string.
   Radish roses.
   Relishes.
   Salted nuts.

APPLE-CELERY SALAD

Amount		Ingredient	Method
1 pt.		Mayonnaise	} Mix.
½ c.		Whipped cream	
		Add	
6 lb.	(E. P.)	Apples, tart	} Dice. Add each apple to dressing as soon as diced.
		Add	
2 lb.	(E. P.)	Celery, chopped	
1	oz.	Salt	
6	oz.	Sugar (may omit)	
			Serving approx. 3 oz.

Note: 8 oz. cut marshmallows added to the dressing will improve the flavor.

SPICED APPLE SALAD

Amount		Ingredient	Method
50 (approx. 12 lb.)		Apples	} Core and peel apples and leave whole.
			Place apples in a flat pan. Pour over them a thin sirup made from
4 lb.		Sugar	
2 qt.		Water	
	½ c.	Vinegar	
	½ t.	Coloring, red	
	1 oz.	Cinnamon (tied in bag)	
		Cook on top of stove.	
		Turn while cooking.	

Note: When cool fill centers of apples with a mixture of 8 oz. celery, 4 oz. English walnuts, ½ t. salt, and 6 oz. mayonnaise.

GINGERED APPLE

Amount	Ingredient	Method
6 lb. 3½ c. 4 oz.	Sugar Water Ginger root	Combine. Heat to boiling point.
	Add	
6 lb.	Apples	Peeled and quartered. Cook until apples are transparent. Yield approx. 4 qt.

Note: Use an apple that will hold its shape when cooked.
Pears may be substituted for apples.

MIXED FRUIT SALAD

Amount	Ingredient	Method
2 lb. 8 oz. 1 lb. 8 oz. 5 lb. 8 oz. 2 lb.	Pineapple, cubed Cherries, Royal Anne, seeded Peaches, cubed Pears, cubed Combine with as few motions as possible. Serving approx. 3 oz.	

Note: Drain all fruit well. Other fruit combinations may be used.

GRAPEFRUIT-ORANGE SALAD

Amount	Ingredient	Method
16 (size 80)	Grapefruit	Pare. Remove white membrane. Cut into sections.
17 (size 126)	Oranges	Pare. Remove white membrane. Cut into 6 uniform sections.
	For each salad use 2 sections of orange and 3 sections of grapefruit arranged alternately on garnish.	

CRANBERRY RELISH (Raw)

Amount	Ingredient	Method
4 (size 150) 4 lb. 6 lb.	Oranges Cranberries, raw Apples (remove cores) } Grind.	
3 lb.	Add Sugar Chill for 24 hr. before using. Serving approx. 3 oz.	

NOTE: May be used as salad if drained before using.

ROYAL CRANBERRY SAUCE

Amount	Ingredient	Method
2 lb. 2 lb. 1 pt.	Cranberries Sugar Water	} Cover and cook (below boiling point) until tender. Cool.
2 1 lb. 1 lb. 1 lb. 4 oz.	Add Oranges, large, chopped Apples, tart, chopped White grapes, seeded Pineapple, diced Pecans, chopped	
		Yield approx. 4 qt.

NOTE: The sauce will keep for several weeks if placed in a covered jar in a cool place.

CRANBERRY SAUCE

Amount	Ingredient	Method
2 lb. 1½ pt.	Sugar Water	} Make a thin sirup.
2 lb. 8 oz.	Add Cranberries	} Cook below the boiling point until transparent.
8 oz.	Purée, and add (while hot) Sugar	} Stir until dissolved. Yield approx. 2½ to 3 qt.

NOTE: Make at least 24 hr. before it is to be used.

FROZEN FRUIT SALAD

Amount		Ingredient	Method
1	oz.	Gelatin, plain	⎫ Sprinkle gelatin over water.
½	c.	Water, cold	⎬ Soak 10 min.
		Add	
1¾	c.	Orange juice, hot	
1¾	c.	Pineapple juice, hot	
		When cold and slightly thickened, Add	
1	c.	Mayonnaise	⎫ Folded together.
1	pt.	Cream, whipped	⎬
		Fold in	
1 lb. 12	oz.	Pineapple, canned, diced, drained	
1 lb. 8	oz.	Orange sections, cut in halves	
1 lb. 8	oz.	Peaches, sliced, drained	
2 lb.		Bananas, diced	
8	oz.	Marshmallows, diced	
12	oz.	Pecans, chopped	
8	oz.	Cherries, maraschino	
		Pour into molds and freeze.	
		Yield 4½ qt.	

Note: Cherries and nuts may be omitted.

CHERRY SALAD

Amount		Ingredient	Method
1 lb. 8	oz.	Gelatin, lemon flavored	⎫ Dissolve gelatin in hot water.
1 qt.		Water, boiling	⎬ Cool.
		Add	
3½ qt.		Water and cherry juice	⎫ Chill.
	2 drops	Coloring, red	⎬
		When gelatin mixture begins to thicken,	
		Add	
2 No. 2½ cans		Cherries, Bing	⎫ Seeded and stuffed with nuts.
12	oz.	Nuts	
	3 c.	Olives, stuffed, sliced	
		Pour into 50 individual molds or a pan 12 in. x 20 in.	

MOLDED SPICED FRUIT SALAD

Amount	Ingredient	Method
2½–3 oz. 1 pt.	Gelatin, plain Water, cold	} Sprinkle gelatin over water. Soak 10 min.
	Add	
2⅔ c. 8 oz. ½ t. ½ c.	Water, boiling Sugar Salt Lemon juice	} Stir until dissolved.
	When cold, add	
2 qt.	Ginger ale	
	Pour over	
50	Peaches, spiced, whole	} Arranged in 50 individual fancy molds.
	Let congeal. Unmold and serve in lettuce cup.	

Note: A bit of coloring may be added to the liquid. Spiced pears may be used in place of peaches.

CIDER FRUIT SALAD

Amount	Ingredient	Method
3 c. 2½– 3 oz.	Water, cold Gelatin, plain	} Sprinkle gelatin over the water. Let stand 10 min.
	Add	
1 qt.	Water, boiling	} Stir until gelatin is dissolved.
	Add	
8 oz. 1 t.	Sugar Salt	} Stir until dissolved.
	Add	
2½ qt.	Cider (or ginger ale)	
	When liquid begins to congeal, Add	
1 lb. 12 oz. 1 lb. (E. P.) 1 lb. 4 oz.	Grapes (or white cherries) Celery, cut fine Apples, cubed Pineapple, diced Lemon juice	
		Serving approx. 2½ oz.

CHEESE-PINEAPPLE SALAD

Amount	Ingredient	Method
1 lb. 8 oz.	Gelatin, pineapple flavored	
2 qt.	Add Water, boiling	}Stir until dissolved.
2 qt.	Add Water, cold (or pineapple juice)	
	When gelatin mixture begins to congeal	
1 lb.	Add Cheese, American, grated	
2 lb.	Pineapple, crushed, drained	
3 oz.	Peppers, green, chopped (or pimiento)	
4 oz.	Celery, finely chopped	
1 t.	Onion juice	
	Place in ice box to congeal.	
		Serving approx. 4 oz.

CARROT-PINEAPPLE SALAD

Amount	Ingredient	Method
2½–3 oz.	Gelatin, plain	} Soak 10 min.
1 pt.	Water, cold	
2 qt.	Add Pineapple juice, hot	} Stir until dissolved.
1 lb. 4 oz.	Add Sugar	
1 oz.	Salt	} Chill.
1 c.	Vinegar	
	When mixture begins to congeal, Add	
2 lb.	Pineapple, crushed, drained	
1 lb. (E.P.)	Carrots, raw, grated	
8 oz.	Nuts, chopped (if desired)	
	Pour into a flat pan 12 in. x 20 in. x 2½ in. and place in refrigerator to congeal.	

PINEAPPLE-CUCUMBER SALAD

Amount		Ingredient	Method
2½–3 oz.		Gelatin, plain	Sprinkle gelatin over water.
1 pt.		Water, cold	Soak 10 min.
		Add	
3 qt.		Pineapple juice, hot	Stir until dissolved.
		Add	
	10 oz.	Sugar	
	1 t.	Salt	Stir until dissolved.
	1 c.	Vinegar	
		When beginning to congeal, Add	
1 lb.	12 oz.	Pineapple, finely diced	
1 lb.	8 oz.	Cucumber, finely diced	
	5 oz.	Pimiento, finely chopped	

Pour into flat pan 12 in. x 20 in.

Serving 3½ oz.

FRUIT SALAD SUGGESTIONS

Apple

1. Apples, celery, walnuts. Chantilly dressing (Waldorf Salad).
2. Apples, celery, diced orange section. Club dressing.
3. Apples, celery, Malaga grapes. Chantilly dressing.
4. Apples, pineapple, cucumber. Mayonnaise dressing.
5. Apples, grapes, bananas, pineapple. Sour cream dressing.
6. Apples, bananas, pineapple. Mayonnaise dressing.
7. Apples, celery, dates. Combination dressing.
8. Apples, pineapple, Tokay grapes. Chantilly dressing.
9. Apples, grapes, bananas, pineapple, oranges, lemon juice. Golden salad dressing and whipped cream.
10. Apples, celery, small amount pimiento. Mayonnaise dressing.
11. Apples, cream cheese, pimiento. Combination dressing.
12. Apples, oranges, dates, marshmallows. Golden or sour cream dressing.
13. Apples, celery, grapefruit. Mayonnaise dressing.
14. Apples, figs, celery, pistachio nuts (dissolve small red cinnamon candies and use to color apples). Mayonnaise dressing.
15. Apples, celery, pears, red and green peppers cut julienne; and mixed with mayonnaise, garnished with pimientos.

16. Apples, celery, chicken, and green pepper cut julienne, or diced and mixed with mayonnaise.

17. Apples, celery, red and green peppers. Mayonnaise dressing.

18. Apples, shredded romaine, celery, and pineapple mixed with mayonnaise.

19. Apples, oranges, pineapple, sliced strawberries. Sour cream dressing.

20. Apple, orange, and pear sections (arranged alternately). French dressing.

21. Apple, orange, and pear mixed with mayonnaise.

22. Apples, diced or julienne, cooked cranberries, drained; halved grapes and pecans, mixed with mayonnaise.

23. Fill half alligator pear with Waldorf salad and garnish with red and green peppers. French dressing.

24. Place apples and celery cut julienne (and marinated) on romaine. Mayonnaise dressing.

25. Mix and place apples and celery cut julienne on lettuce leaf, crisscross top with red and green pepper. Garnish around base with stiff mayonnaise. French dressing.

26. Arrange sections of scored red-skin apples and grapefruit alternately on leaf lettuce. Thick French dressing.

27. Garnish Waldorf salad with three thin sections of marinated bright red apples and whole cloves.

28. Arrange marinated apple balls on lettuce alternately with pimiento cream cheese balls; garnish with pimiento. French dressing.

29. Place chopped apple, grapefruit, and celery on lettuce or romaine, cover with mayonnaise. Decorate with parallel sections of orange and strips of green pepper and pimiento. French dressing.

30. Place mounds of finely chopped tart apples, celery, and carrots on romaine. Thousand Island dressing.

31. Peel half a large apple, scoop out center, fill with diced banana and pineapple mixed with sour cream dressing. Garnish top with tangerine sections in shape of a daisy and place a ripe olive in center.

32. Pare, core, and scoop out tart apple. Spice and cool. Stuff with cream cheese, pears, and pecans. French dressing.

33. Serve celery and apple mixed with mayonnaise on slice of pineapple.

34. Arrange marinated slices of tart apple and avocado alternated with sections of orange. Sprinkle with pistachio nuts. French dressing.

Bananas

1. Bananas, grapes, pineapple, marshmallow. Whipped cream mayonnaise.

2. Diced alligator pear, pineapple, bananas. Sour cream dressing.

3. Cubed bananas, tangerines, pineapple. Whipped cream mayonnaise, paprika garnish.

4. Diced banana, pineapple, pear. Whipped cream dressing with Bar-le-Duc.

5. Banana and orange sections arranged alternately and sprinkled with julienne cucumbers. French dressing.

6. Scoop out half a large banana and fill with finely chopped cucumbers. Sour cream dressing.

7. Cut banana in thirds crosswise and lengthwise, roll in thin boiled dressing, and then in chopped nuts or cornflakes. Arrange with slices of tangerine.

8. On a bed of shredded lettuce place a layer of marinated sliced bananas, top with an apricot half. Boiled dressing.

Grapefruit

1. Grapefruit sections arranged alternately with orange sections. French dressing.

2. Grapefruit sections arranged alternately with apple sections. French dressing.

3. Grapefruit sections arranged alternately with tomato sections. French dressing.

4. Grapefruit sections arranged alternately with tomato sections and ½ slice pineapple. Spiced French dressing.

5. Grapefruit sections arranged on watercress like spokes of a wheel; in center place 4 shrimps. Garnish with mayonnaise and paprika.

6. Grapefruit sections arranged like spokes of a wheel with stuffed prune in center.

7. Grapefruit sections, broken, and thinly sliced kumquats. Golden dressing.

8. Grapefruit sections alternated with julienne celery mixed with mayonnaise and sprinkled with chopped nuts and ripe olives. French dressing.

9. Grapefruit, orange, and pear sections, with strips of red and green pepper placed alternately between slices of fruit. Tarragon dressing.

10. Grapefruit sections, sliced bananas, and pimiento. Mayonnaise.

11. Three grapefruit, 3 pear, and 3 orange sections arranged on lettuce in 3 pyramids, radiating from center; cream cheese in center, topped with cherry. French dressing.

12. Grapefruit and seeded grapes. Chantilly dressing garnished with nut meats.

13. Three sections of grapefruit and orange placed on a lettuce leaf, garnished with green pepper. Roquefort dressing.

Orange

1. Orange, Bermuda onion rings, cream cheese balls. French dressing.

2. Diced orange and cooked chestnuts mixed with whipped cream mayonnaise sprinkled with minced green pepper.

3. Orange, grapefruit, celery, nuts, peach slices. Mayonnaise.

4. Orange and alligator pear sections, and sliced black grapes. French dressing.

5. Diced orange sections, peaches, pears, pineapple, whipped cream, and pistachio nuts. Mayonnaise dressing. Garnish with orange gelatin.

6. Place orange and pineapple cubes mixed with mayonnaise and chopped nuts on a lettuce leaf. Place on the top of this alternate sections of orange, grapefruit, and alligator pear. Top with red and green pepper strips.

7. Place a canned, drained stuffed fig on a bed of lettuce and orange slices. Mayonnaise dressing.

8. Arrange alternately three orange sections and 2 half slices of pineapple and sprinkle with green pepper. French dressing.

9. Arrange orange sections on bed of lettuce like spokes of wheel. Place ripe olive or cream cheese ball in center. French dressing.

10. Arrange orange sections to form a leaf (use thin green pepper strips to form veins of leaves). Thick French dressing.

11. Arrange orange or tangerine sections, grapes stuffed with pimiento, and cheese balls on lettuce leaves. French dressing.

12. Stuff large cooked prunes with orange sections. Mayonnaise dressing.

Peach

1. Stuff half a peach with cream cheese balls, or cottage cheese, shredded American cheese, pineapple or almonds.

2. Spice peach halves and use as plain halves.

3. Soak peach halves in beet colored vinegar to color red.

Pear

1. Stuff half a pear with cream cheese, cottage cheese, or grated American cheese.

2. Spice pear halves, and use as plain halves.

3. Place a pear half on an orange slice, top with lime gelatin and maraschino cherry.

4. Stuff pear half with diced apple and celery mixed with sour cream dressing.

5. Place julienne pear between sections of ripe tomato. French dressing.

6. Mix diced pear, pineapple, and apricots with whipped cream mayonnaise.

Pineapple

1. Mix diced pineapple, marshmallows, white grapes, nuts. Golden dressing.

2. Mix diced pineapple, celery, almonds and mayonnaise. Cheese dressing.

3. Mix diced pineapple, celery, white grapes. Whipped cream dressing.

4. Arrange 8 strips of dates, radiating from center, on a slice of pineapple. Nut mayonnaise.

5. Roll the edge of a slice of pineapple in paprika. Make a cream cheese rosette in center. Use a pastry tube to make spokes of cream cheese mixed with minced green or red pepper.

6. Place in the center of a slice of pineapple a small heart of lettuce. Mayonnaise dressing.

7. Place a small quartered, ripe tomato on top of a slice of pineapple. Cheese dressing.

8. Cut a slice of pineapple in half and place together in an upright position on lettuce leaf. Place 3 long pieces of Cheddar cheese through notch at the bottom of pineapple.

9. Alternate 2 sections of orange and 2 of pear on top of a slice of pineapple. Garnish with cheese rosettes.

10. Place 4 slices of banana around the edge of a slice of pineapple. Garnish each slice with halves of black cherries. Fill center with almonds. Sour cream dressing.

11. Place on slice of pineapple 3 or 4 sections of grapefruit and on top of that 3 sections of orange. Fill center with julienne celery, nuts and mayonnaise.

12. Place diced fresh pineapple and bananas, and tangerine sections on a slice of pineapple. Whipped cream dressing.

13. Place a thin slice of whole orange, scored, on a slice of pineapple, and in the center place chopped pears. Place cream cheese rosettes around orange and on top of pears. Garnish with Bar-le-Duc. French dressing.

TOMATO ASPIC

Amount		Ingredient	Method
	1½ pt.	Water, cold	Sprinkle gelatin over water.
	6 oz.	Gelatin, plain	Let stand 10 min.
		Add	
6 qt.		Tomato juice	
	3	Onions, small	
	3	Bay leaves	
	6	Celery stalks	
12		Cloves	Boiled 5 min. and strained.
	1 T.	Mustard, dry	
1 lb.	8 oz.	Sugar	
	1 oz.	Salt	
		Stir until gelatin is dissolved.	
		Add	
	2¾ c.	Vinegar or lemon juice	
		Pour into ring molds or mold in pan.	
		Place in a cold place to congeal.	

Note: If ring molds are used the recipe will yield approx. 75 servings. Centers may be filled with cole slaw.

PERFECTION SALAD

Amount	Ingredient	Method
3–3¼ oz. 1 pt.	Gelatin, plain Water, cold	} Sprinkle gelatin over water. Soak 10 min.
3 qt.	Add Water, boiling	} Stir until gelatin is dissolved.
1 pt. 1 c. 1 oz. 1 lb.	Add Vinegar, mild Lemon juice Salt Sugar	} Stir until sugar is dissolved.
	Chill. When liquid starts to congeal, Add	
1 lb. 8 oz. (E. P.)	Cabbage, chopped	
10 oz. (E. P.)	Celery, chopped	
4 oz. 4 oz. 1 T.	Pimientos, chopped Pepper, green, chopped Paprika	
	Pour into a flat pan 12 in. x 20 in. Serving 4 oz.	

NOTE: 1 lb. 10 oz. lemon gelatin may be substituted for the 3 oz. gelatin and liquid.

BEET RELISH SALAD

Amount	Ingredient	Method
1 lb. 7 oz.	Gelatin, lemon flavored	
2 qt.	Add Water, boiling	}Stir until dissolved.
1 qt. 1 c. 1½ oz. 3 T.	Add Beet juice Vinegar, mild Salt Onion juice	} Chill.
	When mixture begins to congeal Add	
6 T. 2 lb. 8 oz. 2 lb. 8 oz.	Horseradish Celery, finely diced Beets, diced	
	Pour into two pans 10 in. x 14 in. and place in refrigerator to congeal.	

CABBAGE-PINEAPPLE-MARSHMALLOW

Amount		Ingredient	Method
7 lb. (E.P.)		Cabbage, shredded	
		Add	
2 lb.		Pineapple, diced	
1 lb.		Marshmallows, diced	
	1 pt.	Whipped cream	Mix carefully.
	1 pt.	Mayonnaise	
	1 T.	Salt	

Serving approx. 3 oz.

CABBAGE SPICE

Amount		Ingredient	Method
	9 oz.	Peppers, green	
1 lb.	12 oz.	Carrots	Grind.
6 lb.	(E.P.)	Cabbage	
		Add	
1 qt.		Cream, sour	
	1½ oz.	Salt	
	9 oz.	Sugar	Mixed.
	1 c.	Vinegar	

Serving approx. 3 oz.

CARROT-CELERY SALAD

Amount		Ingredient	Method
2 lb.	(E.P.)	Celery, cut into ¼-in. pieces	
5 lb.	(E.P.)	Carrots, coarsely ground or grated	
	1 oz.	Salt	
	1 c.	Salad dressing	
	1 pt.	Mayonnaise	Mix.
	½ c.	Vinegar	
	2 oz.	Sugar	
		Combine ingredients.	

Serving approx. 3 oz.

COMBINATION VEGETABLE SALAD

Amount	Ingredient	Method
3 lb. (E.P.)	Cabbage, shredded	
3 lb. 8 oz. (E.P.	Celery, chopped	
12 oz.	Green peppers, shredded	Mix.
3 lb.	Tomatoes, cubed	
1 oz.	Salt	
		Serving approx. 3 oz.

NOTE: Serve with mayonnaise.

PICKLED BEETS

Amount	Ingredient	Method
2 qt.	Vinegar, mild	
1 lb.	Sugar, brown	
8 oz.	Sugar, granulated	
1 t.	Salt	Mix. Heat to the boiling
½ t.	Pepper	point. Boil 5 min.
1 t.	Cinnamon	
1 t.	Cloves	
1 t.	Allspice	
	Pour over	
6 lb.	Beets, cooked, sliced	

NOTE: Let stand 24 hr. before using.

CARROT-RAISIN SALAD

Amount	Ingredient	Method
6 lb. 8 oz. (E.P.)	Carrots, coarsely ground	
8 oz.	Raisins	Mix.
1 T.	Salt	
1 qt.	Mayonnaise	
		Serving approx. 3 oz.

NOTE: Marinate 1 hr. before serving. For variety, 1 lb. toasted cocoanut may be substituted for raisins.

CABBAGE SALAD

Amount		Ingredient	Method
5 lb.	(E.P.)	Cabbage, shredded	
1 qt.		Cooked salad dressing	} Mix.
	1 oz.	Salt	
		Serve with a No. 16 dipper (1½-oz. serving)	

POTATO SALAD

Amount		Ingredient	Method
10 lb.	(E.P.)	Potatoes	} Cook and dice.
		Marinate with	
	1½ c.	Salad dressing, French	
1	oz.	Salt, or more	
	½ c.	Vinegar, mild	
		Add	
8		Eggs, hard-cooked, diced	
4	oz.	Peppers, green, chopped	
6	oz.	Pimiento, chopped	
1 lb.	(E.P.)	Celery, cut in rings	
1	c.	Mayonnaise	
		Mix carefully.	
			Serving approx. 4 oz.

Note: The number of eggs may be increased if desired.

BEAN SALAD

Amount		Ingredient	Method
3 lb. 8	oz.	Beans, brown, cooked	
(A.P.)			
		Add	
18		Eggs, hard-cooked, diced	
1 lb.		Pickles, minced	
4	oz.	Onion, minced	
	½ c.	Vinegar	
	2½ oz.	Salt	
1 lb. 4	oz.	Celery, diced	
4	oz.	Pepper, green, chopped	
1 qt.		Salad dressing	
		Marinate before serving.	
			Serving approx. 5 oz.

Note: May use for variety ½ Lima beans and ½ kidney beans.

STUFFED TOMATO SALAD

Amount	Ingredient	Method
50 (approx. 12½ lb.)	Tomatoes	} Peel tomatoes. Remove core and ½ to ¾ oz. of pulp from each.
	Add tomato pulp to	
1 lb. (A.P.)	Cabbage, chopped fine	
1 lb. (A.P.)	Celery, chopped fine	
8 oz.	Pickle, sweet, chopped	} Mixed.
8 oz.	Mayonnaise	
1 T.	Salt	
	Sprinkle in the cavity of the tomatoes	
1 oz.	Salt	
	Stuff each tomato with approx. 2 T. of the vegetable mixture.	

Note: Fish or chicken salad may be substituted for the vegetable mixture.

COTTAGE CHEESE SALAD

Amount	Ingredient	Method
6 lb.	Cheese, cottage, dry	
3 lb.	Tomatoes, raw, peeled, diced	
4 oz.	Peppers, green, chopped	
1 lb.	Celery, diced	
2 oz.	Salt	
1½ pt.	Mayonnaise (less if cream in cheese)	
	May add	
8 oz.	Radishes, diced	
1 lb.	Cucumber, diced	
	Mix carefully.	
	Serve with No. 12 dipper.	

VEGETABLE SALAD SUGGESTIONS
Asparagus
1. Place three asparagus tips through a ring of green pepper. Place on lettuce leaf. Place at one side of asparagus a mound of diced carrots, celery. Mayonnaise dressing.
2. Mix cut asparagus, diced celery, chopped sweet pickle, chili sauce. Mayonnaise dressing.

Green Beans
1. Mix marinated cooked green beans, diced celery, sweet pickle, pimientos, salt, pepper. Mayonnaise dressing.
2. Mix cooked green beans and diced marinated carrots, celery, parsley, and green pepper. Combination dressing.
3. Mix cooked green beans, small chopped green onions, and thinly sliced radishes. Thick French dressing.
4. Mix cooked green beans, shredded cabbage, cubed celery, bit of onion, red or green pepper. Marinate. Boiled dressing.
5. Mix cooked green beans, peas, Lima beans, cauliflower and carrot strips. Marinate. Chiffonade dressing.

Beets
1. Mix diced, marinated cooked beets, chopped celery, pimiento, green pepper, bit of onion, salt and paprika. Combination dressing.
2. Mix chopped marinated cooked beets, chopped celery, cabbage, sweet pickle, salt, paprika. Egg dressing.
3. Mix diced marinated cooked beets, cucumbers, pickle relish, salt, pepper, and a bit of onion. Russian dressing.
4. Stuff large cooked beets with chopped celery, pickle, onion, and mayonnaise. Roquefort dressing.
5. Arrange sliced pickled beets and eggs on lettuce. Garnish with pickle relish. Mayonnaise dressing.
6. Place sliced marinated beets, overlapping each other, in a circle on lettuce leaf, place julienne celery and red peppers in a mound in center. Garnish with watercress. French dressing.
7. Place on endive equal quantities of celery and fine julienne beets. French dressing.
8. Mix diced cooked beets, Bermuda onion rings, quartered hard-cooked eggs, anchovies. Thousand Island dressing.
9. Mix shredded cabbage, diced beets, chopped pickles, horseradish, and salt. Combination dressing.

Broccoli
1. Arrange marinated broccoli and tomato sections on lettuce. Thick French dressing.

Cabbage

1. Mix shredded cabbage, peanuts, paprika, and pimiento. Sour cream dressing.
2. Mix shredded cabbage, hard-cooked eggs, nuts. Combination dressing.
3. Mix shredded cabbage, pimiento, and hot boiled dressing. Chill.
4. Mix shredded cabbage, chopped almonds, and whipped cream dressing.
5. Mix shredded cabbage, green peppers, nuts, pimiento, chili sauce, vinegar, and mayonnaise.
6. Mix shredded cabbage, carrots, green peppers, salt, and mayonnaise.
7. Mix shredded cabbage, grated carrots, diced bananas, salt, and mayonnaise.
8. Mix shredded cabbage, celery, green peppers, peanuts. Chantilly dressing.
9. Mix shredded cabbage, green pepper, and raw shredded beets. Mayonnaise dressing.
10. Mix shredded cabbage with salt, vinegar, and sugar.
11. Mix shredded cabbage, diced apple, and combination dressing.

Carrot

1. Mix diced cooked carrots, chopped celery, cucumber, salt, and a bit of onion. Combination dressing.
2. Cut raw carrots, celery, cucumber, and green peppers into fine strips $1\frac{1}{2}$ inches in length. Mix. Serve with mayonnaise at the side.

Cauliflower

1. Sprinkle raw cauliflowerets with grated cheese. Tarragon dressing.
2. Marinate and arrange raw cauliflowerets and carrot rings on lettuce. Thick French dressing.
3. Marinate and arrange raw cauliflowerets and tomato sections on lettuce. French dressing.
4. Mix cooked cauliflowerets, sliced Spanish stuffed olives, cooked carrot cubes, and peas. Thick French dressing.

Corn

1. Mix drained whole grain corn, chopped pimiento, celery, sweet pickle, salt. Sour cream dressing.

Cucumber

1. Place a mound of 1-inch julienne cucumbers in the center of lettuce leaf. Arrange thinly sliced radishes around the outside of cucumbers. Place julienne strips of pepper on the top. Sprinkle with salt and pepper. Onion dressing.
2. Cut cucumbers in very thin slices and place on watercress in a half circle. Sprinkle with paprika. French dressing.

3. Cut cucumbers into wedges; arrange with tomato sections. French dressing.

4. Place a thin slice of cucumber on a slice of tomato. Arrange three of these on a lettuce leaf. Tarragon dressing.

5. Arrange wedges of cucumber with section of grapefruit and pineapple. Garnish with watercress. French dressing.

6. Scoop out centers of medium peeled cucumbers. Chill. Stuff with whole grain corn and pimiento mixed with Thousand Island dressing.

7. Marinate thin slices of cucumber and Bermuda onion. Vinaigrette dressing.

8. Mix marinated julienne celery, cucumbers, and mushrooms. French dressing.

9. Mix diced cucumber and celery with Thousand Island dressing and endive. Garnish with chopped hard-cooked eggs.

Endive

1. Mix tiny cottage cheese and bacon balls with endive.

Lettuce

1. Place on romaine, shredded green peppers and lettuce. French dressing.

Pea

1. Mix cooked peas, diced cheese, celery, pickle, and pimiento. Combination dressing.

Salad Greens

Cabbage, celery, celery cabbage, chives, chicory, endive, escarole, leaf lettuce, head lettuce, parsley, romaine, spinach, watercress.

Spinach

1. Chop crisp raw spinach leaves. Chiffonade dressing.

Tomato

1. Fill hollowed out tomato with balls of cantaloupe, watermelon, and honeydew. Fruit French dressing.

2. Fill hollowed out tomato with fresh pineapple balls or cubes. Garnish with 3 small cream cheese balls and watercress. Thick French dressing.

3. Stuff hollowed out tomato with green pepper, celery, salt, and mayonnaise. Sour cream dressing.

4. Remove top from tomato and insert a marinated caulifloweret. Thousand Island dressing.

5. Poinsettia Salad. Arrange tomato sections around a pimiento cheese ball. Garnish with green pepper arranged to represent stem and leaves. French dressing.

6. Make 4 incisions in a peeled tomato and insert egg or cheese slices. Mayonnaise dressing.

7. Make a tomato sandwich by placing cream cheese, green pepper, and onion between 2 slices of tomato. Garnish with chopped green pepper. Mayonnaise.

8. Fill hollowed out tomato with Roquefort cheese, celery, and green pepper. Arrange 2 slices of cucumber upright in the tomato. French dressing.

9. Fill hollowed out tomato with cottage cheese. Garnish with celery curl and paprika, or green pepper ring. Sour cream dressing.

10. Mix cubed tomato, cucumber, diced pickle, pimiento, green pepper, and onion. French dressing.

11. Arrange alternately avocado and tomato slices. French dressing.

12. Place a small ripe quartered tomato on lettuce and circle with chopped celery and mayonnaise.

13. Sprinkle watercress over tomato sections. French dressing.

14. Fill molds with alternate layers of chopped green pepper, shredded cabbage, and diced tomatoes mixed with mayonnaise. Unmold. French dressing.

15. Place a thick, small slice of tomato on a lettuce leaf. Place around the tomato, celery, and apple cut julienne and mixed with mayonnaise. Garnish with nuts. French dressing.

16. Hollow out center of a peeled tomato, fill with Parisienne balls of avocado. Fruit French dressing.

SPAGHETTI LUNCHEON SALAD

Amount		Ingredient	Method
2 lb.	2 oz.	Spaghetti	Cook in boiling salted water and wash in hot water. Drain. Chill.
		Add	
2 lb.		Cheese, American, diced or grated	
1 lb.	8 oz.	Pickle, chopped	
18		Eggs, hard-cooked, chopped	
2 lb. (E.P.)		Celery, chopped fine	
1 qt.		Mayonnaise	
	1 oz.	Salt	
		Mix carefully.	
			Serving approx. 5 oz.

Courtesy, Kraft-Phenix Cheese

FIG. VII.—A salad of tomato stuffed with crab meat or shrimp and garnished with ripe olives may be served as a main course for luncheon.

TOMATO SHRIMP SALAD

AMOUNT	INGREDIENT	METHOD
17 lb. (50 medium)	Tomatoes	}Scoop out center of tomato.
	Fill tomato shells with	
2 lb.	Shrimp, cut ½-in. pieces	
1 lb. 4 oz.	Celery, diced	
1 pt.	Cucumber, diced	
2 T.	Lemon juice	}Mixed.
2 t.	Salt	
1 t.	Paprika	
2 t.	Prepared mustard	

NOTE: May be garnished with mayonnaise and whole shrimp and served on lettuce or watercress.

CHINESE SALAD

Amount	Ingredient	Method
1 lb. 4 oz.	Rice	} Cook and wash in hot water. Cool.
6 1-lb. cans	Salmon, red, flaked	
4 oz.	Peppers, green, chopped	
1 lb. (E.P.)	Celery, chopped	
1 lb.	Pickles, chopped	
1½ pt.	Mayonnaise	
1½ oz.	Salt	
2 T.	Paprika	
	Mix carefully.	
		Serving approx. 4 oz.

SALMON SALAD

Amount	Ingredient	Method
7 No. 1 cans	Salmon	
4 lb. 8 oz.	Celery, diced finely	
1 lb.	Peas	
1½ oz.	Salt	} Combine.
1 qt.	Mayonnaise	
8 oz.	Pickles, chopped	
12	Eggs, hard-cooked, chopped	
		Serving approx. 4 oz.

CRAB MEAT SALAD

Amount	Ingredient	Method
8 (6½-oz. cans)	Crab meat, flaked	
30	Eggs, hard-cooked	
1 lb.	Almonds, blanched, shredded	
2 lb.	Celery, chopped	
1 pt.	Olives, ripe, sliced	
	Add	
1 qt.	Mayonnaise	
	Chill.	

Serve with No. 10 dipper.

Note: If desired, omit mayonnaise and marinate with French dressing. Lobster may be substituted for crab.

TUNA FISH SALAD

Amount	Ingredient	Method
8 (13-oz. cans)	Tuna fish, flaked	
1 lb. 8 oz.	Celery, chopped fine	
1 lb. 8 oz.	Cucumbers, diced	} Mix.
2 qt.	Peas	
1 qt.	Mayonnaise	
	Sprinkle with	
3 oz.	Parsley, chopped fine	
		Serving approx. 4 oz.

CHICKEN SALAD

Amount	Ingredient	Method
5 lb. (4 4½- to 5-lb. fowls)	Chicken	Cook and let stand in broth over night. Remove skin and cut chicken meat into ½-in. cubes.
12	Eggs, hard cooked, diced	
4 lb. (E.P.)	Celery, diced	
2 oz.	Salt	
1 t.	Pepper, white	
2½ c.	Mayonnaise	
4 oz.	Pickles, chopped (may be omitted)	
	Season, combine and add mayonnaise.	
	Serve in lettuce cup.	
		Yield approx. 8 qt.

Note: The marinating of cubed chicken with ⅔ c. French dressing for 2 hr. will improve the flavor. 8 oz. toasted almonds may be added just before serving. Pineapple or white cherries may also be added for variety.

MEAT SALAD

Amount	Ingredient	Method
3 oz.	Salt	
4 lb. 12 oz.	Celery, diced	
6 oz.	Pimiento, chopped	} Combine and mix carefully.
10 lb.	Meat, cooked, diced	
1¼ qt.	Mayonnaise	
		Serving approx. 5 oz.

Note: Ham, veal, chicken, or pork may be used.

Courtesy, Kraft-Phenix Cheese

Fig. VIII.—The salad plate may play an important role in luncheon menus.

SALAD DRESSINGS

Variety's the very spice of life
That gives it all its flavor.
—COWPER.

COOKED SALAD DRESSING

Amount		Ingredient	Method
3 lb.		Sugar	
1 lb.	8 oz.	Flour	Sift together.
	6 oz.	Salt	
	4 oz.	Mustard, dry	
		Add	
1 qt.		Water	Stir until a smooth paste is formed.
		Add	
4 qt.		Milk, hot	Stir continuously while adding.
2 qt.		Water, hot	Cook 20 min. in steamer.
		Add	
1 lb.		Butter	Mixed.
3 qt.		Vinegar, hot	
		Add very slowly to	
50 (2 lb. 12 oz.)		Egg yolks, beaten	Stir briskly while adding.

Cook 7 min. in steamer.
Remove from fire and cool.
Yield 3 gal.

VARIATIONS OF COOKED SALAD DRESSING

Variation	Ingredients
	To 4 cups of cooked salad dressing
Creamy-Egg.......	**Add** 1 pt. whipped cream 6 eggs, hard cooked and diced ½ c. fine green pepper strips ½ c. fine pimiento strips
Combination......	Use half mayonnaise and half cooked dressing or use half mayonnaise and half French dressing.
Curry...........	**Add** ½ t. curry powder ½ c. sandwich spread
Egg..............	**Add** 4 eggs, hard cooked, chopped ½ c. pimiento, chopped ¼ c. pickles, chopped
Harlequin........	**Add** 1 pt. whipped cream 4 oz. sugar 1 qt. red cherries 1 qt. green seedless grapes 8 oz. quartered marshmallows
Mustard..........	**Add** ½ c. prepared mustard
Peanut...........	**Add** 1 c. crushed peanuts
Whipped Cream...	**Add** 1 pt. whipped cream

SOUR CREAM DRESSING

Amount	Ingredient	Method
1 qt. 16	Cream, sour Eggs, beaten	} Mix.
	Add to	
2 lb. 1½ oz. 1 c.	Sugar Flour Water	} Mixed.
	Add	
1 pt.	Vinegar	} Stir and cook until thick.

Note: Use heavy cream if possible. This will keep several days. Add whipped cream before serving.

FRENCH DRESSING

Amount	Ingredient	Method
2 oz. 2 T. 2 T. 1 T.	Salt Mustard, dry Paprika Pepper	} Mix.
	Add	
2 qt. 1 qt. 4 t.	Oil Vinegar Onion juice	
	Put into a jar and shake vigorously just before serving, or beat well with a Dover beater.	
	Yield 3 qt.	

Note: An egg white beaten into each quart of dressing just before using will keep it from separating.

VARIATIONS OF FRENCH SALAD DRESSING

VARIATION	INGREDIENTS
	To 3 cups of French dressing
Anchovy..........	Add ½ c. chopped anchovies
Catsup............	Add 1 c. tomato catsup
Chiffonade........	Add 6 T. parsley, chopped 6 T. red pepper, chopped 1 T. onion, minced 1 oz. green pepper, chopped 4 eggs, hard-cooked, chopped (May add shredded beets in place of red pepper)
Chutney..........	Add 1 c. Chutney
Cream............	Add 1 c. heavy cream, beaten or unbeaten
Cucumber........	Add 1½ oz. cucumber, chopped fine
Curry............	Add ½ t. curry powder 8 eggs, hard cooked, puréed
Fruit............	3 c. salad oil ½ c. lemon juice ½ c. orange juice 2 T. sugar, powdered 1 T. salt ½ t. pepper
Mexican..........	Add 2½ oz. green pepper, chopped ¾ c. chili sauce 2 T. onion, chopped
Onion............	Add ¾ c. sweet pickled onions, chopped, or 3 oz. onion rings.

VARIATIONS OF FRENCH SALAD DRESSING (continued)

VARIATION	INGREDIENTS
Parisian..........	Add 3 T. green pepper, chopped 3 T. red pepper, chopped ½ c. celery, chopped 3 T. onion, minced 3 T. pimiento, chopped 1 T. salt ½ c. parsley, minced
Piquante..........	Add 1½ t. mustard, dry ½ t. Worcestershire sauce 1½ t. onion juice 3 drops Tabasco sauce
Roquefort.........	Add 4 oz. Roquefort cheese, riced Whip dressing slowly into cheese. (May also mix 1 c. heavy cream with cheese before French dressing is added.)
Spiced.............	Use spiced vinegar to make regular French dressing.
Spinosa...........	Add 6 T. capers 6 T. stuffed olives, chopped 3 T. parsley, chopped
Tarragon.........	Use tarragon vinegar to make regular French dressing.
Tomato...........	Add 4 oz. sugar 1 t. onion juice 1½ c. tomato soup
Vinaigrette........	Add 5 oz. pickles, sour, chopped

THICK FRENCH DRESSING

Amount	Ingredient	Method
1¼ t.	Onion juice	
1½ oz.	Salt	
4 t.	Mustard, dry	} Mix.
2 T.	Paprika	
2 lb.	Sugar	
	Add	
1⅓ c.	Vinegar	} Mix well.
	Add gradually	
1 qt.	Salad oil	} Stirring constantly. Yield approx. 5 c.

NOTE: If a French dressing of usual consistency is desired use only 8 oz. of sugar.

FRENCH DRESSING, SEMI-PERMANENT

Amount	Ingredient	Method
4 t.	Mustard, dry	
4 t.	Paprika	
2 oz.	Sugar	} Mix.
f.g.	Pepper, red	
1½ oz.	Salt	
	Add slowly	
1 qt.	Salad oil	} Beating continuously.
	Add slowly	
1 c.	Vinegar	} Beat vigorously for 5 min.
	Add	
4 t.	Gelatin	⎱ The gelatin should be previously
4 T.	Water, cold	⎰ soaked in the cold water and dis-
½ c.	Water, boiling	solved in the hot water and chilled. Yield approx. 5 c.

GOLDEN SALAD DRESSING

Amount	Ingredient	Method
5⅓ oz. ½ c.	Cornstarch Water	} Make a paste.
16	Add Eggs, well beaten	
1 qt. 1½ pt. 1 pt. 2 lb.	Add, while stirring Pineapple juice Orange juice Lemon juice Sugar Cook until thick.	} Mixed and heated to the boiling point.
1 qt.	Cool, and add Whipped cream	
		Yield 3 qt.

Note: Serve with fruit salads.

MAYONNAISE

Amount	Ingredient	Method
8 2 oz. 1 t. ⅛ t. 2 T.	Egg yolks (or 4 whole) Salt Paprika Cayenne Mustard, dry	} Mix well.
¼ c.	Add Vinegar	
2 qt.	Add slowly Salad oil	
	Add oil very slowly, beating steadily until an emulsion is formed. (Oil may then be added in amount of ½ c. and later 1 c. at a time, beating well after each addition.)	
¼ c.	Add Vinegar	} Beat well.
2 qt.	Add Salad oil	} Continue beating until oil is emulsified.
		Yield 1 gal.

VARIATIONS OF MAYONNAISE

VARIATION	INGREDIENTS
	To 2 cups of mayonnaise
Campus Dressing......	Add ½ c. tomato purée ½ c. pepper relish 2 T. pimiento
Celery Dressing........	Add 2 T. parsley, chopped 2 oz. green peppers, chopped 3 oz. celery, diced
Club Dressing.........	Add 2 T. currants, chopped 4 T. raisins, chopped 3 T. nuts, chopped
Chantilly Dressing.....	Add ½ c. whipped cream
Egg Dressing..........	Add 2 eggs, hard-cooked, chopped
Egg and Green Pepper Dressing............	3½ c. mayonnaise 6 eggs, hard-cooked, chopped 2 oz. green peppers, chopped fine 1 T. onion, scraped f. g. cayenne Mix carefully
Horseradish Dressing...	Add 2 T. dry horseradish mixed with 4 T. cold water
Indian Dressing........	Add 4 oz. chopped chow-chow pickle
Piquante..............	Add 2 oz. olives, chopped 2 oz. pickles, chopped
Roquefort.............	Add 1 c. French dressing 2 oz. Roquefort cheese 1 t. Worcestershire sauce

VARIATIONS OF MAYONNAISE (continued)

Variation	Ingredients
Russian Dressing......	1½ qt. mayonnaise (stiff) 1¼ c. Chili sauce (thick) ¼ c. Worcestershire sauce Few drops onion juice f. g. cayenne
Savory Dressing.......	Add 3 oz. celery, diced 2 oz. green peppers, chopped 2 t. onion, chopped
Tartar Sauce.........	Add ½ c. pickles, chopped 1 oz. green pepper, chopped 2 T. parsley, chopped ½ c. olives, chopped 4 T. vinegar or lemon juice 2 t. onion, minced Few drops Worcestershire sauce Few drops Tabasco sauce
Thousand Island Dressing............	7 c. mayonnaise ¼ c. onion, minced ½ c. pimiento, chopped 1¾ c. Chili sauce (thick) 10 eggs, hard cooked, chopped ½ c. pickles or olives, chopped f. g. cayenne

MAYONNAISE WITH COOKED BASE

Amount	Ingredient	Method
10 oz. 2 c.	Cornstarch Water, cold	} Make a smooth paste.
2 qt.	Add Water, boiling	} Stirring constantly. Cook until clear.
	Place in bowl of electric mixer. Beat until cool.	
20 (or 12 whole eggs)	Add, ¼ at a time, while beating, Egg yolks	} Mix well.
2½ oz.	Add Salt	} Mix well.
2 c.	Add Vinegar	
1 gal.	Add slowly, beating constantly, Salad oil	
2 c.	Add Vinegar	
1 gal.	Add slowly, beating constantly, Salad oil	
		Yield 3 gal.

Note: If desired add 3 oz. dry mustard and 2 oz. paprika.

SANDWICHES

Sandwiches may be hearty and substantial, approximating a meal, or light and dainty as an accompaniment to tea. They are made of one or more slices of bread, spread with one or more kinds of filling. The closed sandwich is made by spreading one slice of bread with a filling and covering it with a second slice. The open-faced sandwich is made by spreading a slice of bread with filling and decorating it.

Ingredients

1. *Bread.* Any kind may be used with a suitable filling. Cracked wheat, graham, whole wheat, white, or rye are most often used for the substantial type of sandwich. Nut, orange, raisin, date, banana, or rolled oat bread is most often used for plain tea sandwiches.

For most sandwiches the bread should be a Pullman or sandwich loaf, 24 hours old and unsliced. If crusts are to be removed it should be done before the bread is sliced. The bread should be sliced $\frac{1}{8}$- to $\frac{1}{4}$-inch thick, depending upon the type of sandwich to be made.

2. *Butter.* Butter should be creamed so that it is soft and pliable. It is best creamed by placing it in the bowl of the electric mixer, and allowing it to stand at room temperature, until soft enough to mix with the mixer. (A half cup of milk per pound of butter may be added to increase the volume.) Mix first on low speed and then whip on second and high speed until fluffy. Butter need not always be used on sandwiches when a rich filling is used. However, butter helps to prevent fillings from soaking into the bread and improves the flavor. Minced cucumber, spices, onion, or other ingredients may be added to change the flavor of the butter.

3. *Fillings.* Sandwich filling may be made of chopped meats, vegetables, nuts, fish, or fruits. One of these ingredients or a combination of them is usually mixed with mayonnaise, cooked dressing, or cream.

Soft mixed fillings should be measured with a spoon or small dipper to insure a uniform amount in each sandwich.

If slices of meat or cheese are used for filling, the slices should be even in thickness and the same size as the bread upon which they are to be placed.

4. *Garnishes.* The garnishes to be used depend upon the type of sandwich. Lettuce, parsley, watercress and other salad greens, olives, pickles, pimiento, green peppers, and radishes are most often used. Nuts, paprika, cheese, and mayonnaise are also often used as garnishes for various types of sandwiches.

Making Simple Sandwiches.

1. Have filling, garnish, and butter prepared.
2. Allow plenty of work space.
3. Arrange the slices of bread in rows.
4. Spread butter or filling with a pie server or short spatula, having enough butter on spatula to cover 2 or 3 slices.
5. Spread all bread with butter before spreading with filling. Do not pick up bread to spread.
6. Spread from back row of bread to front row.
7. Use dipper or spoon and place a uniform amount of filling on alternating slices of bread.
8. Spread the filling evenly and to the edge of the bread.
9. Cover each slice with corresponding slice of bread.
10. Stack several made sandwiches and cut down through the middle with one stroke of the knife. Stack on a tray and cover with a wet cloth (or wrap in wax paper) to prevent drying.

Simple sandwiches may be made more attractive by cutting into rounds, triangles, or small squares.

Making Tea Sandwiches.

Checkerboard Sandwiches. 1. Cut 3 slices of white and 3 slices of whole wheat bread about half an inch thick.
2. Spread one slice of white bread with a thin spread, place a slice of whole wheat bread on this and spread with butter, and top with another slice of white bread.
3. Use the remaining 2 whole wheat slices and the slice of white bread to make another stack.
4. Wrap in a damp cloth, place under a light weight, and put in a cool place until firm and cooled.
5. Trim, and cut each pile into 3 slices.
6. Spread these slices and combine them crosswise, white and whole wheat squares alternating.
7. Repeat weighting and cooling process for a few hours. When ready to serve, cut in 1/4- to 1/2-inch slices.

Ribbon Sandwiches. Proceed as for checkerboard sandwich to step 5, then slice each pile into desired thickness.

Open Sandwiches. 1. Cut slices of bread 1/4-inch thick into rounds, hearts, stars, diamonds, crescents, squares, or any desired shape.
2. Spread with creamed butter then with filling, and decorate. The filling may be ham and sliced cheese, lettuce and hard-cooked egg, chicken salad, shrimp salad, minced tongue and sliced tomato, sliced cucumber and lettuce, cottage cheese and sliced tomatoes, jam, olives, chopped parsley and pimiento, hard-cooked eggs. (Cut the bread a little thicker and use a little thicker filling than for the simple sandwich.)

a. *Tomato.* Place a thin slice of tomato on a round of buttered bread. Garnish with mayonnaise and a sprig of parsley, or butter the edges of the bread and roll in chopped parsley.

b. *Cream cheese.* Spread bread cut into diamond shapes with butter and cream cheese. Garnish with pimiento or green peppers.

c. *American cheese.* Place thin slices of cheese on crisp crackers. Add a dash of salt and pepper and place under the broiler until the cheese has melted. Garnish with paprika and serve hot.

d. *Cherry-nut.* Spread bread cut in heart shapes with a mixture of chopped almonds, maraschino cherries, and whipped cream.

e. *Ginger-nut.* Mix chopped walnuts, candied ginger, and mayonnaise. Cut bread into tiny squares and garnish with a half walnut and bit of paprika.

f. *Spiced cheese.* Mix ground American cheese, butter, lemon juice, Worcestershire sauce, paprika, cayenne, and onion juice. Spread on rounds of rye bread. Garnish with stuffed olive slices.

Rolled Sandwiches. 1. Slice a sandwich loaf of bread lengthwise into 6 slices.

2. Spread each slice with creamed butter and then with a thin filling of cream cheese.

3. Place a thin strip of pimiento, and chopped parsley across the end of each slice and roll bread around pimiento as you would a jelly roll.

4. Wrap each roll in wax paper, tie, and put in a cool place.

5. When ready to serve, slice thin.

Pinwheel Sandwiches. 1. Remove crusts from half a Pullman loaf of bread and cut into slices 1/4-inch thick.

2. Spread slices with creamed butter and then with pimiento cream cheese to which has been added paprika.

3. Roll like a jelly roll.

4. Cover with a very damp cloth and place in the refrigerator until set.

5. Slice into 1/4-inch slices.

Two-tone Sandwiches. 1. Cut whole wheat and white bread into 2 1/2-inch rounds.

2. Spread with butter or cream cheese or other thin fillings.

3. Use a doughnut cutter and remove the center from half of the whole wheat and half of the white bread.

4. Place the whole wheat round on the white bread and vice versa; fit the white rounds into the whole wheat circles and vice versa.

Toasted Sandwiches. Many ingredients may be combined to make suitable fillings for toasted sandwiches. The outside is often brushed with butter and the sandwich toasted after the filling has been added, although a crisp ingredient like lettuce is added after the sandwich is toasted. Toasted sandwiches may be either closed or open faced. A few suggestions for toasted sandwiches follow:

1. Thinly sliced tomato, broiled bacon, lettuce, and salad dressing.

2. Chicken livers, mashed, crisp bacon, and salad dressing.
3. Sweetbreads and mushrooms browned in butter.
4. Sardine and hard-cooked eggs, mayonnaise and slice of tomato.
5. Sweetbreads, hard-cooked eggs, mayonnaise and lemon juice.
6. Goose liver, mayonnaise, and onion.
7. Sliced cheese, sliced ham, and prepared mustard.
8. Sliced cheese, tomato, and mayonnaise.
9. Chicken salad.

SANDWICH FILLING SUGGESTIONS

1. Dates, figs, raisins, orange, ground.
2. Peanut butter and bananas, mixed.

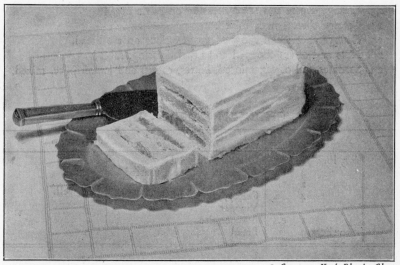

Courtesy, Kraft-Phenix Cheese

FIG. IX.—The cheese sandwich loaf is an unusual and pleasing dish suitable for bridge or buffet suppers.

3. Hard-cooked eggs and olives, chopped.
4. Hard-cooked eggs and olives, chopped, grated cheese and mayonnaise, mixed.
5. Hard-cooked eggs and pickles, chopped, tuna fish and mayonnaise, mixed.
6. Hard-cooked eggs and pimiento, chopped, sweet relish and mayonnaise, mixed.
7. Sliced cold boiled tongue and mayonnaise.
8. Stuffed olives, sliced, and Neufchâtel cheese.
9. Cucumber, chopped and mixed with creamed butter.
10. Dates, lemon juice and nuts, minced.

11. Raspberry jelly or jam and cream cheese.
12. Sliced tomato and mayonnaise.
13. Ground cheese and drief beef, mixed with tomato juice and cooked, then egg yolk added.
14. Cream cheese, chopped red and green peppers, mixed.
15. Cream cheese and chopped dates, mixed.
16. Cream cheese, chopped preserved ginger, mixed.
17. Cabbage and carrot, chopped fine, mixed with salad dressing.
18. Grated carrots, chopped nuts and mayonnaise, mixed.
19. Chopped celery and salad dressing, mixed.
20. Chopped celery, nuts and salad dressing, mixed.
21. Chopped celery, nuts, olives and salad dressing, mixed.
22. Mashed baked beans, sliced tomato and lettuce.
23. Cottage cheese and salad dressing on raisin bread.
24. Cottage cheese, nuts, mixed.
25. Cottage cheese and chopped green onions on rye bread.
26. Nuts and olives chopped and salad dressing, mixed.
27. Sardines and olives, minced, butter, catsup and lemon juice, mixed.

CHICKEN SANDWICHES

Amount		Ingredient	Method
3 lb.	8 oz.	Chicken, chopped	
	4 oz.	Almonds, chopped, toasted	
	2 t.	Salt	
	4 oz.	Celery, chopped fine	} Mix well.
	¼ c.	Vinegar	
	1 c.	Mayonnaise	
100 slices		Bread	

HAM SALAD SANDWICHES

Amount		Ingredient	Method
4 lb.		Ham, cold, boiled, coarsely ground	
	8 oz.	Pickles, chopped	
	2 oz.	Pimientos, chopped	} Mix well.
	1 c.	Boiled dressing	
	1 c.	Mayonnaise	
100 slices		Bread	

TUNA FISH SANDWICHES

Amount	Ingredient	Method
3 lb. (4 13-oz. cans)	Tuna fish, flaked	
¼ c.	Lemon juice	Mix well.
1 t.	Onion juice	
1 c.	Boiled dressing	
1 c.	Mayonnaise	
100 slices	Bread	

MEAT SANDWICHES

Amount	Ingredient	Method
4 lb.	Meat, cold, boiled, finely chopped	
4	Eggs, hard-cooked, chopped	
4 oz.	Celery, chopped fine	
8 oz.	Olives, chopped	
1 pt.	Mayonnaise	Mix well.
¼ c.	Vinegar	
3¼ c.	Boiled dressing	
1 t.	Salt	
100 slices	Bread	

TOMATO AND BACON SANDWICHES

Amount	Ingredient	Method
4 lb.	Bacon, sliced	Place slices in rows in a baking pan. Cook in oven until crisp and brown.
7 lb.	Tomatoes, sliced	
1 c.	Mayonnaise	
100 slices	Bread	
2 heads	Lettuce	

Spread 50 slices of bread with mayonnaise, place bacon slices, thin slices of tomato, and a piece of lettuce on each.

PEANUT SANDWICHES

Amount		Ingredient	Method
1 lb.	8 oz.	Peanuts, shelled	} Grind.
		Add	
	6 oz.	Butter	
		Mix well.	
		Add	
	1 c.	Cream, whipped	
	1 c.	Mayonnaise	} Mixed.
	1 T.	Salt	
2 heads		Lettuce	
		Place a piece of lettuce in each sandwich.	
100 slices		Bread, cracked wheat	

CHEESE SANDWICHES

Amount		Ingredient	Method
3 lb.		Cheese, ground	
	1 pt.	Cream	
	2 t.	Salt	} Mix well.
	f.g.	Cayenne	
	4 oz.	Butter	
100 slices		Bread	

SAUCES

The true essentials of a feast are only fun and feed.
—HOLMES.

CARAMEL SAUCE

AMOUNT	INGREDIENT	METHOD
1 lb. 1⅓ c. ⅔ c.	Sugar, brown Corn sirup Water	} Cook until a soft ball forms (238°F.).
6 oz. 8	Add Butter Marshmallows	} Stir until melted.
1⅓ c.	Cool, then add Milk, evaporated	
		Yield approx. 5 c.

ORIENTAL SAUCE

AMOUNT	INGREDIENT	METHOD
2 lb. 1½ pt.	Sugar Water	} Cook and stir until sugar is dissolved.
1 1 1 1	Add Lemon, juice Lemon rind, cut into long, thin strips Orange, juice Orange rind, cut into long, thin strips	} Cook until clear.
6 oz.	Add Ginger, candied, crystallized	} Cook to 234°F.
4 oz.	Remove from stove, add Almonds, blanched, cut into strips.	
		Yield approx. 1 qt.

NOTE: Serve cold with vanilla ice cream.

227

CHOCOLATE SAUCE

Amount	Ingredient	Method
5 oz. 2½ c.	Cocoa Water, lukewarm	} Mix.
1 qt.	Add Water, boiling	} Stir constantly until it boils.
3 oz. ⅓ c.	Add Cornstarch Water, cold Bring to boiling point.	} Mixed.
1 lb. 8 oz. f.g.	Add Sugar Salt Cook over water 1 hr.	
1 t. 8 oz.	Add Vanilla Butter	Yield 9 c.

Note: Serve hot or cold with pudding or ice cream.

HOT CHOCOLATE SAUCE

Amount	Ingredient	Method
8 oz. 1 lb. 8 oz.	Butter, soft or melted Sugar, powdered	} Cream in top of double boiler.
1¼ c. 8 oz.	Add Milk, evaporated Chocolate, shaved Cook over water 30 min.	Yield approx. 5 c.

Note: This sauce will keep indefinitely. Serve on vanilla or peppermint ice cream. Heat in a double boiler before serving.

PEPPERMINT SAUCE

Amount	Ingredient	Method
2 lb. 4 oz. 2½ c.	Sugar Water	}Boil to a medium sirup (234°F.).
10 oz.	Add Marshmallow, cut	
5	Add gradually to Egg whites, stiffly beaten	
5 drops	Add Peppermint oil	
		Yield approx. 2½ qt.

NOTE: Chill and serve with ice cream or cake.

CUSTARD SAUCE

Amount	Ingredient	Method
14 oz. 2 oz. ½ t.	Sugar Cornstarch Salt	}Mix.
1 pt.	Add Milk, cold	}Stir until smooth.
3 qt.	Add Milk, hot	}Stirring constantly.
10	Add Egg yolks, beaten	}Blend well.
2 T.	Cook over water, add Vanilla	
		Yield 5 qt.

NOTE: Cool and serve with pudding or over cubed oranges.

LEMON SAUCE

Amount	Ingredient	Method
2 lb.	Sugar	⎫
3 oz.	Cornstarch	⎬ Mix.
½ t.	Salt	⎭
	Add	
2 qt.	Water, boiling	} Cook until clear.
	Add	
5 oz.	Lemon juice	
	Add	
2 T.	Butter	
		Yield 2 qt.

Note: Serve hot with steamed bread or rice pudding.

HARD SAUCE I

Amount	Ingredient	Method
8 oz.	Butter	} Cream well.
	Add	
2 T.	Water, boiling	} Stir until creamy.
	Gradually add	
1 lb. 3 oz.	Sugar, powdered	
1 t.	Lemon extract	

Note: Serve with Christmas Pudding.

HARD SAUCE II

Amount	Ingredient	Method
12 oz.	Butter, creamed	⎱ Add sugar gradually. Cream
1 lb. 4 oz.	Sugar, brown, sifted	⎰ well.
	Fold in	
¾ c.	Cream, whipped	
2 t.	Vanilla	

HOLLANDAISE SAUCE

Amount	Ingredient	Method
2 oz.	Butter	
	Add	
1½ T.	Lemon juice	} Place over low flame and cook
3	Egg yolks	} slowly, beating constantly.
	When first portion of butter is melted, add	
2 oz.	Butter } Continue cooking and beating.	
	Beat until mixture thickens, add	
2 oz.	Butter	} Stirring constantly. Cook until } thickened.
	Remove from flame, add	
f.g.	Salt	
f.g.	Cayenne	
	Serve immediately.	
		Yield 12 servings.

Note: If sauce tends to curdle, add hot water, a teaspoon at a time, stirring vigorously.

MOCK HOLLANDAISE SAUCE

Amount	Ingredient	Method
1½ qt.	Milk, hot	
6 oz.	Butter, melted	
3 oz.	Flour	} Make a white sauce.
1 t.	Salt	
½ t.	Pepper	
f.g.	Cayenne	
	Add	
12	Egg yolks, unbeaten	Add 1 egg at a time, a little
1 lb.	Butter	butter, and a little lemon
½ c.	Lemon juice	juice until all are added. Beat well.
		Yield approx. 2 qt.

HOT VEGETABLE SAUCE

Amount	Ingredient	Method
1 lb.	Bacon, cubed (or butter) } Fry crisp.	
	Add	
4 oz.	Flour	} Stir until smooth and flour browned.
	Add	
1 lb. 4 oz.	Sugar	
2½ oz.	Salt	} Mixed and heated to boiling point.
1½ pt.	Vinegar, mild	
1½ pt.	Water	
	Cook over water.	
		Yield 2½ qt.

Note: Use to wilt lettuce, spinach, or for hot potato salad.

RAISIN SAUCE

Amount	Ingredient	Method
4 oz.	Sugar	} Bring to boiling point.
1 pt.	Water	
	Add	
1 lb.	Raisins, cooked	
⅓ c.	Vinegar	
2 oz.	Butter	
1 T.	Worcestershire sauce	} Let simmer gently about 5 min. or until jelly is dissolved.
1 t.	Salt	
¼ t.	Pepper, white	
½ t.	Cloves	
⅛ t.	Mace	
1 lb.	Currant jelly	
		Yield 1½ qt.

Note: Red coloring may be added. Serve with ham.

KENTUCKY LAMB SAUCE

Amount	Ingredient	Method
4 oz.	Butter	
½ c.	Jelly, apple	
½ c.	Catsup	} Thoroughly blend.
1 t.	Sugar	
1 t.	Allspice	
		Yield approx. 1¼ c.

Note: Fresh mint may be added.

MUSTARD SAUCE

Amount	Ingredient	Method
1 oz.	Sugar	⎫
½ t.	Salt	⎬ Mix.
2 t.	Mustard, dry	⎭
	Add	
2	Eggs, beaten	⎫
2 T.	Water	⎬ Mixed.
4 T.	Vinegar	⎭
	Cook in double boiler until thick.	
	Add	
1 oz.	Butter	} Stir until melted.
	When cold, fold in	
1 pt.	Cream, whipped	
		Yield approx. 2½ c.

NOTE: Serve cold with pork, beef, or ham roasts.

SPANISH SAUCE

Amount	Ingredient	Method
3 oz.	Onion, chopped	⎫ Fry until brown.
4 oz.	Butter	⎭
	Add	
2 qt.	Tomatoes, canned	⎫
1 lb.	Celery, diced	⎪
4 oz.	Green pepper, chopped	⎬ Let simmer slowly until all
6 oz.	Pimiento, chopped	vegetables are tender.
1 T.	Salt	⎪
½ t.	Pepper	⎭
f.g.	Cayenne	
		Yield 2½ qt.

BARBEQUE SAUCE

Amount	Ingredient	Method
¾ c.	Vinegar	⎫
3 oz.	Sugar	⎪
2¾ c.	Catsup	⎬ Mix.
1 oz.	Salt	⎪
2 T.	Onion, grated	⎭
		Yield approx. 1 qt.

BÉCHAMEL SAUCE

AMOUNT			INGREDIENT	METHOD
1½ qt.			Stock, white	Cook together 20 min. Strain.
	4		Onion slices	(There should be 1 qt. of
	2	T.	Peppercorns	liquid.) Use in the prepara-
	3	oz.	Carrots, chopped	tion of sauce.
	1		Bay leaf	
	8	oz.	Butter, melted	
	4	oz.	Flour	
1 qt.			Liquid (prepared above)	Use same procedure as for
1 qt.			Milk, hot	white sauce.
		½ t.	Salt	
		¼ t.	Pepper, white	
		f.g.	Cayenne	
				Yield approx. 2 qt.

NOTE: Serve with meat timbales or soufflé.

WHITE SAUCE

SAUCE I	SAUCE II	SAUCE III	SAUCE IV	INGREDIENT METHOD
8 oz.	10 to 12 oz.	12 to 16 oz.*	1½ to 2 lb.*	Fat, melted, hot
4 oz.	6 oz.	8 oz.	1 lb.	Remove from fire, add Flour }Stir until smooth.
1 T.	1 T.	1 T.	1 T.	Add Salt
1 t.	1 t.	1 t.	1 t.	Pepper, white
4 qt.	4 qt.	4 qt.	4 qt.	Add gradually, stirring constantly Milk, scalded Cook until smooth and thick. Yield 1 gal.

NOTE: If more than 4 qt. of white sauce are made, add approx. ¼ of the milk to the fat-flour mixture; stir until smooth; add this mixture to the remaining milk.

* May be reduced to 8 to 12 oz. If fat is reduced combine flour and salt with ¼ of the milk. Add flour-milk paste to remainder of milk that has been scalded. Cook to desired consistency. Add fat.

WHITE SAUCE VARIATIONS

Variation	Ingredients
	To 2 quarts White Sauce No. III
Caper Sauce.........	Add 1½ c. capers, drained
Celery Sauce........	Add 8 oz. celery, diced, cooked
Cheese Sauce........	Add 12 oz. cheese, grated
Egg Sauce...........	Add 8 eggs, hard-cooked, chopped
Horseradish Sauce...	Add (just before serving) 1½ c. horseradish, drained
Parsley Sauce........	Add 1 c. parsley, minced
Pimiento Sauce......	Add 6 oz. pimiento, chopped
Pepper Sauce........	Add (just before serving) ¼ c. red peppers, chopped ½ c. green peppers, chopped ½ c. pickle relish ¼ t. mustard seed ¼ t. celery seed

CHEESE SAUCE

Amount	Ingredient	Method
2 qt. 3 oz. 1 T. f.g.	Milk, hot Flour Salt Cayenne	} Make a sauce.
1½ to 2 lb.	Add Cheese, ground	} Mix. Yield approx. 3 qt.

Note: Do not cook after cheese is added.

SOUPS

Beautiful Soup, so rich and green,
Waiting in a hot tureen!
Who for such dainties would not stoop?
Soup of the evening, beautiful Soup.
                    —*Alice in Wonderland.*

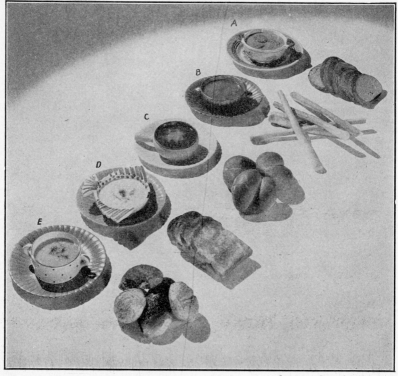

FIG. X.—The right accompaniment may determine the success of the soup course. (a) Potage St. Germaine calls for rye bread, (b) Minestrone for Italian bread sticks, (c) Onion soup au gratin for hard crusted rolls, (d) Clam chowder for lightly buttered toast, and (e) Navy bean soup for the hearty plain roll.

WHITE STOCK

Amount	Ingredient	Method
5 lb. 2 lb.	Veal knuckle Beef shank, lean	} Cut meat into small pieces and put bone and meat into kettle.
1½ gal.	Add Water, cold	} Bring to boiling point.
3 2½ oz. 2½ oz. ½ t. 1 2 oz.	Add Onions, chopped Celery, chopped Carrots, chopped Peppercorns Bay leaf Salt	} Let simmer until meat leaves bone (about 4 hr.)
	Remove meat, strain and skim off fat.	
4 4	Add Egg whites, beaten Egg shells, crushed	} Boil 5 min.
	Let simmer 15 min. Strain through cheese cloth. Yield 1 gal.	

Note: This stock may be used for fine soups. Chicken may be used for part of the meat in making this stock.

BROWN STOCK

Amount	Ingredient	Method
8 lb.	Brisket	} Wipe off meat with damp cloth. Dice.
	Put ⅔ of meat into stock pot.	
1½ gal.	Add Water, cold	} Let stand 30 min.
	Heat slowly to boiling point. Let simmer 2 hr.	
1 1 t. 1 1 T. 6 ⅓ above amount	Add Onion Celery seed Bay leaf Salt Cloves Beef	} Braised.
	Let simmer 3 hr.	
		Yield 1 gal.

VARIATIONS OF STOCK SOUP

Variation	Ingredients
	To 3 gallons meat stock
Alphabet Soup......	Add 2 T. celery salt ¼ t. pepper 4 oz. onion, grated 6 oz. carrots, grated 10 oz. alphabets
Barley Soup.........	Add 1 lb. 12 oz. barley
Bean Soup..........	Add 4 lb. 8 oz. navy beans, cooked 1 c. celery leaves, chopped 4 oz. onion
Beef Soup...........	Add 3 lb. beef, ground, fresh 5 oz. celery, chopped 5 oz. carrots, chopped 3 oz. onions, chopped 12 oz. peas 8 oz. rice (if desired)
Creole Soup.........	Add (use 3 qt. less stock) 1 No. 10 can tomatoes 1 lb. green peppers, shredded 1 lb. onion, chopped 1 lb. macaroni, cooked 2 oz. salt (may vary) ¼ t. pepper 4 bay leaves
Julienne Soup.......	Add 2 T. celery salt 1 lb. carrots, cut long, thin 1 lb. green beans, cut long, thin 12 oz. celery, cut long, thin 2 oz. onions, cut long, thin 2 oz. salt (may vary)
Noodle Soup........	Add 6 oz. (A.P.) noodles
Oyster Bouillon.....	Add 5 oz. carrots 4 oz. onions

VARIATIONS OF STOCK SOUP (continued)

Variation	Ingredients
	10 oz. green peppers 2 qt. strained tomatoes 6 oz. flour } Blended 6 oz. butter 2 oz. salt (may vary) 2 qt. oysters
Rice Soup..........	Add 1 lb. 8 oz. (A.P.) rice
Spaghetti Soup...... (or Vermicelli)	Add 12 oz. (A.P.) spaghetti
Split Pea Soup.......	Add 2½ lb. split peas 1 qt. tomatoes 2 oz. salt (may vary) 1 lb. salt pork, diced 1 c. celery leaves 1 pt. cream, thin
Tomato Bouillon....	Add (omit 6 qt. broth) 2 No. 10 cans tomatoes, strained 1 oz. onions, chopped 2 oz. sugar 2 oz. salt (may vary) ½ t. pepper ½ t. cloves 2 bay leaves ¼ T. peppercorns ½ t. soda
Vegetable Soup......	Add 3 qt. vegetables, cooked, mixed or 4 qt. vegetables, raw, mixed
Velouté Soup........	10 oz. flour } Blended 6 oz. butter Add Stock 6 oz. onions 1 oz. or more salt ½ T. peppercorns Vegetables, as desired

BOUILLON

Amount	Ingredient	Method
4　lb.	Bone	⎫ Crack the bone and add to the
3½ gal.	Water	⎭　　to the water.
	Add	
8　lb.	Beef, lean, seared	⎱ Let stand 1 hr.
	Let simmer for 3 to 4 hr.	
	Add	
8 oz.	Carrots, diced	⎫
8 oz.	Celery, chopped	⎪
2 oz.	Onion, chopped	⎬ Cook 1 hr. Strain. Chill over
1	Bay leaf	⎪　　night. Remove fat.
1 T.	Peppercorns	⎪
5 oz.	Salt	⎭
	To clear the broth, add	
3	Egg shells, crushed	
3	Egg whites, beaten	

Bring slowly to the boiling point, stirring constantly. Let boil 15 to 20 min. without stirring. Strain through a cloth.

VEGETABLE SOUP

Amount			Ingredient	Method
1	lb.	8　oz.	Carrots, diced	⎫
1	lb.		Turnips, diced	⎪
1	lb.		Cabbage, diced	⎬ Cook in 2 qt. boiling water
		8　oz.	Onions, diced	⎪　　until tender.
		2　oz.	Salt	⎭
			Add	
		4　oz.	Tapioca, minute	
			Add to	
2½ gal.			Stock, brown, hot	
			Add	
1	qt.		Tomato purée	
		¼ t.	Pepper	

PEPPER POT SOUP

Amount			Ingredient	Method
	2	oz.	Onions, chopped fine	
	8	oz.	Peppers, green, chopped fine	
	6	oz.	Celery, chopped	Fry vegetables in butter approx. 15 min.
3 lb. (E.P.)	8	oz.	Potatoes, diced	
	12	oz.	Butter	
			Add	
	5	oz.	Flour	Stir until well blended.
			Add	
7½ qt.			Stock, hot	
	1½	pt.	Milk, hot	Keep just below the boiling point for 30 min.
	1	oz.	Salt	
	2	T.	Pepper, red, chopped	

TOMATO RICE SOUP

Amount			Ingredient	Method
2 gal.			Soup stock	
1 gal.			Tomatoes, puréed	Heat to boiling point.
	1	oz.	Salt	
			Add	
	2	oz.	Onions, chopped	
	4	oz.	Green peppers, chopped	Cooked until rice is tender.
	8	oz.	Rice	
			Add	
	6	oz.	Fat, melted	Mix.
	3	oz.	Flour	

RICE SOUP

Amount	Ingredient	Method
8 lb. 1½ gal. 1 lb.	Soup bone and meat Water, cold Celery, diced	Make soup stock. There should be 4½ to 5 qt. when cooked.
	Add	
13 oz.	Rice	Cooked in 6 qt. of boiling water.
	Add	
1 gal.	Milk, hot	
1 t.	Onion juice	
2½ oz.	Salt	
1 t.	Pepper	
¼ c.	Parsley, chopped	

Note: Garnish with toast rings sprinkled with chopped parsley and Parmesan cheese.

SPLIT PEA SOUP

Amount	Ingredient	Method
4 lb. 2 gal.	Peas, split Water	Wash and soak over night.
	Add	
1	Ham bone (or 2 lb. salt pork) Cook in water in which peas were soaked. Cook 4 or 5 hr. or until peas are soft. Strain.	
	Add to peas	
4 oz.	Butter, melted	
2 oz.	Flour	
1 oz.	Onion, chopped	Made into a white sauce.
1½ oz.	Salt	
½ t.	Pepper	
2 qt.	Milk, hot	
	Bring to boiling point. Serve at once.	

Note: It may be necessary to add more salt. If soup becomes too thick add hot milk to bring to proper consistency.

SPANISH BEAN SOUP

Amount	Ingredient	Method
5 lb. 1 lb. 4½ gal.	Beans, kidney Onions, chopped Water	Cook until beans are tender. Strain.
	Add	
8 oz. 2 oz. 2 oz.	Onions, chopped Green peppers Butter or bacon fat	Fried until onions are slightly browned.
	Add	
1½ gal. 3 oz. 1¼ T.	Tomatoes, strained Salt Pepper	Heat about 10 min. Add to bean purée.
	Cook 5 min. to blend thoroughly the ingredients. Serving approx. 6 oz.	

Note: Baked bean purée may be substituted for kidney bean purée.

ORANGE SOUP (CH'EN TZU KENG)

Amount	Ingredient	Method
2 c. 6 oz. 1 t.	Water Sugar Salt	Heat to the boiling point.
	Add	
2 oz. ½ c.	Cornstarch Water, cold	Made into a paste.
6 qt. 2 oz.	Cook until clear, add Orange juice Butter Heat and serve at once.	

Note: Foundation may be made and kept covered. Reheat before adding fruit juice.

BASIC CREAM SOUP

Amount	Ingredient	Method
9 qt.	Milk, hot	
12 oz.	Butter, melted	
6 oz.	Flour	} Make a white sauce.
2 oz.	Salt	
½ t.	Pepper, white	

VARIATION

Asparagus Soup........
Add

6 lb. 8 oz. asparagus, cut and cooked
Strain after it has been added to the white sauce. Serve immediately.

Celery Soup..........
Add

1 lb. 8 oz. celery stalks, chopped
8 oz. carrots, diced
2½ oz. onions
1½ gal. water
Cook vegetables in the water for about 1 hr. Add to white sauce. Heat, then strain.

Corn Soup...........
Add

3 qt. corn
1 oz. onions, chopped
Strain after the corn has been added.

Pea Soup............
Add

3 qt. pea purée
2 oz. onions, minced
1 oz. sugar

Spinach Soup.........
Add

2½ to 3 qt. spinach purée
2 oz. onions, grated (optional)

CREAM OF POTATO SOUP

Amount		Ingredient	Method
12 lb.		Potatoes	Cook until the potatoes are soft. Purée or mash without draining.
	6 oz.	Onion, chopped	
9 qt.		Water	
		Add to	
9 qt.		Milk, whole, hot	
	12 oz.	Butter	
	3 oz.	Flour	Made into a white sauce.
	1½ t.	Pepper, white	
	3 oz.	Salt	

Bring to boiling point.
Sprinkle with parsley and serve.
Yield approx. 3 gal.

NOTE: 12 eggs beaten and added to the soup just before serving will improve the flavor.

CREAM OF TOMATO SOUP

Amount		Ingredient	Method
1½ gal.		Tomato purée, thin	Heat to boiling point.
	1 oz.	Onion, chopped	
	½	Bay leaf	
		Add	
	2 t.	Soda	Mix well.
		Just before serving, pour slowly into	
1½ gal.		Milk, hot	
	10 oz.	Butter, melted	
	6 oz.	Flour	Made into a white sauce.
	2 oz.	Salt	
	1 t.	Pepper	
	4 oz.	Sugar	

Yield approx. 3 gal.

NOTE: Chopped parsley and 1 t. whipped cream may be used as a garnish for each serving.

CREAM OF VEGETABLE SOUP

Amount	Ingredient	Method
1 lb. (E.P.)	Celery, chopped	
4 oz.	Onion, chopped	
1 lb.	Carrots, diced	Mix. Cook until vegetables are soft.
2 lb.	Potatoes, diced	
1 gal.	Water	
2 oz.	Salt	
	Add to	
9 qt.	Milk, hot	
5 oz.	Fat, melted	Made into a white sauce.
2⅔ oz.	Flour	
		Yield approx. 3 gal.

CREAM OF CHICKEN SOUP

Amount	Ingredient	Method
1 gal.	White Sauce No. I	Substitute chicken fat for butter in making the white sauce.
	Add	
2 gal.	Chicken stock	
2 t.	Celery salt	
¼ t.	Pepper, white	
		Yield 3 gal.

NOTE: 2 c. of chopped chicken and 2 c. of cooked rice may be added to the above recipe. Sprinkle chopped parsley over the top just before serving.

CORN CHOWDER

Amount	Ingredient	Method
1 lb.	Salt pork, cubed	Fry until crisp.
	Add	
12 oz.	Onions, chopped	Cook slowly 5 min.
	Pour into kettle	
5 lb. (E.P.)	Potatoes, cubed, cooked	
	Add	
1 No. 10 can	Corn	
	Add	
	Fat, tried from pork	
2 oz.	Flour	
7 qt.	Milk, hot	Made into a white sauce.
1 t.	Pepper, white	
2 oz.	Salt	
		Serving 6 oz.

CLAM CHOWDER

Amount	Ingredient	Method
2 qt. (8 9-oz. cans)	Clams	Clean. Steam until tender. Drain and chop (save juice).
	Add	
2 oz.	Onions, chopped	Fried together 5 min.
4 oz.	Salt pork	
	Add	
5 lb. (E.P.)	Potatoes, cubed, cooked	
1 T.	Salt	
	Add	
2 gal.	White Sauce No. I	
		Serving approx. 8 oz.

Note: Juice drained from clams may be substituted for an equal quantity of the milk in white sauce.

POTATO CHOWDER

Amount	Ingredient	Method
6 slices	Bacon, cubed	Fry together until onions are tender.
5 oz.	Onions, chopped	
	Add	
3 oz.	Flour	
	Add	
6 qt.	Milk, hot	
	Add	
5 lb.	Potatoes, cubed, cooked	Heat.
2 oz.	Salt	
1 t.	Pepper	
		Serving approx. 6 oz.

ACCOMPANIMENTS FOR SOUP

Bacon Square, broiled
and diced

Celery

Cheese Sticks

Cheese, grated on toast

Crackers, toasted

Crisped Bread

Croutons

Custard Cubes

Dumplings

Eggs, poached

Egg Balls

Julienne Vegetables

Melba toast

Olives

Parsley

Pickles

Radishes

Toast Sticks

Vegetables, crisp

Whipped Cream

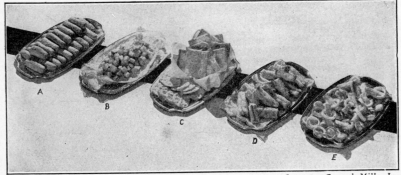

Courtesy, General Mills, Inc.

FIG. XI.—Pleasing accompaniments for the soup course.
(a) New style bread sticks, (b) croutons, (c) Melba toast, (d) toasted cheese rolls,
(e) toasted rings.

VEGETABLES

By the lamplit stall I loitered, feasting my eyes
On colors ripe and rich for the heart's desire—
Tomatoes, redder than Krakatoa's fire,
Oranges like old sunsets over Tyre,
And apples golden-green as the glades of Paradise.
—W. W. GIBSON, *Sight.*

VEGETABLE COOKERY

The amount of time required to cook any given vegetable will depend upon:

1. Method of cookery.
2. Age and condition of vegetable.
3. Preparation of the vegetable (large or small pieces).
4. The amount of water used and the temperature.
5. The amount of vegetable cooked at one time.
6. Chemical composition of the water.
7. The size and shape of container used.
8. Altitude.
9. Preference of clientele served.

DRIED VEGETABLES

A greater yield and a more satisfactory product is obtained from dried vegetables if they are soaked several hours before they are to be used.

Vegetable	Lbs.	Method	Approximate Cookery Time*
Asparagus..........	5	Steamer	8 to 10 minutes**
Asparagus..........	5	Stove	15 to 20 minutes
Green Beans........	5	Steamer	25 to 35 minutes
Green Beans........	5	Stove	45 to 55 minutes
Beets, unpeeled, old.	Up to 30	Steamer	1½ to 2 hours
Beets, peeled, shredded.........	5	Steamer	3 to 4 minutes**
Broccoli, stems split.	5	Steamer	6 to 8 minutes**
Broccoli............	5	Stove	12 to 15 minutes
Brussels Sprouts....	5	Steamer	6 to 8 minutes**
Brussels Sprouts....	5	Stove	15 to 20 minutes
Cabbage, cut.......	5	Steamer	6 to 8 minutes**
Cabbage, cut.......	5	Stove	15 to 20 minutes
Cabbage, shredded..	5	Steamer	5 minutes**
Carrots, quartered..	5	Steamer	15 to 20 minutes**
Carrots, quartered..	5	Stove	25 to 35 minutes
Cauliflower.........	5	Steamer	6 to 8 minutes**
Cauliflower.........	5	Stove	15 to 20 minutes
Onions.............	5	Stove	15 to 20 minutes
Parsnips, quartered..	5	Steamer	20 minutes**
Peas, fresh.........	5	Steamer	8 to 10 minutes**
Peas, fresh.........	5	Stove	20 to 25 minutes
Potatoes, sweet.....	Up to 30	Steamer	30 to 40 minutes
Potatoes, white.....	Up to 30	Steamer	20 to 30 minutes
Potatoes, white.....		Stove	30 to 45 minutes
Spinach............	5	Steamer	5 minutes**
Spinach............	5	Stove	18 to 25 minutes
Squash, summer....	5	Steamer	12 to 15 minutes**
Squash, summer....	5	Stove	20 to 30 minutes
Turnips, cut........	Up to 30	Steamer	15 to 20 minutes**
Turnips, cut........	5	Stove	20 to 30 minutes
Tomatoes, whole...		Oven	18 to 25 minutes

* If a steam jacketed kettle is used for cooking vegetables the cooking time required will be comparable to the time given for steaming.

** Arranged in a thin layer, preferably in the serving pan.

SUMMARY OF A STUDY OF THE WASTE AND TIME
OF PREPARATION OF CERTAIN FRESH
FRUITS AND VEGETABLES*

	Average Percentage of Waste	Time of Preparation Minutes per lb.
Vegetables:		
Beans, string....................	10.48	6.6
Cabbage........................	28.08	1.2
Carrots.........................	21.42	2.0
Cauliflower, untrimmed...........	72.89	0.5
Cauliflower, trimmed.............	53.58	0.7
Celery..........................	38.55	5.4
Cucumbers......................	25.54	2.7
Onions.........................	6.85	2.2
Peppers, green..................	28.11	—
Potatoes........................	27.67	1.1
Spinach........................	37.78	3.5
Sweet Potatoes..................	26.15	1.1
Tomatoes.......................	14.46	1.4
Fruits:		
Apples, unpeeled................	14.24	1.8
Apples, peeled..................	27.89	2.0
Bananas........................	33.44	—
Strawberries....................	18.43	7.3

* Lillian H. Johnson: "A Study of the Waste in and the Time of Preparation of Certain Fresh Fruits and Vegetables." Unpublished thesis (1931), Kansas State College.

CANNED VEGETABLES

Vegetable	Creamed Amount		Buttered Amount	
	Vegetable	White Sauce II	Vegetable	Butter
Asparagus........	2 No. 10 cans	2 qt.	2 No. 10 cans	8 oz.
Beans, wax.......	2 No. 10 cans	2 qt.	2 No. 10 cans	8 oz.
Beans, Lima......	1½-2 No. 10 cans	2 qt.	2 No. 10 cans	8 oz.
Carrots, diced.....	1½ No. 10 cans	2 qt.	2 No. 10 cans	8 oz.
Hominy..........	1½ No. 10 cans	2 qt.	2 No. 10 cans	8 oz.
Peas..............	1½ No. 10 cans	2 qt.	2 No. 10 cans	8 oz.
Tomatoes.........			2 No. 10 cans	8 oz.

CREAMED OR BUTTERED VEGETABLES

Vegetable	Creamed Amount		Buttered Amount	
	Vegetable	White Sauce II	Vegetable	Butter
Asparagus, tip..............	20 lb.	2 qt.	21 lb.	8 oz.
Asparagus, cut..............	10 lb.	3 to 3½ qt.	15 lb.	8 oz.
Broccoli....................			21 lb.	8 oz.
Cabbage....................	10 lb.	2 to 3 qt.	12 lb.	8 oz.
Carrots.....................	10 lb.	2½ to 3 qt.	12½ lb.	8 oz.
Cauliflower.................	10 lb. E.P.	2 to 3 qt.	10 lb. (E.P.)	8 oz.
Celery.....................	7 lb. E.P.	2 qt.		
Onions.....................	8 lb. E.P.	2 to 3 qt.	13 lb.	8 oz.
Potatoes....................	12 lb. E.P.	3 qt.	12 lb. (E.P.)	8 oz.
Peas.......................	25 lb.	2 qt.	25 lb.	8 oz.
Squash.....................			12 lb.	8 oz.
Tomatoes, whole............			18 lb.	8 oz.
Turnips, diced..............	10 lb.	2 qt.	10 lb.	8 oz.

NOTE: For scallop vegetables, place cooked vegetables in baking pan, cover with White Sauce No. II, and top with buttered crumbs. Bake.

MASHED POTATOES

Amount	Ingredient	Method
12 lb. (E.P.)	Potatoes	} Place in large kettle.
	Add	
1½ gal.	Water, boiling	⎫ Cook until tender.
3 oz.	Salt	⎭ Drain.
	Mash, and add	
2½ qt.	Milk, hot	
8 oz.	Butter	
2 oz.	Salt	
		Serving approx. 5 oz.

NOTE: Whip until light and creamy. Potatoes may be cooked in the steamer.

SCALLOPED POTATOES

Amount	Ingredient	Method
11 lb. (E.P.)	Potatoes	⎫ Slice. Place in 2 baking pans.
2 oz.	Salt	⎭
	Pour over potatoes	
1 gal.	White Sauce No. II, hot	
	Bake 1 hr., then cover potatoes with	
6 oz.	Bread crumbs	⎫ Mixed.
2 oz.	Butter, melted	⎭

Bake approx. 2 hr. 350°F.   Serving 5 oz.

NOTE: If a shorter cooking time is desired the sliced potatoes may be steamed until tender.

FRENCH FRIED POTATOES

Amount	Ingredient	Method
10 lb. (E.P.)	Potatoes	
		Cut into long narrow pieces. Cover with cold water. Let stand 1 hr. or longer. Drain. Place in wire basket and fry in deep fat about 2 min.
		Drain on brown paper. This may be done before serving time. At serving time fry the potatoes again until brown and tender.
		Serving approx. 3 oz.

NOTE: If raw, fry in deep fat approx. 4 min. 375°F.

SCALLOPED SWEET POTATO AND APPLE

Amount	Ingredient	Method
15 lb.	Sweet potatoes	Cook potatoes in skins. Peel and slice.
5 lb.	Apples, peeled and sliced	
	Place alternate layers of sweet potatoes and apples in baking pan.	
	Add	
1 lb.	Sugar, brown	
8 oz.	Sugar, white	
1½ oz.	Salt	Made into a sirup.
8 oz.	Butter	
2 qt.	Water	

Bake 45 min. 350°F.
NOTE: During the last 5 min. of baking, place 1 lb. of marshmallows on the top.
For Cranberry-Sweet Potato casserole substitute 7 lb. uncooked cranberries for apples, omit brown sugar, and add 4 lb. of granulated sugar.

GLAZED SWEET POTATOES

Amount	Ingredient	Method
20 lb.　(A.P.)	Sweet potatoes	Pare potatoes, then cook; or cook, then pare. Arrange in shallow pans.
	Pour over potatoes	
1 lb.　12　oz.	Sugar, brown	
1　pt.	Water	Mixed and heated to the boiling point.
4　oz.	Butter	
½ t.	Salt	

Bake approx. 15 to 20 min. 400°F.　　　　Serving approx. 4 oz.
NOTE: Baste frequently with sirup.

APPLES (Buttered)

Amount	Ingredient	Method
13 lb. (E.P.)	Apples	Cut apples into sections. Remove core. Arrange in pan.
	Add	
8 oz.	Butter	
1 pt.	Water, hot	Mixed.
1 lb. 8 oz.	Sugar	
1 oz.	Salt	
	Cover and let simmer until apples are tender.	

Cook approx. 1 hr.   Serving 4 oz.

Note: A more attractive product is obtained if apple sections are arranged in a serving pan and steamed until tender, butter and sugar sprinkled over the top, and then placed in the oven for 15 to 20 min.

Apples may be cut into rings and cinnamon drops "red-hots" added for flavor and color.

CABBAGE (Buttered)

Amount	Ingredient	Method
9 lb. (E.P.)	Cabbage	Remove outer leaves. Cut into quarters and remove stalk. Cut quarters in several pieces or shred. Cook in boiling salt water until tender.
4 gal.	Water, boiling	
4 oz.	Salt	
	Drain and add	
8 oz.	Butter, melted	

Cooking time approx. 20 min.   Serving 3 oz.

Note: Cabbage will cook in a shorter time if shredded and will yield a more desirable product.

SPINACH (Buttered)

Amount	Ingredient	Method
10 lb. (E.P.)	Spinach	Remove roots, wilted leaves, and coarse stems. Weigh. Wash first in warm water then in cold water until free from soil. Enough water will cling to the leaves so it is not necessary to add water to cook. Cook in uncovered kettle, stirring frequently with a fork until leaves are wilted. Drain if necessary.
	Add	
1 oz.	Salt	
8 oz.	Butter	

Cooking time approx. 20 min.   Serving 3 oz.

HOT SLAW

Amount			Ingredient	Method
1 lb.	5	oz.	Sugar	
	1	oz.	Salt	
	4	oz.	Flour	} Mix.
	2	t.	Mustard, dry	
			Add	
1 qt.			Milk, hot	
1 qt.	1	c.	Water, hot	} Stir and cook until thick.
			Add	
	8		Eggs, beaten	} Stirring constantly.
			Add	
	2⅔ c.		Vinegar, hot	
			Pour sauce over	
9 lb. (E.P.)			Cabbage, raw, shredded	
	4	t.	Celery seed	
				Serving approx. 3 oz.

Note: Do not pour hot sauce over cabbage until ready to serve. The sauce will yield 4 qt. This sauce may also be used as a cooked salad dressing.

VEGETABLE MACÉDOINE

Amount		Ingredient	Method
1 lb.	8 oz.	Celery	} Dice and cook together in
	6 oz.	Onion	juice drained from peas and
2 lb.		Carrots	enough water to make 5 c.
		When partially cooked, add	
1 lb.	8 oz.	Potatoes, diced	
2 lb.	8 oz.	Peas, canned	
3 lb.	4 oz.	Tomatoes, cooked	
	1 T.	Salt	
		When all vegetables are tender, add	
	4 oz.	Butter or bacon fat	} Creamed.
	1 oz.	Flour	

Cook approx. 45 min.   Serving approx. 3 oz.

SPANISH GREEN BEANS

Amount	Ingredient	Method
8 oz. 6 oz. 4 oz.	Bacon, diced Onion, chopped Green pepper, chopped	} Fry until onions are browned.
4 oz.	Add Flour	} Stir until smooth.
1 No. 10 can (or 6 lb.)	Add Tomatoes, hot	} Stir well.
2 No. 10 cans (or 10 lb.)	Add Green beans, drained Pour into a flat pan. Let simmer approx. 30 min.	

GERMAN CARROTS

Amount	Ingredient	Method
1 qt. 2 t. 2 oz. 2 lb.	Vinegar, dilute Salt Cornstarch Sugar	Make into a sauce. Cook 5 min.
8 oz.	Add Butter	} Stir until melted.
10 lb.	Add Carrots, cooked, diced	}Let simmer 15 min.

When ready to serve, sprinkle with chopped parsley.
Serving approx. 3 oz.

NOTE: Use the water in which the carrots were cooked to make the sauce, if possible; if this water is used omit salt from sauce.

BRAISED CELERY

Amount	Ingredient	Method
8 lb. (E.P.)	Celery	} Use outside stalks and cut into 1½-in. pieces.
1 gal.	Cook until tender in Broth	
6 oz. 1 c.	Add Flour Broth, cold	} Made into a thin paste.
1 t.	Add Salt (or more)	

Cook approx. 1 hr.   Serving approx. 3 oz.

SCALLOPED CUCUMBERS

Amount	Ingredient	Method
14 lb.	Cucumbers	} Pare. Slice lengthwise and remove hard seeds. Steam 3 min. Drain.
	Arrange in oiled baking pan.	
1 oz. 1 t.	Sprinkle with Salt Pepper	
2½ qt. 6 oz.	Pour over the cucumbers White Sauce No. IV Pimiento, chopped	} Mixed.
8 oz.	Sprinkle over the top Buttered bread crumbs	

Bake approx. 30 min. 350°F.
Note: For variety cheese may be added to white sauce.

HOT POTATO SALAD

Amount	Ingredient	Method
1 lb.	Bacon	}Dice and fry.
1½ pt. 1 pt.	Add Mayonnaise Cooked salad dressing	
15 lb. (E.P.)	Add Potatoes	}Diced and steamed until tender.
3 oz. 6 oz. 12	Add Onion Green pepper, chopped Eggs, hard-cooked	

Combine all ingredients just before serving.
Serving approx. 4 oz.

Note: Bacon and salad dressing may be omitted and one recipe of hot vegetable sauce added.

HARVARD BEETS

Amount	Ingredient	Method
10 lb	Beets, fresh	

Cut tops from beets, leaving 2-in. stems. Weigh.
Do not remove roots.
Wash and cook until tender. Plunge into cold water.
Remove skins. Cut into ½-in. cubes. (May use 2
No. 10 cans of beets in place of fresh beets.)
Raw beets may be peeled, shredded and cooked 4
min. in steamer.

SAUCE

Amount	Ingredient	Method
12 oz. 1 oz. 8 oz.	Sugar Salt Cornstarch	}Mix.
2 qt.	Add Water, hot	} Stirring constantly.
4 oz. 1½ c.	Cook until thick; add Butter Vinegar	

Add the sauce to the beets and reheat.

Note: If the beets are canned, use the beet juice in place of water.

BAKED TOMATOES

Amount	Ingredient	Method
50	Tomatoes (4 to 5 oz. each)	} Wash. Cut cone-shaped piece from center.
3 oz.	Add Salt Allow to stand 1 hr.	}¼ t. in center of each tomato.
2 oz. 6 oz.	Add Bread crumbs, coarse Onions, chopped fine	} Place 1 t. crumbs and 1 t. onion in each tomato.

Bake 15 to 20 min. 400°F.

SAUTÉED TOMATOES

Amount	Ingredient	Method
15 lb.	Tomatoes	}Wash. Cut into ½-in. slices.
3½ oz.	Season with Salt	
1 lb. 2 oz. 12 oz.	Dredge in Bread crumbs, dry Flour	} Mixed.
1 lb.	Sauté in Butter	

STUFFED BAKED ONIONS

Amount	Ingredient	Method
50	Onions (4 oz. each)	} Peel. Scoop out center. Steam until tender.
1 lb. 1 oz. 1½ qt. 1 lb. 6	Fill with Bread crumbs, dry Salt White Sauce No. I Butter Egg yolks, beaten	} Mixed with onion centers cooked and chopped.

Cover tops with buttered crumbs.

Bake 400°F. until browned.

NOTE: For variation 1 lb. chopped almonds may be added to filling. For plain baked onions, make a small cavity in each onion; steam. Sprinkle salt in each onion and fill with buttered crumbs. Bake until brown.

BAKED BEANS

Amount			Ingredient	Method
5 lb.			Beans, navy	Weigh, wash and soak over night. Drain.
			Add	
1 gal.	1	pt.	Water	}Cook until tender.
			Add to beans	
	2	oz.	Salt	
	6	oz.	Sugar, brown	
	1	t.	Mustard, dry	
	1	oz.	Vinegar	
	8	oz.	Molasses	
	2½	c.	Catsup (optional)	
1 lb.			Salt pork, cubed	
			Pour into baking pan.	

Bake 4 hr. 350°F.   Serving approx. 3 oz.

NOTE: If necessary more water may be added to beans while cooking.

BAKED LIMA BEANS

Amount		Ingredient	Method
6 lb.		Beans, Lima	Soak beans in cold water. Drain. Add boiling water; cook until tender.
1 gal.		Water, boiling	
		Add to beans	
	4 oz.	Pimiento, chopped	
	8 oz.	Fat, bacon	}Mixed.
	1 oz.	Salt	
	1 c.	Molasses	
		Pour beans into a baking pan.	
		Place on the top of beans	
1 lb.	8 oz.	Salt pork, sliced	
		Bake until tender and brown.	

Bake approx. 2 hr. 350°F.   Serving approx. 5 oz.

CURRIED RICE

Amount	Ingredient	Method
12 oz. 12 oz.	Onion, minced Butter	} Cook until onions are slightly browned.
3 lb.	Add Rice, washed	} Stir until butter is absorbed.
½ oz. 1½ oz. 2½ qt.	Add Curry powder Salt Water, boiling	} Boil 10 min.
	Pour rice mixture into double boiler. Add	
3 qt.	Milk, hot	} Cook until rice is tender. Serving 5 oz.

Note: Serve with veal stew.

SPANISH RICE

Amount	Ingredient	Method
2 lb. 4 oz.	Rice	} Wash in cold water. Cook in 8 qt. boiling water until tender. Drain and wash with hot water.
4 lb. 2½ oz. 2 oz.	Add Tomatoes, canned Pimiento, chopped Salt	
1 lb. 8 oz. 4 oz.	Add Bacon, chopped Onion, chopped Green pepper, chopped	} Fried together.
	Pour into oiled pan.	

Bake approx. 1 hr. 350°F.   Serving approx. 5 oz.

SWEET POTATO AND ALMOND CROQUETTES

Amount	Ingredient	Method
10 lb. (E.P.)	Sweet potatoes	} Cook and mash.
	Add	
16	Egg yolks, beaten	} Mix well.
1 c.	Cream	
	Add	
2 t.	Nutmeg	
5 T.	Sugar	} Mix well.
1 T.	Salt	
1 lb.	Almonds, chopped	
	Measure with a No. 12 dipper.	
	Let stand in ice box 2 hr.	
	Remove ½ hr. before frying.	
	Dip in egg mixture.	
	Roll in	
1 lb.	Cornflakes	
	Shape. Place a few croquettes in wire basket.	

Fry in deep fat 3 to 4 min. 375°F.
NOTE: Sweet potato puffs for a large number may be made by placing them on an oiled pan, and baking them 30 to 45 min. 350°F.

RICE CROQUETTES

Amount	Ingredient	Method
2 lb. 4 oz.	Rice	} Wash with cold water.
	Add to	
3 qt.	Milk, hot	
1½ qt.	Water, hot	} Cook until tender.
2 oz.	Salt	
	Add	
16	Eggs, beaten	} Cook until eggs are done.
2 oz.	Butter	
	Measure with a No. 12 dipper. Let cool 2 hr. Shape.	
	Egg and crumb, using	
1 c.	Milk	
3	Eggs	
12 oz.	Crumbs, bread	

Fry in deep fat approx. 3 to 4 min. 375°F.
NOTE: Serve with cheese sauce or apricot sauce.

HOT CORN SANDWICH

Amount		Ingredient	Method
3 qt.		Tomato purée	
2 qt.		Corn	
1 lb.		Butter	Make as white sauce.
	4 oz.	Pimientos, chopped	
	2 oz.	Salt	
	8 oz.	Flour	
		Add	
1 lb.	8 oz.	Cheese, ground	When cheese is melted add
	2 T.	Paprika	eggs.
20		Egg yolks, beaten	
		Heat over water until yolks are cooked, stirring constantly.	

Note: Serve immediately on a split toasted bun.

VEGETABLE PIE

Amount		Ingredient	Method
3 lb. (E.P.)		Carrots, raw, diced	
2 lb. (E.P.)		Potatoes, diced	
	2 oz.	Onion, chopped	Cook vegetables until tender.
	2 oz.	Pepper, green, chopped	
2 qt.		Water, or more	
		Add	
2 lb.		Peas	Drain liquid from peas and
4 lb.		Tomatoes	tomatoes and use with other
	3 oz.	Flour	ingredients to make a sauce.
	1 oz.	Salt	Add this to peas and to-
	1 t.	Pepper	matoes.
	6 oz.	Fat, bacon	
		Pour into 2 pans 12 in. x 20 in.	
		Cover with biscuit dough.	

Bake 20 min. 400°F.
Note: Use ½ of biscuit recipe and roll to ½-in. thickness, rectangular shape.

VEGETABLE TIMBALES

Amount		Ingredient	Method
2 qt.	1 c.	Vegetable, finely chopped or puréed	
18		Eggs, beaten	
		Add	
1½ qt.		Milk, hot	
	6 oz.	Butter, melted	Made into a white sauce.
	3 oz.	Flour	
	1½ oz.	Salt	
		Pour into 50 custard cups.	
		Place cups in pans of hot water.	

Bake 30 min. 350°F.
NOTE: Use carrots, cabbage, asparagus, spinach, or chard.

PREPARATION AND ADDITIONAL SUGGESTIONS FOR SERVING VEGETABLES

1. *Artichokes.* Cut off stem close to leaves and 1 in. off from the top. Cook in a large quantity of boiling, salted water 30 min. to 1 hr., depending on size.

2. *Fresh Asparagus with Cheese Sauce.* Place 5 or 6 stalks of cooked asparagus on each plate and garnish with a tablespoon of cheese sauce and riced egg yolk.

3. *Broccoli.* Remove only large outer leaves and tough part of stem. Cover with rapidly boiling, salted water. Cooked in uncovered utensil 12 to 15 min. Serve with lemon or Hollandaise sauce.

4. *Brussels Sprouts.* Trim outer leaves from sprouts and a little off stem. Cook in a large quantity of boiling, salted water 10 to 15 min. in uncovered kettle.

5. *Julienne Carrots and New Peas.* Cut carrots into long narrow strips, cook, and add butter. Place 4 or 5 strips on each plate and place a tablespoon of buttered peas in the center.

6. *Buttered, Latticed Carrots.* Cut the carrots with a lattice slicer and cook until tender; serve with melted butter.

7. *Carrots O'Brien.* Cut carrots into long narrow strips, cook, and add butter in which pepper strips have been cooked. Cook a few minutes and add pimiento strips before serving.

8. *Corn with Green Pepper Ring.* Place a ring of green pepper on each serving of buttered, whole grain corn.

9. *Green Peppers Stuffed.* Remove fresh corn from cob. Season with salt, pepper, and sugar, and cook partially. Stuff peppers with this mixture and bake in milk.

10. *Green Peppers Stuffed.* Stuff green peppers with macaroni or mashed potatoes.

11. *Egg in Green Pepper Rings.* Cut peppers into wide rings, parboil, and arrange in oiled baking pans. In each ring place an egg. Bake until firm.

12. *Broiled Tomatoes.* Select firm ripe tomatoes. Slice, dip in egg, and then

in flour. Place in pan, dot each piece with butter. Cook under broiler or in a very hot oven. Tomatoes may also be broiled whole. Cut off top, dot with butter, and place under broiler.

13. *Celery and Rice.* Cook celery and when tender add cooked rice. Let simmer 20 min. Add butter. Garnish.

14. *Stuffed Turnips.* Remove the center from a medium-sized cooked turnip. Fill with buttered peas or baked beans.

15. *Apple Rings.* Cut rings of unpeeled apple, steam until tender, add sugar and butter, and bake 15 min. Garnish with jelly.

16. *French Fried Squash.* Use a French vegetable cutter to make balls from squash. Steam until tender, roll in batter, then in crumbs, and fry.

17. *French Fried Pineapple Rings.* Bread pineapple rings and fry in deep fat.

18. *Spinach and Beets.* Serve spinach with sliced new beets.

19. *Stuffed Tomatoes.* Stuff tomatoes with cooked rice, cover with buttered bread crumbs, and broil.

20. *Stuffed Tomatoes.* Stuff broiled tomatoes with cooked cauliflower. Serve with cheese sauce.

21. *Stuffed Beets.* Stuff cooked beets with a mixture of bread crumbs, onion juice, beet pulp, salt, and pepper. Bake.

22. *Rice (Oriental).* Boil 4 lb. of rice in 3 qt. of water, to which 1½ oz. of salt has been added, until nearly all the water has evaporated. Cover and place over very low flame. Steam until water is absorbed, about 30 min. Remove cover and let rice dry. If brown rice is used, time for cooking is approx. 1 hr.

23. *Mushrooms.* Clean thoroughly. Peel all but tender young caps.

To fry: Add whole sliced mushrooms to butter (2 oz. butter to 1 lb. mushrooms). Cover and cook over low heat until tender, approx. 10 min.

To cream: Proceed as for frying; when cooked 2 min. add flour (2 T. to 1 lb. mushrooms). Blend, add 1 pt. thin cream. Cover and cook 5 min. Season.

To broil: Remove and chop stems. Season. Use these to fill hollows of caps. Place in shallow pan. Dot with butter. Broil.

24. For variety, use:
    a. Creamed fresh peas and mushrooms.
    b. Scalloped peas and onions.
    c. Scalloped or creamed carrots and onions.
    d. Corn and tomatoes.
    e. Lima beans and corn (succotash).
    f. Scalloped cauliflower and apples.
    g. Carrots and celery.
    h. Scalloped cucumbers with tomatoes, green peppers and onions.
    i. Scalloped spinach with tomato.
    j. Scalloped celery and peas.
    k. Peas cooked in water containing mint leaves and sugar. Lemon juice and butter added before serving.
    l. Tomatoes and celery stewed.

PART III

MENU PLANNING

The initial step toward a successful meal is a carefully planned menu. The usual dietetic principles and menu-planning suggestions should be followed with special emphasis upon the following points:

1. *The age, sex, and occupation of the group to be served.* In most cases, the type of food suitable for a men's civic club would not be enjoyed by a group of high-school girls, nor would the luncheon considered by the high-school girls as "perfectly delicious" be fully appreciated by the men's club. Food preferences are definitely influenced as are food needs, by the age, sex, and occupation of the persons comprising the group being served.

2. *The income and cost dispersion.* The amount paid for a meal and the number of guests served determine to a great extent the type of meal that can be served. Within limits, the larger the number served, the better the quality and the wider the variety which can be served for a given price.

3. *The number to be served.* Besides affecting the variety of food that can be served for a given price, the number to be served also influences the method of preparing the food. For example, it would be difficult, under usual institutional conditions, to prepare grilled tomatoes or stuffed baked potatoes for a large group.

4. *Climate and season.* The climate and season must be considered in the choice of foods. Plan cool, crisp, fresh foods for hot weather. In cold weather the heavier foods high in caloric value may be used. Use foods which are in season; they are less expensive and of a better quality. Certain foods are especially enjoyed at holiday times, such as turkey at Thanksgiving and plum pudding at Christmas.

5. *Equipment needed.* There is a definite relation between the menu and the equipment available for its preparation. The menus should be planned so that the preparation will require only the available equipment. The dining room equipment (dishes, linen, and silver) also limits the extent of the menu, the table setting, and the type of service.

6. *Type of kitchen employees and time for preparation.* If the food is to be prepared by inexperienced class girls or untrained employees, the menu must be kept simple in detail and foods selected that do not require special skill or extra time for preparation. It is always advisable to have a minimum amount of last-minute preparation so that all hot foods may be served *hot* and cold foods *cold.*

7. *The place of service and the number of waitresses.* It is obvious that the place of service and the number of waitresses available should influence the kind and extent of the menu. An elaborate menu consisting of many

courses and requiring an elaborate form of service should not be used when the number of waitresses is limited and the space between the tables is small.

8. *Appearance of the plate.* It is important that the plate present an inviting appearance. Harmonious colors and dainty, attractive arrangement of food play a large part in a successful meal. One should avoid uninteresting meals that are drab in color. Foods that clash in color, such as beets and radishes, or carrots and tomatoes, should not appear on the plate together.

9. *Variety.* Variety should be introduced not only in the kind of food but in the preparation, texture, flavor, and garnish. See that no one food predominates in the meal. Do not serve two foods prepared in the same manner, such as two creamed, two buttered, or two fried foods. The texture of the food should vary. Have a good balance between the soft and the solid foods. Avoid serving, at the same time, two dishes of similar flavor or two of pronounced flavors. There should be a definite contrast in flavor and texture between the foods of different courses.

10. *Recipes.* Many a well-planned menu has been a failure because sufficient thought was not given to the selection of recipes. The cooks should be familiar with the recipes so there will be no question as to the yield or quality of the finished product. If deviations from the original recipes are necessary great care should be used in making substitutions in any formula, as both the quality and yield may be affected.

Menus as commonly written may include a first course, such as a canapé, a fruit drink, vegetable juice, fruit cup, sea-food cocktail, chowders. In some dinners both a cocktail and a soup are served. These are usually selected after consideration of the main course, which, as has been said, is centered about the main dish or meat. The choice of the meat suggests, if it does not prescribe, the vegetables to be served with it, the character of the course or courses preceding it, the salad found most palatable with it, and the type of dessert to be used.

Menu Forms. The recording of menus on a menu-planning sheet will be found helpful. The procedure often followed in preparing this sheet is to fill out the meat column for the three meals a day for the entire time for which the menus are being planned, whether eight weeks or one week, and then to evolve the rest of each meal about the meat or main dish chosen.

Listed in steps the menu planning and its recording are about as follows:

1. Plan meat or other main dish.
2. Plan vegetables, including potatoes.
3. Plan salad.

4. Plan hot bread.
5. Plan dessert.
6. Plan first course, if one is to be served.
7. Plan beverage.
8. Plan cereals, if used.
9. Plan breakfast fruits.

On the following pages there are given lists of meat arranged according to their suitability for dinner menus or luncheon menus. There are also lists of vegetables, salads, garnishes, breads, and desserts. These lists, although not complete and exhaustive, are fairly comprehensive. Reference to them should afford suggestions for varying menus. Further suggestions for salads and vegetables are given under these headings in the recipe section of this manual.

MENU PLANNING SUGGESTIONS, LIST I: MEATS

DINNER MEATS	LUNCHEON MEATS	DINNER OR LUNCHEON MEATS
Chicken	Beef and Veal	Chicken
Baked	Browned Beef Stew	and Rice Casserole
Broiled	Beef Stew with	à la King
Fricasseed	Dumplings	Creamed
Fried	Meat Balls with	Croquettes
Maryland	Spaghetti	Cutlets
Beef and Veal	Meat Patties, Braised	Pie
Corned Beef	Beef Steak Pie	Scalloped
Steaks, Beef, Broiled	Beef Upside Down	Stewed
Chops	Pie	Timbales
Minute	Spanish Meat Balls	Turnovers
Fillet Mignon	Meat Croquettes	With dumplings
Sirloin	Meat Turnovers	With noodles
Steaks, Veal, Braised	Chop Suey	With waffles
T-bone	Chili, Mexican	With biscuits
Steaks, Round	Chow Mein	In patty shells
Braised	Meat Loaf	Fish
Country Fried	Creamed Beef	Baked in Milk
Cubed	Creamed Dried Beef	Broiled
Swiss	Baked Hash	Steamed
Spanish	Beef Rolls	à la Creole
Roast Beef	Beef Ragout	à la Newburg
Roast Veal	Meat Pie	Frog Legs, fried
Stuffed Flank Steak	Beef Shortcake	Clams, creamed
Veal Cutlets	Stuffed Peppers	Clams, scalloped
Breaded	Hungarian Goulash	Clams, fried
Baked in Sour	Italian Spaghetti	Crab, à la King
Cream	Shepherds' Pie	Crab, deviled
Veal Birds	Veal à la King	Lobster, à la New-
Veal Birds with	Veal Croquettes	burg
Mushroom Stuffing	Veal Pie	Oysters, fried
Fish	Veal Patties	Oysters, scalloped
Baked	Veal Soufflé	Scallops, creamed
Baked, Stuffed	Veal Stew with	Scallops, fried
Broiled	Vegetables	Scallops and Mush-
Boiled	Creamed Veal in	rooms, baked
Ham (cured)	Patty Cases	Shrimp Creole
Baked	Curried Veal with	Shrimp, scalloped
Boiled	Rice	Ham
Spiced	Ragout of Veal	Ham Loaf
Virginia Baked	Fish	Lamb
	Casserole of Rice	Loin Chops
	and Tuna	Pork
	Codfish Balls	Spare Ribs with
	Creamed Tuna	Dressing
		Veal
		Fricassee

Dinner Meats	Luncheon Meats	Luncheon Dishes
Baked Veal, Ham, Apricots	Creamed Salmon	Cheese Rarebit
Ham and Sweet Potato en Casserole	Fish Soufflé	Cheese Balls
Fried Ham	Salmon Croquettes	Cheese Croquettes
Lamb	Salmon Loaf	Cheese Soufflé
Chops	Salmon and Potato Chip Casserole	Cheese Fondue
Roast	Tuna and Noodles	Macaroni and Cheese
Pork	Ham	Scalloped Macaroni
Baked Ham	Creamed Ham	Creole Spaghetti
Breaded Pork Tenderloin	Creamed Ham and Celery	Baked Rice and Cheese
Pork Chops	Ham à la King	Spanish Rice
Pork Chops, deviled	Ham Croquettes	Rice Croquettes with Cheese Sauce
Pork Chops, stuffed	Ham Soufflé	Egg-Rice Casserole
Roast Pork	Ham Timbales	Chinese Omelet
Miscellaneous	Ham and Egg Scallop	Fried Mush
Braised Tongue	Lamb	Fried Scrapple
Liver and Bacon	Creole Lamb	Baked Eggs and Bacon Rings
Liver, Braised	Curried Lamb with Rice	Baked Eggs with Cheese
Liver and Onions	Lamb Fricassee with Noodles	Curried Eggs
Stuffed Baked Heart	Lamb Stew	Creamed Eggs
Mock Drum Sticks	Pork	Egg Cutlets
Flank Steak, stuffed	Pork and Noodle Ring	Hot Stuffed Eggs
	Pork Pie (biscuit)	Eggs à la King
	Pork Pie (pie crust)	Scalloped Eggs and Cheese
	Sausage Cakes	Plain Omelet
	Link Sausage Rolls	Spanish Omelet
	Sausage and Dressing	Fruit Omelet
	Rice, Sausage, and Tomato	Potato Omelet
	Sweetbreads	Hot Potato Salad
	Creamed	Vegetable Pie
	Cutlets	Baked Lima Beans
	à la King	Baked Navy Beans
	Timbales and Ham, creamed	Vegetable Timbales
		Fried Potatoes with Cheese
		Spinach Timbales with Poached Egg
		Mushroom Soufflé
		Spoon Bread with Bacon
		French Toast
		Scrambled Eggs

MENU PLANNING SUGGESTIONS, LIST II:
VEGETABLES

Potatoes or Substitute	Other Starchy	Green
Potatoes, Irish	Corn	Apples
Au Gratin	In Cream	Buttered Apple
Baked	Balls or Fritters	Rings
Browned in oven	Creole	Hot Baked
Browned in deep fat	Squaw	Buttered Sections
Buttered	Scalloped	Artichoke
Chips	Pudding	With Butter
Creamed	With Celery and	With Mayonnaise
Croquettes	Bacon	Asparagus
Duchess	With Green Pepper	French Fried
Fried	Rings	Buttered
French Fried	Succotash	With Cream
Hot Potato Salad	Carrots	With Hollandaise
Latticed	Creamed	With Cheese Sauce
Lyonnaise	Scalloped	On Toast
Potato Curls	Stuffed	Beans, Green
Potato Cakes	Timbales	Buttered
O'Brien	Molded Ring	With Hollandaise
Potato Omelet	O'Brien	With Cheese
Rissolé	Bananas	With Tomato Sauce
Riced	French Fried	With Celery Strips
Scalloped	Baked	Beets
Spanish	Green Peppers	Buttered
Stuffed Baked	Stuffed with Maca-	Harvard
Rice	roni	Harvard with
Buttered	Stuffed with Corn	Raisins
Creamed	Lima Beans	Pickled
Curried	Baked	Broccoli
Cooked in Broth	Buttered	Buttered
With Tomato Sauce	Creole	With Cheese Sauce
Noodles	Onions	With Hollandaise
Cooked in Broth	Creamed	Brussels Sprouts
Creamed	French Fried	Buttered
With Tomato Sauce	Stuffed with Crumbs	With Cheese Sauce
Macaroni	Stuffed with Baked	With Hollandaise
Cooked in Broth	Beans	Cabbage
Creamed	Peas	Au Gratin
With Tomato Sauce	Creamed	Buttered
Spaghetti	Scalloped	Polonaise
Cooked in Broth	Squash	Hot Slaw
Creamed	Baked	Carrots
With Tomato Sauce	Mashed	Glazed
Sweet Potatoes	French Fried	Mint Glazed
Au Gratin	Baked Stuffed	

MENU PLANNING SUGGESTIONS, LIST II:
VEGETABLES (continued)

Potatoes or Substitute	Other Starchy	Green
Baked Candied Scalloped Fried Glazed Mashed Sweet Potato and 　Almond Croquettes	Turnips 　Creamed 　Scalloped	German 　Buttered, strips 　Buttered, rounds 　Buttered, latticed Cauliflower 　Au Gratin 　Buttered 　Creamed 　French Fried 　With Hollandaise

OTHER GREEN VEGETABLES

Celery
　Braised
　Buttered
Celery-Cabbage
　Buttered
Corn on Cob
Cucumbers
　Scalloped
　French Fried
Egg Plant
　Fried
　French Fried
　Scalloped
　Soufflé
Kale
　Buttered
Mustard Greens
　With Ham
Lettuce
　Stewed with
　　Spanish Sauce
　Wilted
Mushrooms
　Broiled
　Creamed
　Fried
Onions
　Baked
　Buttered
　In Cream
　Stuffed
　With Spanish Sauce
　French Fried

Peas
　Buttered
　With Hollandaise
　With Diced Celery
　Served in Rosettes
Parsnips
　Buttered
　Cooked in Meat
　　Broth
　Browned
Pineapple Ring
　Fried
　Breaded
Radishes
　Raw
　Buttered
Spinach
　Buttered
　Molded in Ring with
　　Hard-Cooked Egg
　With Tomato

Squash
　Baked
　Baked Half Acorn
　　with Broiled
　　Tomato
　Mashed
　French Fried
　Buttered
Tomato
　Baked, Stuffed
　Broiled with
　　Hollandaise
　Creole
　Croquettes
　Fresh, stewed
　Fried
　Green Tomatoes,
　　fried
　Grilled
　Scalloped
　Tomato and Corn
Turnips
　Buttered
　In Cream
　Mashed

MENU PLANNING SUGGESTIONS, LIST III: SALADS*

Fruit	Vegetable	Gelatin	Ices	Main Dish
Apple	Asparagus	Apple-Nut Gelatin	Apricot	Brown Bean
Balls	Tips with pimiento	Apple-Cheese Gelatin,	Banana	Cottage Cheese
Diced	In green pepper ring	layered	Cherry	Cheese-Pea-Pickle
Julienne	Bean, green	Cabbage, Celery in	Cider	Chicken-Celery
Sections	Marinated	tomato jelly	Cranberry	Chicken, Celery, Ham
Spiced	In combination	Carrot-Pineapple	Currant	Chicken, Celery, Almonds
Apricot	Beet	Carrot, Peas, Cabbage	Gooseberry	Chicken, Celery, Peas
Stuffed with pineapple	Cups	Cheese	Grapefruit	Chicken, Celery, Veal
With pears	Pickled	Cherry-Olive	Lemon	Crab
In combination	In combination	Chicken	Lime	Egg
Banana	Broccoli	Cranberry	Mint	Stuffed
In combination	With tomato section	Cucumber, Pineapple	Orange	with celery
Wedges	Cabbage	Beet	Pineapple	pimiento
Cherries	Shredded	Pickled	Raspberry	green pepper
Stuffed	In combination	In combination	Rhubarb	With tomato
With pear ball	With sugar and vinegar	Fruit Combination	Strawberry	In combination
With peach ball	Carrot	Ginger Ale Fruit	Tomato	Lobster
In combination	Diced, raw	Perfection		Macaroni
Cranberry	Strips, raw	Prune, Orange Sections, jellied		Meat
Raw with orange	Rings, raw	Salmon		Potato
With grape and pineapple	Shredded, raw	Spiced Fruit Combination		Salmon
With applesauce	Cooked and raw	Tomato Aspic Rings		Shrimp
Frozen Fruit	In combination	Tomato-Cheese		Tuna Fish
Fruit, combination	Cauliflower	Vegetable Combination		
Grapefruit	Raw with carrots			
Sections	Raw with tomatoes			
In combination	Raw with oranges			
Orange	In combination			
Sections	Celery			
Sliced	Curls			
In combination	Hearts			

Peach
Halves
In combination
Spiced halves
Pineapple
Slices
In combination
Prune
Spiced
Stuffed
(See Fruit Salad Suggestions)

Stuffed
In combination
Celery Cabbage
Shredded
Corn
Relish in cucumber boats
Cucumber
Cups
Sliced
Sections
In combination
Lettuce
Head lettuce section
Head lettuce slices
Shredded lettuce
With tomato
Peas
In combination
With cheese and pickles
Radish
Strips
Slices
In combination
Salad Greens
Spinach, raw
Tomato
Sliced
Sections
Stuffed
In combination
Turnip
Watercress
(See Vegetable Salad Combination)

* For more detailed salad suggestions, see p. 192 and p. 202.
The ices may be used in place of a salad with the dinner course.

MENU PLANNING SUGGESTIONS, LIST IV: GARNISHES

Yellow-Orange	Red	Green	White	Brown-Tan	Black and Miscellaneous
Cheese	Fruit	Fruit	Fruit	Breads	Caviar
Balls	Cherries	Avocado	Apple rings	Tiny biscuits	Chocolate-covered mints
Grated	Cinnamon apples	Cherries	Apple balls	Croustades	Chocolate sprill
Strips	Cranberries	Green plum	Grapefruit sections	Croutons	Chocolate, shredded
Piped on with pastry tube	Strawberries	Honeydew melon	Gingered apple	Cheese straws	Chocolate sauce
Egg.	Red raspberries	Preserves and Other Sweets	White raisins	Fritters, tiny	Dates, raw
Sliced hard-cooked eggs	Maraschino cherries	Angelica	White grapes	Noodle rings	Dates, spiced
Deviled egg halves	Watermelon cubes	Candied mint leaves	Pear balls	Noodle flowers	Dates, stuffed
Hard-cooked egg sections	Watermelon balls	Citron	Pear sections	Toast	Olives, ripe
Hard-cooked egg arranged as flowers	Preserves and Other Sweets	Green sugar	Vegetables	Cubes	Prunes
Riced egg yolk	Apple jelly	Gelatin cubes	Cabbage, shredded	Points	Prunes, spiced
Fruit.	Cranberry glacé	Mint jelly	Cauliflowerets	Strips	Pickled walnuts
Apricot halves	Cranberry jelly	Mint pineapple	Celery-Cabbage flowerets	Rings	Raisins
Apricot sections	Cherry jelly	Mints	Celery curls	Waffled	Truffles
Cantaloupe balls	Currant jelly	Turkish paste	Celery hearts	Timbales	Candy silver balls
Grapefruit baskets	Gelatin cubes	Vegetables	Celery strips	Waffles	Cake confetti
Lemon sections	Loganberry jelly	Asparagus tips	Cucumber rings	Cinnamon	
Lemon slices	Raspberry jelly	Broccoli	Cucumber strips	French fried cauliflower	
Orange sections	Red sugar	Brussels sprouts	Cucumber wedges	French fried onions	
Orange slices	Turkish paste	Endive	Cucumber cups	Meringue shells	
Orange rind	Vegetables	Green pepper	Mashed potato piped on with pastry tube	Mushrooms	
Peach slices	Beets, pickled, cut in fancy shapes	Strips	Onion rings	Nutmeats	
Peach balls	Beet hollowed out to form cup	Chopped	Onions, tiny	Nut-covered cheese balls	
		Green onions	Onions, pickled	Potato chips	
		Lettuce cups		Rosettes	
		Lettuce, shredded			
		Mint leaves			

Peach halves with jelly	Beet relish	Olives	Radishes, white	Toasted cocoanut
Spiced peaches	Beets, julienne	Parsley	Miscellaneous	
Persimmons	Peppers, red	Sprig	Sliced hard-cooked egg white	
Tangerines	Rings	Chopped	Shredded cocoanut	
Preserves and Other Sweets	Strips	Pickles	Marshmallows	
Apricot preserves	Shredded	Burr gherkins	Almonds	
Orange preserves	Pimiento	Strips	Mints	
Peach preserves	Chopped	Fans	Small dumplings	
Peanut brittle, crushed	Cut in fancy shapes	Rings	Whipped cream	
Sugar, yellow	Radishes, red	Spinach leaves	Rice	
Sugar, orange	Sliced	Miscellaneous	Powdered sugar	
Turkish paste	Roses	Cocoanut, tinted	White meat of chicken	
Vegetables	Stuffed olives	Mayonnaise, tinted		
Carrot, shredded	Sliced	Pistachios		
Carrot strips	Tomato			
Carrot rings	Aspic			
Carrot, cut in fancy shapes	Catsup			
Carrot cubes	Cups			
Carrot, spiced	Chili sauce			
Squash strips, steamed	Sections			
Squash balls, steamed	Slice, raw			
Miscellaneous	Slice, broil			
Butter balls	Miscellaneous			
Cocoanut, tinted	Paprika			
Gelatin cubes	Tinted cocoanut			
Mayonnaise	Mayonnaise, tinted			
	Cinnamon drops "red-hots"			

MENU PLANNING SUGGESTIONS, LIST V: DESSERTS

Cake and Cookies	Pie and Pastry	Puddings	Frozen	Miscellaneous
Cake	One Crust	Apple Dumplings	Bisque	Cheese
Angel Food	Apricot Cream	Apricot Bavarian	Almond	American
Applesauce	Banana Cream	Apricot Whip	Pistachio	Camembert
Apricot, upside down	Butterscotch	Apple Brown Betty	Walnut	Cheddar
Banana	Caramel	Apple Tapioca	Ice cream	Cottage
Burnt Sugar	Cherry Cream	Apple Snow	Apricot	Cream
Caramel	Chocolate Chiffon	Baked Custard	Banana	Gruyère
Caramel-Nut	Cocoanut Cream	Caramel	Butter Brickle	Roquefort
Chocolate Angel Food	Cocoanut Custard	Coffee	Caramel	Stilton
Chocolate Chip	Custard	Chocolate	Chip Chocolate	Swiss
Chocolate, layer	Date Custard	Date	Chocolate	Fruit, Baked
Chocolate, loaf	Deep Dish Apple	Pumpkin	Coffee	Apples
Chocolate, nut	Lemon Fluff	Plain	Grapenut	Pears
Chocolate, roll	Orange Cream	Rice	Lemon Custard	Dutch Baked Apple
Cocoanut	Pecan Cream	Banana Whip	Macaroon	Fresh, Stewed
Coffee-Walnut	Pineapple Cream	Boston Cream Roll	Peach	Apples
Cup Cakes	Pumpkin	Bread Pudding	Peanut Brittle	Apricots
Fruit	Pumpkin Chiffon	Chocolate	Pecan	Blackberry
Fudge	Squash	Nut Bread	Peppermint Stick	Cherries
Gingerbread	Strawberry	Orange	Philadelphia	Dewberries
Golden Angel Food	Bavarian Cream	Vanilla	Pineapple	Figs
Jelly Roll	Vanilla Cream	Caramel Tapioca	Pistachio	Grapes
Maple-Nut	Vinegar	Cherry Bavarian	Prune	Loganberries
Marble	Two Crust	Cherry Tapioca	Raspberry	Peaches
Marshmallow	Apple	Chocolate Cream Pudding	Strawberry	Pears
Mocha	Apricot	Christmas Pudding	Toffee	Pineapple
Nut	Blackberry	Cornstarch	Tutti Frutti	Plums
Poppyseed	Blueberry	Caramel	Ice	Raspberries
Ribbon	Cherry	Chocolate	Apricot	Rhubarb
Spice	Cranberry	Cocoanut	Cherry	Strawberries
Sponge	Gooseberry	Date	Cranberry	Stewed or Canned
White	Grape		Crème de Menthe	Apples
Yellow	Loganberry		Gooseberry	Apricots
Cookies	Mince Meat		Grape	Blackberries
Brownies	Peach			
	Pineapple			

Brokaw Ice Box
Butterscotch
Chocolate Crunch
Cocoanut Cookies
Cocoanut Macaroons
Cornflake Kisses
Date bars
Drop Cookies
 Fudge
 Molasses
 Oatmeal
 Rocks
Ginger
Krispie Marshmallow
 Squares
Ice Cream Wafers
Nut Marbles
Oatmeal Cookies
Peanut Butter
Plain Cookies
 (fancy shapes)

Plum
Prune
Raisin
Rhubarb
Strawberry
Cobblers
 Apple
 Apricot
 Berry
 Cherry
 Gooseberry
 Peach
 Plum
 Rhubarb
Gelatin
Apricot Chiffon
Chocolate Cream
Chocolate Sundae
Coffee Chiffon
Lemon Chiffon
Orange Chiffon
Pumpkin Chiffon
Strawberry Chiffon
Tarts and Individual Pies
 Apple
 Apricot (fresh)
 Banbury
 Blackberry
 Blueberry
 Cherry
 Lemon
 Mince Meat
 Orange
 Strawberry
Transparent Pudding

Maple
Nut
Strawberry
Vanilla
Cottage
Cream Puffs
Dainty Rice Pudding
Date Pudding
Date Roll
Divinity Pudding
Fruit Gelatin
Fruit Tapioca
Graham Cracker Betty
Graham Cracker Pie
Ice Box Cake
Junket
Lemon Snow
Marshmallow Pudding
Meringue Shells
Norwegian Prune Pudding
Oatmeal Bars
Old English Apple Pie
Pineapple Bavarian
Prune Whip
Raspberry Whip
Rice Pudding
Shortcake
Steamed Pudding
Zweibach Cheese Cake

Green Gage Plum
Ginger Ale
Lemon
Lime
Mint
Orange
Raspberry
Rhubarb
Mousse
Bisque
Chocolate
Grape
Maple
Strawberry
Parfait
Angel
Apricot
Bar-le-Duc
Caramel
Chocolate
Coffee
Pineapple
Strawberry
Sherbet
Apricot
Cherry
Cranberry
Gooseberry
Grape
Lemon
Lime
Mint
Pineapple
Plum
Orange
Raspberry
Rhubarb
Sorbet

Blueberries
Cherries
Dewberries
Figs
Gooseberries
Grapes
Huckleberries
Loganberries
Peaches
Pears
Pineapple
Plum
Prunes
Raspberries
Rhubarb
Strawberries
Raw Fruit
Apples
Bananas
Blackberries
Blueberries
Cherries
Dewberries
Figs
Grapefruit
Grapes
Loganberries
Melon
 Cantaloupe
 Casaba
 Honeydew
 Watermelon
Oranges
Peaches
Pears
Pineapple
Plums
Prunes
Raspberries
Strawberries

MENU PLANNING SUGGESTIONS, LIST VI: BREADS

Biscuits	Rolls	Loaf	Muffins	Toast	Miscellaneous
Biscuits, plain	All Bran	Banana	All Bran	Cheese Bread	Cornbread
Butterscotch	Braids	Brown	Apple-Bran	Cinnamon	Cornmeal Pan
Cheese	Butterhorn	Bread,	Apricot	Cracked	Cakes
Cinnamon	Caramel	baked	Bacon	Wheat	Crullers
Drop	Caraway	steamed	Blackberry	Raisin	Doughnuts,
Filled	Cheese	Cheese	Blueberry	White	plain
Fruit	Cinnamon	Date	Cheese	French	chocolate
Graham	Cloverleaf	French	Coffee Cake	French Cheese	Fritters
Orange	Cornmeal	Nut	Cornmeal	Melba	Griddle Cakes
Pecan	Crescent	Orange	Cornmeal-	Milk	Popovers
	Currant	Oatmeal	Bran		Scones
	Date	Potato	Cranberry		Spoon Bread
	Finger	Raisin	Currant		Waffles
	French	Rye	Date		Waffles with
	Graham	Salt Rising	Date-Nut		Pecans
	Hard		English		
	Hot Cross		Fig		
	Ice Box		Graham Gems		
	Orange		Honey Corn-		
	Parkerhouse		flakes		
	Pecan		Jelly		
	Plain		Nut		
	Poppyseed		Orange		
	Raisin		Plain		
	Rolled Oat		Raisin		
	Sesame		Raisin-Nut		
	Swedish Tea		Rice		
	Twin		Spiced		
	Twists		Vanilla		
	White				
	Whole				
	Wheat				

Mechanics of writing menu cards, as cited in "Practical Cookery,"[1] include the following:

1. Use capitals for all words except prepositions and conjunctions.

2. Arrange food in order of service.

3. Write the main dish of each course across the center of the sheet.

Write one accompaniment on the line below, on the right hand or in the center. If two accompaniments, write one at the right and one at the left on the line below.

---

[1] "Practical Cookery and the Etiquette and Service of the Table." Department of Food Economics and Nutrition, Kansas State College. Department of Printing, 1939.

Example:

Cream of Tomato Soup
Croutons

Cream of Tomato Soup
Celery   Croutons

4. If more accompaniments are served, balance on sheet, thus:

Example:

Breaded Veal
Stuffed Baked Potato   Buttered Asparagus
Carrot and Pea Salad
Graham Bread   Butter
Cake   Apricot Sherbet
Coffee

5. Write beverage at the bottom of the menu or with the course with which it is to be served.

6. Do not write accompaniments as cream and sugar on menu for guests.

MENUS

School Lunch. The most simple of all menus to plan is that of the school lunch room. This institution usually serves one meal a day for five days a week to school children. The menu then must provide, wholly or in part or both, for the food needs of a growing child. In many schools, it is not the custom to bring food from home, and hence the menus are planned to provide a complete meal. In other schools, a lunch bag or box containing the major part of the lunch is brought by the child, and the lunch room then makes provision for a supplementary luncheon item, as soup, cocoa, and various luncheon dishes served piping hot.

If a complete meal is served, the director of the lunch room in a small school usually lists, as the feature of the menu, a plate lunch, offered at a set price and including the foods necessary for a balanced meal. Luncheon dishes, vegetables, bread, butter, milk, and a dessert are often included in the plate lunch. Usually the small school lunch room offers few, if any, dishes in addition to the plate lunch.

When all the factors to be considered in planning menus are taken into consideration, the food suitable for a school lunch group themselves into the following classifications: soups, hot dishes, vegetables, salads, beverages, sandwiches, breads, and desserts. The following is a suggested list of suitable foods which may be served:

SOUPS

Cream of tomato; cream of spinach; cream of potato; corn chowder; split pea; vegetable.

HOT DISHES

Creole spaghetti; Spanish rice, creamed chipped beef; stuffed tomatoes with ham; vegetable stew; noodles and stew; cottage pie; shepherds' pie; scalloped salmon; macaroni and cheese; baked Lima beans; scalloped corn and bacon; baked beans, scalloped potatoes, and ham; scrambled bacon and eggs; macaroni à la king.

VEGETABLES

Peas; carrots; green and wax beans; beets; spinach; tomatoes; cabbage; asparagus; corn; potatoes. These various vegetables may be creamed, buttered, or scalloped to offer variety.

SALADS

Fruit Salads. Peach, pear, pineapple, orange, and apple; apple, pineapple, and marshmallow; Waldorf; stuffed prune, apple, and banana; banana and nut; apple, grape, and banana; raisin and carrot; raw cranberry; combination salad; grapefruit.

Vegetable Salads. Sliced tomato; head lettuce; stuffed celery; vegetable combination; spring salad; stuffed tomato; carrot and celery; cole slaw; cabbage and pineapple; asparagus.

Heavy Salads. Kidney bean; potato; cottage cheese; deviled eggs; potato and egg; salmon.

Gelatin Salads. Perfection; jellied Waldorf; pineapple-carrot; jellied fruit; jellied vegetable.

SANDWICHES

Cold meat; ground meats moistened with salad dressings; cottage cheese and nut; pimiento cheese; lettuce and tomato; nut bread; chicken salad; peanut butter and raisin; raisin and date; date and nut; egg and bacon; egg and celery; rye bread and jelly; prune and cottage cheese; peanut butter and cheese.

DESSERTS

Tapioca. Caramel tapioca; tapioca cream; tapioca with fruit; chocolate.

Puddings. Dainty rice; custard; bread; divinity; caramel blanc mange; Brown Betty.

Fruit. Fruit ambrosia; orange, banana, cocoanut combination; fruit cup; stuffed dates; baked apples; prune soufflé; raw fruit.

Gelatin. Fruit gelatin; fruit whip; Bavarians.

Pastry. Washington pie; cottage pudding; chocolate cup cakes; cherry cakes; cream puffs; cake delight; cobblers; cookies; jelly roll; gingerbread; upside-down cake; pastry.

BEVERAGES

Chocolate and plain milk; malted milks; cocoa; tomato juice; fruit juices.

West and Wood suggest an eight-day cycle of menu planning as an efficient means of securing meals of maximum interest and economy in the school lunch room if the director has but little time to devote to the menu planning. Provision in such a plan should of course be made for the use of seasonal foods, for the use of left-over foods, and for meals for special occasions.

The menus on the following page, planned on an eight-day cycle, may be found to provide, with the desirable changes, satisfactory daily menus for a small school lunch.

College Commons. The college commons presents one of the most interesting but difficult menu-making problems of all the types of services included in the simpler meal services. The factors which contribute to the complications are:

1. Faculty and students are both served from one menu.

2. The food is usually sold at a low cost.

3. The food must meet nutritional needs, yet also offer variety.

4. A major part of food preparation may be in hands of inexperienced student help.

5. There is often an unexpectedly small volume of business and an attendant problem of left-overs.

6. The uncertainty of numbers complicates the food cost control.

An eleven-day cycle similar to the eight-day cycle suggested for the school lunch room might be of value in some situations. However, the problem of the use of left-overs and the desirability of the inclusion of seasonable foods available on the market lead many directors to plan for periods as brief as one week.

SUGGESTED SCHOOL LUNCH ROOM MENUS FOR AN EIGHT-DAY CYCLE*

Soup	Tomato and Barley	Corn Chowder	Pepper Pot	Cream of Celery	Noodle	Cream of Tomato	Vegetable	Cream of Spinach
Meat or Main Dish	Creamed Dried Beef	Scalloped Eggs	Macaroni and Cheese	Meat Patties—Brown Sauce	Baked Lima Beans	Meat Roll	Spanish Rice	Stuffed Peppers
Vegetables	Buttered Carrots Baked Potato	Buttered Cabbage Buttered Peas	Buttered Apple Celery Curls	Mashed Potatoes Buttered Spinach	Macédoine of Vegetables Glazed Sweet Potato	Creamed Potatoes German Carrots	Sweet Potato Puffs Buttered Green Beans	Stewed Tomatoes Mashed Potatoes
Salads	Head Lettuce Pear Combination Vegetable	Pineapple-Cheese Potato	Tomato Stuffed Egg	Fruit Gelatin Carrot-Raisin	Cranberry Stuffed Celery	Stuffed Prune Perfection	Apple-Celery Cottage Cheese	Peach Cabbage
Desserts *Fruit*	Apples, raw	Fruit Cup	Stewed Prunes	Baked Apple	Canned Peaches	Orange Cup	Sliced Bananas	Royal Anne Cherries
Pudding	Chocolate Cream Pudding	Divinity Pudding	Cocoanut Blanc Mange	Apricot Tapioca	Baked Custard	Brown Betty	Cherry Whip	Tapioca Cream
Pastry *Ice Cream*	Poppyseed Cake	Cherry Cobbler	Pumpkin Pie	Gingerbread	Chocolate Roll	Oatmeal Cookies	Doughnuts	Fudge Cake
Breads	Whole Wheat White	Whole Wheat Raisin	Cracked Wheat White	Rye Rolls	Date Bread White	Whole Wheat White	Whole Wheat Muffins	Cracked Wheat White
Sandwiches	Egg Salad Lettuce	Peanut Butter and Jelly Ham Salad	Raisin-Nut Sardine	Date-Nut Cheese	Nut Bread Meat Salad	Celery-Nut Egg-Pickle	Orange Bread Ham Salad	Tuna Fish Grated Carrot-Nut
Plate Lunch	Creamed Chipped Beef Baked Potato Combination Vegetable Salad Bread Beverage	Corn Chowder Buttered Peas Pineapple-Cheese Salad Bread Beverage	Macaroni and Cheese Tomato Salad Pumpkin Pie Bread Beverage	Meat Patties—Brown Sauce Buttered Spinach Gingerbread Bread Beverage	Baked Lima Beans Macédoine of Vegetables Head Lettuce Salad Bread Beverage	Meat Roll Creamed Potatoes Orange Cup Bread Beverage	Spanish Rice Apple-Celery Salad Sliced Bananas Bread Beverage	Stuffed Pepper Peach Salad Fudge Cake Bread Beverage

Beverages
Milk
Chocolate Milk or Cocoa
Fruit or Tomato Juice

* Bessie Brooks West and LeVelle Wood. "Food Service in Institutions." John Wiley and Sons, Inc., New York. 1938.

MENUS FOR A COLLEGE COMMONS*

MONDAY BREAKFAST

	Week I	Week II
Fruit:	Orange Juice	Orange Juice
	Cantaloupe	Tomato Juice
	Pears (Canned)	Grapefruit
	Stewed Prunes	Peaches (Canned)
Hot Cereal:	Wheatena	Rolled Oats
Prepared Cereal:	Assorted	Assorted
Hot Bread:	Blackberry Muffins	Cinnamon Rolls
Beverages:	Coffee, Cocoa	Coffee, Cocoa
Miscellaneous:	Bacon	Bacon
	Eggs	Eggs
	Jam or Jelly	Jam or Jelly

MONDAY LUNCHEON

	Week I	Week II
Hot Bread:	Plain Pan Rolls	Baking Powder Biscuits
Soup:	Cream of Vegetable	Consommé julienne
Meat:	Roast Veal	Cheese Soufflé
	Ham à la King	Meat Loaf
	Chinese Omelet	Baked Ham
Potatoes:	Browned Potatoes	Mashed Potatoes
Vegetables:	Buttered Asparagus	Creamed Fresh Peas and Mush-
	Glazed Carrots	rooms
	Buttered Green Beans	Buttered Carrots and Celery
	Egg Plant Soufflé	Buttered Cauliflower
		Fried Egg Plant
Salads:	Cole Slaw	Stuffed Apricot
	Tomato-Cucumber	Diced Banana, Pineapple, Pear
	Pineapple-Pickle Gelatin	Beet, Cucumber, Pickles, Relish
	Banana-Nut	Cabbage, Peanuts, and Pimientos
Cake:	Angel Food	Prune Cake—Sour Cream Filling
Pies:	Caramel	Green Gage Plum
	Apple	Orange Chiffon
Other	Cherry Tapioca	Marshmallow Pudding
Desserts:	Iced Cantaloupe	Berry Cobbler

* The following items are always available: Whole Wheat Bread, Cracked Wheat Bread, White Bread, Cottage Cheese, Lettuce, Ice Cream, Coffee, Tea, and Milk.

MENUS FOR A COLLEGE COMMONS (*continued*)

MONDAY DINNER

	Week I	*Week II*
Hot Bread:	Poppyseed Rolls	Graham Muffins
Soup:	Barley	Split Pea
Meat:	Welsh Rarebit	Lamb Chops
	Beef Pie	Stuffed Flank Steak
	Pork Cutlets	Creole Spaghetti
Potatoes:	Mashed Potatoes	Browned Potatoes
Vegetables:	Spiced Apple Sauce	Scalloped Cucumbers with Tomatoes, Green Pepper, and Onions
	Mashed Summer Squash	
	Baked Tomato	Wilted Spinach
	Buttered Cauliflower	Buttered Green Beans
		Whole Grain Corn
Salads:	Carrot-Raisin	Sliced Orange—Onion Ring
	Vegetable Combination	Pineapple with Cheese
	Stuffed Pear	Perfection
	Frozen Fruit	Carrot-Cocoanut
Cake:	Fudge Cake—Ice Cream Frosting	Yellow Sponge
Pies:	Lemon	Peach
	Apricot	Cream
Other	Graham Cracker Brown Betty	Brownies
Desserts:	Stewed Figs	Cherry Tapioca
		Pears

TUESDAY BREAKFAST

	Week I	*Week II*
Fruit:	Orange Juice	Orange Juice
	Grapefruit	Cantaloupe
	Figs	Prunes
	Stewed Dried Apricots	Pears
Hot Cereal:	Rolled Oats	Cream of Wheat
Prepared Cereal:	Assorted	Assorted
Hot Bread:	Baking Powder Biscuits	Filled Biscuits
Beverages:	Coffee, Cocoa	Coffee, Cocoa
Miscellaneous:	Bacon	Bacon
	Eggs	Eggs
	Jam or Jelly	Jam or Jelly

MENUS FOR A COLLEGE COMMONS (*continued*)

TUESDAY LUNCHEON

	Week I	*Week II*
Hot Bread:	Ice Box Twin Rolls	Parkerhouse Rolls
Soup:	Rice	Cream of Chicken
Meat:	Roast Beef	Pot Roast of Beef
	Meat Croquettes	French Fried Liver—Bacon
	Hot Stuffed Eggs	Beef Biscuit Roll
Potatoes:	Lyonnaise Potatoes	Parsley Buttered Potatoes
Vegetables:	Buttered Peas	Fresh Asparagus—Cheese Sauce
	Baked Onions	Macédoine of Vegetables
	Macédoine of Vegetables	French Fried Onions
	Shredded New Beets	Lima Beans
Salads:	Stuffed Celery (cheese)	Spiced Apple
	Raw Spinach—Chiffonade Dressing	Peach, Pineapple, Royal Anne Cherries
	Apricot-Cottage Cheese	Tomato Sandwich Salad
	Diced Apple-Pineapple-Cherry	Stuffed Celery
Cake:	Spice Cake—Caramel Frosting	White Cake—Fluffy Frosting
Pie:	Banana Cream	Plum
	Blackberry	Pumpkin Chiffon
Other	Chocolate Cream Pudding	Apricot Bavarian
Desserts:	Green Apple Sauce	Chocolate Pudding
		Royal Anne Cherries

TUESDAY DINNER

	Week I	*Week II*
Hot Bread:	Pecan Rolls	Orange Rolls
Soup:	Pepper Pot Soup	Corn Chowder
Meat:	Stuffed Flank Steak	Baked Stuffed Pork Chops
	Baked Ham	Swedish Meat Balls
	Creole Spaghetti	Scalloped Macaroni
Potatoes:	Parsley Buttered Potatoes	Lyonnaise Potatoes
Vegetables:	Cauliflower au Gratin	Hot Slaw
	German Carrots	Tart Applesauce
	Wilted Spinach	Broiled Tomatoes
	Whole Grain Corn	Buttered Peas
Salads:	Cabbage-Pineapple-Marshmallow	Prune and Cottage Cheese
	Mixed Cooked Vegetable	Jellied Fruit
	Jellied Fruit	French Green Beans—Onion Dressing
	Stuffed Prune	Raw Spinach—Chiffonade Dressing
Cake:	White Cake—Cocoa-Mocha Frosting	Chocolate Cake—Fluffy Frosting
Pie:	Orange Crumb	Apple
	Cherry	Pecan
Other	Cream Puffs	Washington Cream Pie
Desserts:	Meringue Pears	Banana Whip
		Stewed Prunes

MENUS FOR A COLLEGE COMMONS (*continued*)

WEDNESDAY BREAKFAST

	Week I	*Week II*
Fruit:	Orange Juice	Orange Juice
	Bananas	Bananas
	Green applesauce	Grapes, fresh
	Sliced Orange	Raspberries (canned)
Hot Cereal:	Cream of Wheat	Wheat Grits
Prepared Cereal:	Assorted	Assorted
Hot Bread:	Whole Wheat Muffins	Pecan Rolls
Beverages:	Coffee, Cocoa	Coffee, Cocoa
Miscellaneous:	Ham	Bacon
	Eggs	Eggs
	Jam or Jelly	Jam or Jelly

WEDNESDAY LUNCHEON

	Week I	*Week II*
Hot Bread:	All Bran Rolls	Caramel Rolls
Soup:	Potato	Vegetable
Meat:	Sweetbread Cutlets	Braised Tongue
	Country Fried Steak	Beef Croquettes
	Vegetable Pie	Ham and Egg Scallop
Potatoes:	Mashed Potatoes	Mashed Potatoes
Vegetables:	Buttered Apple Sections	Green Beans with Hot Vegetable
	Buttered Cabbage	Sauce
	Stewed Tomato and Corn	Harvard Beets
	Lima Beans in Cream	Buttered Squash (baked)
		Cabbage Polynnaise
Salads:	Celery-Carrot Strips	Peas, and Tomato Sections
	Spiced Beet	Banana Nut
	Combination Fruit	Corn, Pimiento, Celery, Pickle
	Sliced Pineapple	Cauliflower, Olive, Carrot, Peas
Cake:	Prune Cake—Sour Cream Filling	Ribbon Cake
Pie:	Custard	Raisin
	Plum	Butterscotch
Other	Divinity Pudding	Baked Custard
Desserts:	Fresh Bing Cherries	Graham Cracker Betty

MENUS FOR A COLLEGE COMMONS (*continued*)

WEDNESDAY DINNER

	Week I	*Week II*
Hot Bread:	Blackberry Muffins	Nut Bread
Soup:	Celery	Broth with Alphabets
Meat:	Pot Roast of Veal	Roast Veal
	Beef Patties	Chop Suey
	Potato Omelet	Meat Turnovers
Potatoes:	Creamed Potatoes	Oven Browned Potatoes
Vegetables:	Creamed Asparagus	Scalloped Egg Plant
	Fried Egg Plant	Buttered Turnips
	Stewed Tomatoes	Corn and Tomatoes in Cream
	Scalloped Peas and Onions	German Carrots
Salads:	Radishes	Spiced Peach
	Lettuce Hearts—Thousand Island Dressing	Grapefruit, Green Pepper
	Pineapple-Cheese	Cabbage Salad—Vinegar Dressing
	Orange and Fig	Pineapple-Pickle, Gelatin
Cake:	White Cake—Nut Frosting	Maple Nut Cake—Mocha Frosting
Pie:	Chocolate	Loganberry
	Peach	Angel Lemon
Other	Apricot Bavarian	Fig Mousse
Desserts:	Grapefruit Halves	Jelly Roll

THURSDAY BREAKFAST

	Week I	*Week II*
Fruit:	Orange Juice	Orange Juice
	Honeydew Melon	Oranges and Bananas
	Pears	Figs
	Cherries	Fresh Pineapple
Hot Cereal:	Cracked Wheat	Hominy Grits
Prepared Cereal:	Assorted	Assorted
Hot Bread:	Cinnamon Roll	Plain Muffins
Beverage:	Coffee, Cocoa	Coffee, Cocoa
Miscellaneous:	Bacon	Bacon
	Eggs	Eggs
	Jam or Jelly	Jam or Jelly

MENUS FOR A COLLEGE COMMONS (*continued*)

THURSDAY LUNCHEON

	Week I	*Week II*
Hot Bread:	Baking Powder Biscuits	Spiced Muffins
Soup:	Asparagus	Rice
Meat:	Chicken Pie	Swiss Steak
	Stuffed Peppers	Veal à la King
	Casserole of Corn	Baked Lima Beans with Salt Pork
Potatoes:	Mashed Potatoes	Steamed and Browned Potatoes
Vegetables:	Buttered Cauliflower	Baked Stuffed Onions
	Buttered Squash	Buttered Peas
	Carrots in Cream	Steamed Tomatoes
	Green Beans with Hot Vegetable Sauce	Wilted Leaf Lettuce
Salads:	Tomato Aspic Ring	Peas, Pineapple, Apricots—Whipped Cream Dressing
	Combination Fresh Vegetable	
	Perfection	Banana-Nut
	Apple-Celery	Spiced Beet
		Carrot, Celery, Cucumber, and Green Pepper Strips
Cake:	Orange Sponge	White Cake—Caramel Frosting
Pie:	Cream	Gooseberry
	Raisin	Cocoanut Cream
Other	Lemon Snow	Baked Apple Tapioca
Desserts:	Watermelon	Ice Box Cake
		Cherries

THURSDAY DINNER

	Week I	*Week II*
Hot Bread:	Baked Brown Bread	All Bran Ice Box Rolls
Soup:	Bouillon	Cream of Tomato
Meat:	Broiled Tenderloin Tips	Roast Pork
	Vegetable Meat Loaf	Stuffed Green Peppers
	Link Sausage Rolls	Baked Eggs with Cheese
Potatoes:	Scalloped Potatoes	Creamed Potatoes
Vegetables:	Cabbage Polynnaise	Baked Squash
	Spinach with Sliced New Beets	Buttered Shredded Beets
	Hot Baked Apple	Buttered Cabbage
	Buttered Squash	Black-eyed Peas with Bacon
Salads:	Raw Cauliflower-Carrot	Marshmallow Fruit
	Shredded Lettuce with Egg Dressing	Combination Fresh Fruit
	Peach with Whipped Cream Dressing	Pea, Celery, and Carrot Mounds
	Tomato-Cucumber-Pineapple	Head Lettuce, Roquefort Cheese
Cake:	Ribbon Cake—Fluffy Frosting	Gingerbread
Pies:	Butterscotch	Cherry
	Raspberry	Chocolate Chiffon
Other	Dainty Rice Pudding	Blueberry Tarts
Desserts:	Stewed Prunes	Tapioca Cream Pudding
		Cantaloupe

MENUS FOR A COLLEGE COMMONS (*continued*)

FRIDAY BREAKFAST

	Week I	*Week II*
Fruit:	Orange Juice	Orange Juice
	Grapefruit	Honeydew Melon
	Stewed Prunes	Blackberries
	Loganberries	Prunes
Hot Cereal:	Wheat Grits	Rolled Oats with All Bran
Prepared Cereal:	Assorted	Assorted
Hot Bread:	Bacon Muffins	Cinnamon Rolls
Beverage:	Coffee, Cocoa	Coffee, Cocoa
Miscellaneous:	Pecan Waffles—Sirup	Bacon
	Eggs	Eggs
	Jam or Jelly	Jam or Jelly

FRIDAY LUNCHEON

	Week I	*Week II*
Hot Bread:	Cornmeal Rolls	Raisin Bran Rolls
Soup:	Cream of Vegetable	Lima Bean
Meat:	Fried Whiting	Baked Halibut
	Ham Loaf	Creamed Sweetbreads—Toast
	Meat Turnovers	Points
		Cheese Croquettes
Potatoes:	Browned Potatoes	Mashed Potatoes
Vegetables:	Breaded Pineapple Ring	Applesauce
	Buttered Peas	Spanish Green Beans
	Braised Celery	Buttered Cauliflower
	Spanish Lima Beans	Corn in Cream
Salads:	Cabbage-Green Pepper	Cherry Gelatin
	Stuffed Tomato	Pear with Orange Slices
	Honeydew and Cantaloupe Balls	Sliced Cucumber and Tomato
	Grapefruit and Spiced Apple Sections	Celery Hearts
Cake:	Cocoanut Layer	Spice Cake—Maple Frosting
Pie:	Lemon Fluff	Rhubarb
	Cherry	Chess
Other Desserts:	Ice Box Cake	Bread Pudding
	Fresh Raspberries	Divinity Pudding

MENUS FOR A COLLEGE COMMONS (*continued*)

FRIDAY DINNER

	Week I	*Week II*
Hot Bread:	Plain Rolls	Plain Rolls
Soup:	Oyster Stew	Vermicelli Broth
Meat:	Veal Birds	Fried Ham
	Baked White Fish	Lamb Chops
	Spanish Rice	Salmon Timbales
Potatoes:	Mashed Potatoes	Scalloped Potatoes
Vegetables:	Buttered Asparagus	French Fried Bananas
	Harvard Beets	Scalloped Peas
	Creamed Onions	Stewed Tomatoes
	Buttered Green Beans	Buttered Spinach
Salads:	Cauliflower-Pea-Celery	Pineapple, Celery, Almond
	Spring Salad	Cantaloupe Ring—Melon Balls
	Orange and Green Pepper	Endive and Julienne Beets
	Pear-Banana-Pineapple	Carrot and Asparagus Tips
Cake:	Burnt Sugar	Orange Cup Cakes
Pie:	Orange Chiffon	Green Gage Plum
	Apple	Lemon
Other	Caramel Tapioca	Divinity Pudding
Desserts:	Fresh Pineapple Shredded	Jellied Fruit

SATURDAY BREAKFAST

	Week I	*Week II*
Fruit:	Orange Juice	Orange Juice
	Cantaloupe	Sliced Peaches
	Sliced Pineapple	Applesauce
	Banana	Pineapple
Hot Cereal:	Rolled Oats	Steamed Rice
Prepared Cereal:	Assorted	Assorted
Hot Bread:	Raisin Toast	Doughnuts
Beverage:	Coffee, Cocoa	Coffee, Cocoa
Miscellaneous:	Bacon	Bacon
	Eggs	Eggs
	Jam or Jelly	Jam or Jelly

MENUS FOR A COLLEGE COMMONS (*continued*)

SATURDAY LUNCHEON

	Week I	*Week II*
Hot Bread:	Nut Muffins	Cinnamon Rolls
Soup:	Split Pea	Chicken
Meat:	Baked Heart	Creamed Chicken—Waffles
	Stuffed Meat Cakes	Beef Pie
	Creamed Dried Beef	Egg Cutlets
Potatoes:	Hashed Brown Potatoes	Steamed Potatoes
Vegetables:	Hot Slaw	Vegetable Timbales
	Buttered Green Beans	Buttered Carrot Strips
	Stewed Tomatoes	Green Pepper stuffed with Spanish Rice
	Vegetable Timbales	
		Buttered Green Beans
Salads:	Asparagus-Watercress	Banana and Orange Sections
	Pickled Beets	Molded Cheese Ring with Fruit
	Cheese Gelatin	Turnip Salad
	Apple-Nut Gelatin	Stuffed Tomatoes
Cake:	Cup Cakes—Fluffy Frosting	White Cake—Fig Filling
Pie:	Chocolate Gelatin	Youngberry
	Apricot	Chocolate
Other	Norwegian Prune Pudding	Caramel Tapioca
Desserts:	Sliced Oranges	Cream Puffs

SATURDAY DINNER

	Week I	*Week II*
Hot Bread:	Oatmeal Biscuits	Biscuits
Soup:	Pepper Pot	Navy Bean
Meat:	Corned Beef	Spanish Steak
	Meat Pie	Savory Meat Loaf
	Baked Beans	Creamed Dried Beef and Egg
Potatoes:	Parsley Buttered Potatoes	Mashed Potatoes
Vegetables:	Buttered Shredded Cabbage	Squash (baked) with Tomatoes
	Creamed Asparagus	Creamed Onions with Pimiento
	Buttered Green Beans	Spinach with Hard-cooked Egg Slices
	Mashed Squash	
		Succotash
Salads:	Carrot-Cocoanut	Fresh Pineapple—White Grapes
	Pea-Pickle-Cheese	Apricot
	Stuffed Grape and Olive	Egg-Celery
	Sliced Pineapple	Cabbage, spice
Cake:	Golden Cake—Orange Filling	Ice Box Cookies
Pie:	Pecan	Blackberry
		Sour Cream
Other	Jellied Fruit Cup	Chocolate Soufflé
Desserts:	Peach Halves	Jelly Roll

The Residence Hall Menu. The daily menu in the residence hall must be adequate to meet the nutritional needs of the residents. The number to be served is fairly constant so amounts may be carefully planned, resulting in little or no waste. Although there are many halls that still serve a "fixed" or complete meal three times a day, others are finding the use of selective menus for breakfast, or lunch or both, popular and advantageous. In this case the selective menus are simplified cafeteria menus and cafeteria style of service is used for breakfast and lunch, and a more formal type of service for dinner.

MENUS FOR A WOMEN'S RESIDENCE HALL

MONDAY BREAKFAST

Week I

Stewed Rhubarb
Bacon Rings
Buttered Toast
Wheat Krispies
Coffee or Cocoa

Week II

Sliced Oranges
Milk Toast
Poached Eggs
Cornflakes
Coffee or Cocoa

MONDAY LUNCHEON

Spanish Rice
Raw Vegetable Salad
Bran Muffins
Banana Whip
Wafers
Milk

Baked Lima Beans with Salt Pork
   and Pimiento
Cole Slaw
Green Pepper Ring
Cornmeal Muffins
Tapioca Cream
Milk

MONDAY DINNER

Roast Leg of Veal
Browned Potatoes
Creamed Shredded Cabbage
Orange Salad
Angel Food Pie
Coffee or Milk

Vegetable Meat Loaf
Scalloped Potatoes
Spiced Peach
Buttered Peas
Whole Wheat Bread
Date Torte with Whipped Cream
Coffee or Milk

TUESDAY BREAKFAST

Baked Apple and Raisins
Broiled Link Sausages
Cinnamon or Plain Toast
Dwarfies
Coffee or Cocoa

Grapefruit
Bacon
Plain Muffins
Bran Flakes
Coffee or Cocoa

MENUS FOR A WOMEN'S RESIDENCE HALL (*continued*)

TUESDAY LUNCHEON

Week I

Baked Eggs with Cheese
Head Lettuce, Parisian Dressing
Whole Wheat Rolls
Fresh Pineapple
Drop Cookies
Milk

Week II

Creamed Dried Beef with Rice
Raw Vegetable Salad Bowl
Whole Wheat Raisin Bread
Chocolate Pie
Milk

TUESDAY DINNER

Braised Liver with Onions
Parsley Buttered Potatoes
Harvard Beets
Stuffed Celery
Ice Cream with Oriental Sauce
Coffee or Milk

Roast Pork—Gravy
Spiced Apple Salad
Mashed Potatoes
Buttered Wax Beans
Frosted Strawberry Short Cake
Coffee or Milk

WEDNESDAY BREAKFAST

Oranges
Scrambled Eggs
Toast
Shredded Wheat Biscuits
Coffee or Cocoa

Bananas
Doughnuts
Krumbles
Coffee or Cocoa

WEDNESDAY LUNCHEON

Tamale Pie
Cabbage Slaw
Rye Bread
Dutch Apple Cake
Milk

Meat Croquettes
Dill Pickle
Creamed Peas
Biscuits
Pears, Wafers
Milk

WEDNESDAY DINNER

Broiled Ham
Breaded Pineapple Slice
Scalloped Potatoes
Raw Spinach Salad, Chiffonade
   Dressing
Whole Wheat Pan Rolls
Lemon Ice Box Cake
Coffee or Milk

Braised Beef Tongue
Browned Potatoes
Fresh Asparagus—Drawn Butter
Carrot Salad
Plain Rolls
Marshmallow Pudding
Coffee or Milk

MENUS FOR A WOMEN'S RESIDENCE HALL (*continued*)

THURSDAY BREAKFAST

Week I   *Week II*

Stewed Prunes   Tomato Juice
Fried Scrapple   Bacon
Puffed Wheat   Toast
Coffee or Cocoa   Cream of Wheat with Dates
                                 Coffee or Cocoa

THURSDAY LUNCHEON

Rice Croquettes with Cheese Sauce   Stuffed Eggs
Beet and Celery Salad   Baked Potatoes
Whole Wheat Bread   Philadelphia Relish
Fruit Cup   Cucumber Butter Sandwiches
Plain Cake   Blanc Mange with Cream
Milk   Milk

THURSDAY DINNER
(Guest Night)

Filet Mignon—Mushrooms   Spanish Steak
Stuffed Baked Potatoes   Mashed Potatoes
Buttered New Asparagus   Frosted Peas
Chiffonade Salad   Waldorf Salad
Parkerhouse Rolls   Hot Cinnamon Twists
Blueberry Tarts   Cream Puffs with Ice Cream
Coffee or Milk   Coffee or Milk

FRIDAY BREAKFAST

Grape Fruit   Stewed Dried Apricots
Biscuits   Muffins
Scrambled Eggs   Jam
Krumbles   Krispies
Coffee or Cocoa   Coffee or Cocoa

FRIDAY LUNCHEON

Tuna à la King   Cheese Soufflé
Lettuce Salad   French Fried Potatoes
Nut Bread   Raw Spinach Salad
Dainty Rice Pudding   Cracked Wheat Bread
Milk   Fruit Cup
                                 Milk

MENUS FOR A WOMEN'S RESIDENCE HALL (*continued*)

FRIDAY DINNER

Week I	*Week II*
Baked Salmon—Lemon	Baked Halibut
Creamed Parsley Potatoes	Mustard Sauce
Buttered Peas	Scalloped Tomatoes
Emerald Salad	Parsley Buttered Potatoes
Potato Bread	Pineapple Salad
Apricot Sherbet	Whole Wheat Biscuit
Wafers	Date Pudding
Coffee or Milk	Whipped Cream
	Coffee or Milk

SATURDAY BREAKFAST

Tomato Juice	Grapefruit
Creamed Beef on Toast	Rolled Oats
Bran Flakes	Pecan Rolls
Coffee or Cocoa	Coffee or Cocoa

SATURDAY LUNCHEON

Spaghetti and Celery Salad	Potato Omelet
Buttered Carrots	Buttered String Beans
Vienna Rolls	Radishes
Peaches	Pan Rolls
Cookies	Hot Norwegian Prune Pudding
Milk	Milk

SATURDAY DINNER

Saratoga Chops	Beef Stew with Dumplings
Mashed Potatoes	(Vegetables cooked with Stew,
Buttered String Beans	Onions, Carrots, Turnips, Potatoes)
Cucumber Salad	Cole Slaw with Sour Cream Dressing
Ice Box Rolls	Hard Rolls
Currant Jelly	Boston Cream Roll
Chocolate Cream Cake	Coffee or Milk
Coffee or Milk	

SUNDAY BREAKFAST

Grapefruit	Combination Fruit: Bananas, Pine-
Bacon Rolls	apple, Oranges
Jelly	Pancakes
Pettijohns	Sirup
Coffee or Cocoa	Puffed Wheat
	Coffee or Cocoa

MENUS FOR A WOMEN'S RESIDENCE HALL (*continued*)
SUNDAY DINNER

Week I	*Week II*
Bouillon with Whipped Cream	Pineapple Mint Cocktail
Rolled Rib Roast	Fricasseed Chicken
Cucumber Slices	Gravy
Mashed Potatoes	Rice Timbales
Brown Gravy	Glazed Carrots
Buttered Celery Hearts	Olives
Grapefruit Section Salad	Head Lettuce with Roquefort Cheese
Cloverleaf Rolls	Dressing
Peanut Brittle Fluff	Parkerhouse Rolls
Coffee	Graham Cracker Pie
	Coffee

SUNDAY EVENING MEAL

Buffet Service	Picnic Lunch
Chicken Salad	Cottage Cheese Salad in Cups
Waffled Potatoes	Meat Sandwiches
Bread and Butter Sandwiches	Celery Hearts
Pecan Pie	Picnic Oranges
Lemonade	Chocolate Cup Cakes

SPECIAL DINNERS FOR RESIDENCE HALLS

Thanksgiving Dinner

Consommé
Toast Ring with Parmesan Cheese Garnish
Celery and Olives

Roast Turkey   Brown Rice and Almond Stuffing
Giblet Gravy
Brussels Sprouts   Mashed Hubbard Squash
Cranberry Ice   Ice Box Rolls

Mince Meat Tarts with Hard Sauce
Coffee

Christmas Dinner

Iced Tomato Juice

Roast Duck with Chestnut Stuffing
Scalloped Sweet Potatoes and Apples   Broccoli
Lettuce Hearts with Roquefort Dressing   Cranberry Jelly
All Bran Rolls
Celery and Olives

Pumpkin Chiffon Pie   Whipped Cream
Coffee

Tea Room Menus. Menu planning for a tea room has much in common with menu planning for special occasions. Consideration must be given the ten basic points of successful meal planning and, in addition, provision must be made to emphasize some one or more dishes for which the tea room is or may become noted. One tea room always includes in its menus orange rolls, justly popular. Another always includes a favorite salad bowl and a third provides at each luncheon and dinner an opportunity for the guests to have ice cream with a famous chocolate sauce. Repetition of these items leads to heightened satisfaction of the clientele rather than to boredom. Effective use may be made of the featuring of certain foods on certain days, as, for example, chicken and waffles on Monday night and baked beans and cod fish balls on Saturday night. However, the use of features should be restricted so that the menu does not become limited by the routine established. One may go to Ye Rocking Horse Inn some one night each week happy in knowing what the menu will be. Such satisfaction passes if a definitely known menu is established and maintained for each night of the week.

In general, tea room prices are higher than those charged in cafeterias and cafés. This difference in price cannot be regarded as an increase in profit margin, as the guests usually demand highly palatable food, an atmosphere of charm and interest, and daintiness and attractiveness in the service. Usually the menu offered on any one day is restricted to a limited number of choices, often in two or more price levels; but it is expected that the menu will vary markedly from day to day so that interest may be maintained.

The following menus have been successfully used in one small tea room. In the spring and fall respectively they show the differences in dishes characterizing menus popular in certain seasons as well as the differences made in any one day in menus, one of which is offered at a cost fifty per cent greater than the other. In these lists, the more expensive dinners appear in Menu No. I, the less expensive in Menu No. II.

TEA ROOM MENUS FOR SPRINGTIME
MENU NO. I

Monday (May Day)
Broiled Minute Steaks
French Fried Potatoes   Grilled Tomatoes
Iceberg Lettuce   Chiffonade Dressing
Butter Buns
Meringue Shell Baskets with Ice Cream
(Tiny Colored Candies)
or
Hot Chocolate Sundae
Beverage

Tuesday
Chicken Turnovers
Creamed New Potatoes   Pickled Peach
Buttered Carrots
Spring Salad   French Dressing
Honey-Bran Muffins
Rhubarb Sauce   Cookies
or
Chocolate Sundae
Beverage

Wednesday
Baked Ham   Mustard Sauce
Scalloped Potatoes   Buttered Broccoli
Filled Cucumber Salad   Cream Dressing
Baking Powder Biscuits
Fresh Strawberry Bavarian Cream Pie
or
Hot Chocolate Sundae
Beverage

Thursday
Broiled Lamb Chops   Kentucky Lamb Sauce
Franconia Potatoes   Buttered Fresh Peas
Spiced Fruit Salad
Poppyseed Rolls
Green Apple Pie
or
Hot Chocolate Sundae
Beverage

TEA ROOM MENUS FOR SPRINGTIME (*continued*)

Friday

Baked Fish Fillets   Piquante Sauce
Lemon Parsley Buttered Potatoes   Fresh Asparagus
Julienne Vegetable Salad   French Dressing
All Bran Twin Rolls
Chilled Fresh Fruit Cup
or
Hot Chocolate Sundae
Beverage

MENU NO. II

Monday (May Day)

Ham and Egg Scallop
Baby Lima Beans   Raw Carrot Strips
Pineapple-Celery Salad
Plain Rolls
Washington Cream Pie
Beverage

Tuesday

Cheese Soufflé   Béchamel Sauce
Buttered Fresh Spinach   Apple Ring Garnish
Perfection Salad
Blueberry Muffins   Preserves
Cherry Pie
Beverage

Wednesday

Egg and Mushroom Casserole
Buttered New Asparagus   German Carrots
Romaine Salad   French Dressing
Baking Powder Biscuits
Chilled Fruit Cup
Beverage

Thursday

Assorted Cold Meat   Spiced Apricot Garnish
Creamed New Potatoes
Combination Vegetable Salad
Poppyseed Rolls
Caramel Tapioca   Whipped Cream
Beverage

TEA ROOM MENUS FOR SPRINGTIME (*continued*)

Friday
Salmon and Potato Chip Casserole
Buttered Green Beans   Watermelon Pickles
Citrus Fruit Salad
All Bran Twin Rolls
Strawberries   Cookies
Beverage

TEA ROOM MENUS FOR FALL

MENU NO. I

Monday
Stuffed Pork Chops
Sweet Potatoes and Apples en Casserole
Buttered Cauliflower
Lettuce Hearts   Thousand Island Dressing
Orange Rolls
Frozen Fruit Dessert   Wafers
or
Hot Chocolate Sundae
Beverage

Tuesday
Broiled Steak   Celery Curls
Whole Grain Corn   Baked Tomato
Grapefruit Section Salad   French Dressing
Cinnamon Rolls
Ice Box Cake
or
Hot Chocolate Sundae
Beverage

Wednesday
Breaded Veal Cutlets   Orange Garnish
Parsley Buttered Potatoes   Stuffed Baked Onion
Frozen Fruit Salad
Butterhorn Rolls
Poppyseed Cake
or
Hot Chocolate Sundae
Beverage

TEA ROOM MENUS FOR FALL (*continued*)

Thursday

Fried Chicken Spiced Apricot
Mashed Potatoes Gravy
Buttered Broccoli
Lime Ice
Baking Powder Biscuits Jam
Cream Puffs
or
Hot Chocolate Sundae
Beverage

Friday

Broiled Fish Lemon Sauce
Creamed Potatoes Buttered New Peas
Stuffed Spiced Peach Salad Mayonnaise
Orange Rolls
Cranberry Shortcake
or
Hot Chocolate Sundae
Beverage

MENU NO. II

Monday

Stuffed Green Peppers Creamed Potato
Tomato Aspic Ring Salad with Cole Slaw
Plain Rolls
Oranges Soft Custard Sauce
Beverage

Tuesday

Beef Stew Curried Rice
Beet Relish
Shredded Lettuce Salad
Raised Muffins
Apricot Whip
Beverage

Wednesday

Rice Croquettes with Cheese Sauce
Tomato Section Salad Fresh Buttered Peas
All Bran Rolls
Baked Custard
Beverage

TEA ROOM MENUS FOR FALL (*continued*)

Thursday

French Fried Deviled Eggs   Raw Carrot Strips
Scalloped Cabbage
Apple Salad
Baking Powder Biscuits   Jam
Pumpkin Pie
Beverage

Friday

Creamed Tuna Fish in Noodle Ring
Buttered Beets
Shredded Spinach Salad   Chiffonade Dressing
Plain Rolls
Fudge Cake
Beverage

Menus for Children's Homes and Other Philanthropic Institutions. The characteristic problem of the menu planning for an institution of this type is that food needs of the group often must be met at a per capita cost at or below what has been termed the irreducible minimum. The group is served three meals a day. The low cost foods commonly used tend to fall in a monotonous pattern, unless the greatest care is taken to introduce variety and interest in every possible way. The wise use of the cycle method of planning greatly lessens the heavy load of menu planning under the trying conditions often imposed on the director of food services of these institutions. The type of food is the same as that included in the school lunch room menus. Care must be taken to include milk, fresh fruits, and vegetables in various forms to meet the needs of the growing children.

The Hospital Menu. The hospital menu or menus must be planned according to basic principles with food selected so as to meet the needs of its patients, staff members, and employees.

Special food preparation will be reduced to a minimum if the general or house diet is well-planned. All hospital diets are normal diets that have been changed in consistency (liquid, soft or light), energy value (high or low calories), or ratio of food nutrients (low carbohydrates, protein, or high iron). The diets with a modified ratio of constituents are the therapeutic diets. They are either weighed or carefully calculated and will not be considered in this book.

Hospital dietaries may be classified as:

1. Regular, general, or house. These menus are for doctors, nurses, and a few patients. They include a wide range of foods with a few restrictions for patients.

2. Light or convalescent. This diet is given before the patient is ready for a general diet. It must be easily digested, high in protein and nutritive value.

3. Soft. The soft diet is given before the patient may be given a light diet. Restrictions are made for surgical and medical cases.

4. Liquid. A liquid diet may be adapted for either a medical or surgical case.

The following general classification of hospital diets is often used. However, the limitations vary with the hospital.

General	Light	Soft	Medical Liquid	Surgical Liquid
Any well prepared food that is easily digested	Any food allowed on soft diet plus: chicken, broiled lamb or steak, potatoes, vegetables	Any medical liquid plus: cooked cereals, puddings, most strained vegetables, baked potatoes, custards, rice, ice cream, toast, egg, cooked fruit	Milk in any form, cream, broth, milk soup, strained gruel, eggs beaten, malted milk, fruit juice, tea, coffee, sugar, gelatin, junket, custard (sometimes)	Clear broth, tea, coffee, gelatin, fruit juice (no milk products)

Special Occasions. The planning, preparing and serving of meals for special occasions is usually an important part of the program of all institutional management departments in colleges, public schools, and commercial food units. The hospital, too, being a temporary home for large groups of people, must meet the problem of providing festive meals for the holiday-tide as well as that of providing special meals for various other occasions.

The following menus have been formulated and successfully used for special occasions in one institution. The ten points cited as basic to all menu planning would have to be given consideration before these menus could be used successfully in another institution.

American Association of University Women
Assorted Canapés
Fried Spring Chicken
Browned New Potatoes　　Asparagus Tips with Hollandaise Sauce
Creole Baked Tomato
Rhubarb Ice
Ice Box Rolls　　　　　　　　　Butter
Spring Salad　　Salted Wafers
Frosted Strawberry Meringue
Coffee
Nuts　　Mints

Mother-Daughter Luncheon
Chilled Fruit Juice
Jellied Chicken Loaf
Shoe String Potatoes　　Stuffed Tomato Salad
Hot Finger Rolls　　Butter
Apricot Bavarian Cream
Coffee

Business and Professional Women's Luncheon
Bouillon
Creamed Ham with Mushrooms
on Toast Points
French Fried Egg Plant　　Broiled Stuffed Tomato (small)
Celery Strips
Muffins　　　　　Butter
Graham Cracker Pie

School Board Dinner
Hot Tomato Juice　　Cheese Puffs
Veal Birds
Browned Potatoes　　Buttered Latticed Carrots
Jellied Vegetable Salad
Whole Wheat Rolls　　　Butter
Fudge Cake à la Mode

Civic Club Luncheon
Baked Virginia Ham   Mustard Sauce
Sweet Potato Croquettes   Buttered Green Beans
Cabbage-Pineapple Salad
Parkerhouse Rolls
Pumpkin Pie with Whipped Cream
Coffee

Women's Panhellenic Luncheon
Lime Ice Cocktail
Chicken Turnovers   Béchamel Sauce
New Potatoes Persillade   New Peas in Drawn Butter
Pickled Peach
Cucumber, Pineapple, and Almond Salad
Dinner Rolls
Ice Box Cake with Whipped Cream
Coffee

High School Literary Club
Country Fried Steak   Gravy
Oven-browned Potatoes   Buttered Green Beans with Pimiento Strip
Apple and Celery Salad
Pan Rolls
Lemon Chiffon Pie
Coffee

Junior-Senior High School Banquet
Grape Juice Cocktail
Breaded Veal Cutlets with Orange and Celery Garnish
Creamed New Potatoes with Parsley
Buttered Fresh Asparagus
Head Lettuce   Thousand Island Dressing
Hard Rolls   Butter
Special Brick Ice Cream   White Cake
Coffee

Alumni Luncheon
Grapefruit, Orange and Avocado Salad   Cheese Straws
Scalloped Chicken   Gravy
Shoe String Potatoes   Buttered Peas
Celery   Olives
Apricot Ice
Cloverleaf Rolls   Butter
Individual Cherry Pie

Founders' Day Dinner
Mint Cocktail
Mock Drum Sticks with Mushrooms
Browned New Potatoes   Cauliflower with Cheese Sauce
Head Lettuce   Chiffonade Dressing
Finger Rolls   Currant Jelly
Fresh Strawberry Sundae
Coffee

Faculty Club Dinner
Orange Cup
Roast Lamb   Kentucky Lamb Sauce
Parsley Buttered Potatoes   Julienne Carrots with Peas
Combination Vegetable Salad
Celery   Olives
Cloverleaf Rolls
Pecan Ice Cream Balls with Caramel Sauce
Coffee

PART IV

SERVING MEALS FOR SPECIAL OCCASIONS

Wherever or whatever the occasion for which a special meal is planned, there must be a temporary organization which differs in many ways from that established for the usual routine of daily food preparation. For many, the organization and administration of these unusual meals are tasks to be dreaded and, if possible, to be avoided. This attitude is often common among persons without institutional training; although it is not infrequently found among trained food directors whose busy lives seem completely occupied with necessary daily tasks.

Suggestions for the organization and administration of a typical simple meal for 50, such as might be prepared by a high school class, are offered here as an aid for inexperienced teachers and others who are untrained in the institutional field. As will be readily seen the plan can be adjusted to meet changes in the menu or in the number served. These suggestions may be helpful also to the food director in a college commons or residence hall who must assume the responsibility of special meal service in addition to an already full schedule. Here the problem is somewhat different in that the preparation, at least, is usually assigned to experienced workers. However, a temporary organization must be set up for the unusual task. Usually untrained students are employed as waiters or waitresses. In many situations the employment of college men as waiters is the custom.

The responsibilities of the manager in charge of a special meal are as follows:

1. Plan the menu and other details with representative of organization to be served.

2. Determine quantity, quality, and cost of food to be purchased.

3. Make plans for preparation of the food.

4. Make plans for serving of the food.

5. Supervise the preparation and serving of the food.

BANQUETS

Preliminary Procedures

Menus. It is desirable that the food director, or the person acting as manager for the special meal, confer with an authorized representative of the group to be served to work out the details of the plan for the special meal. Such a conference provides not only the basic facts essential to menu planning, as the number to be served, the price per service, and the date and time of service, but also information concerning the type of menu preferred and any items particularly desired.

Duplicate copies of the menu plans should be signed and kept by the representative of the organization and the food director. This confirms the agreement and may prevent a misunderstanding of details and avoid last minute changes, so often made by the thoughtless host or hostess.

The recording of menu plans may be satisfactorily done on such a blank as the following:

CLARK HIGH SCHOOL

		Menu
Date to be served	*Nov. 15*	
Dining Room	*East*	*Swiss Steak*
Time	*6 P. M.*	*Scalloped Potatoes (pimiento)*
Organization	*Athletic Club*	*Buttered Peas*
Plates estimated	*50*	*Olives Celery*
Plates guaranteed	*45*	*Cranberry Salad*
Price per plate	*50¢*	*Ice Box Rolls*
Number served		*Hot Chocolate Sundae*
Amount paid		
Cash		
Charge		

Representative of Organization___*J. B. Arnold*___Signed___*M. Bryant*___

Representative of Institution___*H. Barber*___   Manager

Remarks:

Quantity and Cost. The next step, after the menu has been planned, is to determine the kind and amount of food to purchase and prepare. The amount to prepare will depend largely upon the group to be served, the method of preparation, the form of service, and the experience of the servers.

QUANTITIES OF FOOD

Menu	Materials	Amount	Unit Cost	Total Cost
Swiss Steak.........	Round of beef	12½ lb.		
	Fat	1 lb.		
	Flour	2 c.		
	Salt	4 T.		
	Onion	1		
Scalloped Potatoes with Pimiento....	Potatoes	15 lb.		
	White Sauce	4 qt.		
	Salt	2½ T.		
	Butter	4 T.		
	Bread crumbs	6 oz.		
	Pimiento	1 No. 1 can		
Buttered Peas.......	Peas	8 No. 2 cans or 2 No. 10 cans		
	Butter	½ lb.		
Celery..............	Celery	3 bunches		
Olives..............	Olives	2 qt.		
Butter (for table)....	Butter	1½ lb.		
Rolls..............	Rolls	10 doz.		
Cranberry Salad.....	Cranberries	4 lb.		
	Sugar	3 lb.		
	Jonathan apples	6 lb.		
	Oranges	4 (No. 150)		
Mayonnaise.........	Salad oil	1 qt.		
	Eggs, whole	1		
	Paprika	¼ t.		
	Cayenne	f.g.		
	Mustard	½ T.		
	Vinegar	2 T.		
	Cream, 40 per cent	1 pt.		
Chocolate Sundae....	Ice Cream	2 gal.		
	Butter	½ lb.		
	Powdered sugar	6 c.		
	Chocolate	½ lb.		
	Evaporated milk	1¼ c.		

Food Preparation. The following summary work sheet is adequate for the direction of personnel if the food is largely prepared by regular cooks and the other employees are familiar with the routine and practices involved. This work sheet should be posted in the kitchen at least 2 days before the banquet is to be served. A time interval of 2 days permits familiarity with the details by all concerned.

SUMMARY WORK SHEET

Preparation:

Swiss Steak	Cook
Scalloped Potatoes with Pimiento	Cook
Buttered Peas	Cook
Ice Box Rolls	Pastry Cook
Chocolate Sauce	Pastry Cook
Cranberry Relish Salad	Salad Maid
Celery Curls	Salad Maid
Mayonnaise	Salad Maid
Cut Butter	Ellen
Send up dishes 3:30 P. M.	Paul
Arrange tables	John
Set up tables 4:30 P. M.	Eloise, Irma
Food porter	John
Set up salads and relish dishes 5:30 P. M.	Eloise, Irma

Serve plates 6 P. M.		Heat rolls	John
Meat	Eloise	Pass rolls	Alice
Potatoes	Irma		
Peas	Ellen		
Check plates	Miss Mayer		
Waitresses 5:45 P. M.			
	Edna		
	Blanche		
	Mary		
	Ann		

Clear and stack dishes		Dish desserts	
(in kitchen)	Eloise		Ellen
	Alice		John
	Irma		
Clean kitchen and dining room after banquet			John

The following detailed work schedule for the organization of a high school banquet has been worked out in order to serve as an example for those unfamiliar with banquet organization and who must work with inexperienced helpers.

DETAILED WORK SCHEDULE

Organization Athletic Club

Number to be served 50   Date November 15

Price per place 50¢   Time 6 P.M.

MENU

Swiss Steak

Scalloped Potatoes with Pimiento   Buttered Peas

Olives   Celery Curls

Cranberry Salad

Ice Box Rolls

Vanilla Ice Cream   Hot Chocolate Sauce

PREPARATION

Work	Amount	Time	Class Girl
Make raw cranberry and orange salad	1 x recipe	Day before	
Make ice box roll dough..............	1½ x recipe	Day before	
Make mayonnaise....................	1 qt.	Day before	
Make hot chocolate sauce............	1 x recipe	Day before	
Peel potatoes and slice...............	12 lb. (E.P.)	Before 3 P.M.	
Prepare white sauce No. I..........	1 gal.	3:00 P.M.	
and scalloped potatoes..............	1 x recipe		
Light 2 ovens......................	350°F.	3:15	
Pound flour into steak and cut into serv-	14 to 16 lb.		
ings..............................		3:15	
Brown steak.......................			
Shape rolls and place in pans.........	10 doz.	3:30	
Wash lettuce for salad and crisp if neces-			
sary..............................	5 heads		
Prepare celery curls and place in ice			
water.............................	3 bunches		
Measure out olives, place in refrigerator.	2 qt.		
Count dishes.......................	See dish list		
Fold napkins.......................	See dish list		
Fill salts, peppers, and sugars.........	See dish list		
Put potatoes in oven to cook.........		3:45	
Put steak in oven to cook............		3:55	
Set tables (2 workers)...............	50 places	4:30	
Cut butter and place in refrigerator....	1½ lb.	4:30	
Prepare ice water...................	5 gal.	4:45	
Whip cream and mix with	1 c.	5:00	
mayonnaise.......................	1 qt.		

PREPARATION (*Continued*)

Work	Amount	Time	Class Girl
Put rolls in warm place, if necessary, to rise..........................		5:00	
Set up salads and place..............	50	5:30	
Heat chocolate sauce.................	1 x recipe	5:00	
Open peas, heat and season...........	2 No. 10 or 8 No. 2 cans	5:30	
Bake rolls..........................		5:40	
Pour ice water......................		5:45	
Place relishes and butter on table......		5:45	
Assemble serving utensils.............	See dish list	5:45	
Place food in serving counters........		5:55	

Serving the Food. A list including the amount and kind of linen, dishes, silver, glassware, and serving utensils should be made by the manager and given to the person responsible for the assembling of these, at least one day before they are to be used.

DISH LIST—ATHLETIC CLUB BANQUET

Name	Number	Size
China:		
Service plates	50	6 in.
Dinner plates	54	9 in.
Salad plates	50	6 in.
Bread-and-butter plates	50	5½ in.
Dessert plates	50	6 in.
Cups	—	
Saucers	—	
Relish dishes	6 to 8	Oval
Glassware:		
Water glasses	50	
Stemmed sherbets	50	
Sugar bowls	6 to 8	
Creamers	6 to 8	
Salts and peppers	6 to 8	
Water pitchers	4	
Linen:		
Table cloths	—	
Napkins	54	
Silverware:		
Knives	50	
Forks	54	
Teaspoons	58	
Extra silver on trays	10 each	
Miscellaneous:		
Serving fork	1	
Turner	1	
Large slotted spoons	2	
Soup spoons	2	
No. 16 dipper	1	
No. 12 dipper	1	
Hot pan holders	2	
Dish towels	2	

Preparation of the Dining Room. Class girls or employees assisting with the food service should be given dèfinite instructions.

A mimeographed sheet of personal qualifications and detailed procedures should be given to everyone new on a job.

The first step toward the service of a meal is the preparation of the room. It should be thoroughly cleaned, lighted, ventilated, and the temperature should be regulated, if possible. The tables and chairs must be placed so there will be adequate space for serving after the guests are seated. Usually serving stands, conveniently placed, make service faster. Such provision is especially important when the distance to the kitchen is great.

Arrangement of the Table.[1] In order that the food may be properly served great care must be taken to follow certain accepted rules for table setting. The physical set-up, help available, or other conditions may demand some deviation from the rules given. However, there is often more than one right way.

1. *Silence cloth.* Lay the silence cloth, which is usually of felt or of quilted or double-faced cotton material made for this purpose. It should have a drop of about three inches. Fit it over the table tightly. The corners may be folded, if the table is square, and pinned or tied tightly beneath the table. The silence cloth serves three purposes: it prevents noise, protects the table, and improves the appearance of the table cloth.

2. *Table cloth.* Lay the table cloth, unfolding it carefully on the table to avoid creases. Place the cloth upon the table so that the center, lengthwise fold comes exactly in the middle of the table and the four corners are an equal distance from the floor. The cloth should extend over the table top at least a quarter of a yard at each end. The table cloth should be ironed with one lengthwise fold down the center, the cloth opened up, and each side folded to the center crease, to make 3 lengthwise creases. Because of its length it is usually necessary to fold institutional linen crosswise to facilitate handling and storage.

3. *Table covers, runners, centerpieces, and doilies.* Lace covers and embroidered linen cloths are often used for formal luncheons. Table runners, or a centerpiece and doilies, are suitable for use at breakfast

---

[1] Adapted from Department of Food Economics and Nutrition: "Practical Cookery and the Etiquette and Service of the Table." Kansas State College, Department of Printing, 1939.

and luncheon. Paper doilies are often used in institutions where the linen doilies are not a part of the table appointments. Rectangular doilies may be sufficiently large that a single one will provide protection for the entire cover. If the doilies are small, however, it is necessary to have enough of them, of assorted sizes, to put under glasses, cups and saucers, bread-and-butter plates, and dishes containing food. In many institutions polished wood, lacquered, glass, or attractive composition table tops are used so the cover may be laid without cloth or doilies.

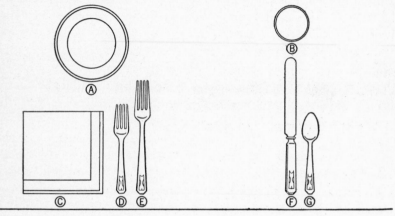

Fig. XII.—A cover for a simple meal.

a. bread and butter   e. fork
b. water glass   f. knife
c. napkin   g. spoon
d. salad fork

4. *The cover.* The plate, silver, glasses, and napkin to be used by each person are called a cover. Consider twenty inches of table space as the smallest permissible allowance for each cover. Twenty-five or thirty inches is better. Arrange covers as symmetrically as possible. Place all silver and dishes required for one cover as close together as possible without crowding, for the appearance of the table is much improved if the covers are compactly laid.

5. *Silver.* Place the silver about one inch from, and at right angles to, the edge of the table. If the table is round, only the outside pieces can be thus arranged. Place knives, forks, and spoons in the order of their use, those first used on the outside with the possible exception of the dinner knife and fork which may be placed immediately to the

right and left of the plate, thus marking its position. Some prefer to place the salad or dessert fork next to the plate as the menu dictates.

Place the knives at the right of the plate with the cutting edge turned inward. If the menu requires no knife omit it from the cover. Place the spoons, bowls up, at the right of the knives. Place the forks, tines up, at the left of the plate. The oyster and cocktail forks are exceptions to this rule. Place these at the extreme right of the cover beyond the spoons.

The fork may be substituted for the knife at a luncheon where no knife is needed. Place it on the right side of the plate with the spoon beside it, if one is used. If more than one spoon is needed, the balance is better if the fork is placed to the left of the plate. With two forks and a spoon it also is probably better to place the forks in the usual position.

Lay the butter spreader across the upper right hand side of the bread-and-butter plate, with the cutting edge turned toward the center of the plate. It may be placed straight across the top of the plate or with the handle at a convenient angle. The butter spreader is sometimes placed with the other knives at the right of the plate beyond the spoons. This practice is followed chiefly in public places.

Do not place the dessert silver on the table when the cover is laid except when the amount of silver required for the entire meal is small. Never lay covers with more than three forks or a total of six pieces of silver. If a dinner is sufficiently elaborate to require too much silver to be put on at one time, place that needed for the later courses quietly at the covers just before the course is served.

If it is necessary to wash silver for use in the later courses, see that it is chilled before returning it to the table. Bring in the extra silver needed during the meal on a serving tray unless it is brought in with the course.

6. *Service plate.* Use a service plate only with a formal service. The service plate is supposedly very handsome and is usually about ten inches in diameter. Place the service plate at each cover when the table is laid. It should be one inch from the edge of the table. Place the plates containing the early courses of the meal, such as fruit, oysters, and soup, on the service plate. Never place food directly upon it. Do not remove the service plate until it is exchanged for the heated plate, upon which the first hot course after the soup is served.

This custom of the use of the service plate has arisen because of the fact that, on formal occasions, it is considered good form never to leave the guest without a plate before him until the table is cleared for dessert.

7. *Napkin.* Place the napkin at the left of the forks or at the right of the spoons, on the service plate, or between the knife and fork if the service plate is not used. It should be so placed that it brings the embroidered initial or monogram, if there is one, in a legible position.

8. *Glass.* Place the glass at the tip of the knife or slightly to the right. Goblets and footed tumblers are often preferred for luncheon or dinner and should be used at a formal dinner.

9. *Bread-and-butter plate.* Place the bread-and-butter plate at the tip of the fork or slightly to the left. At formal dinners, bread-and-butter plates are usually omitted since butter is not served. (Some hostesses, however, prefer to have them placed on the table as a convenient receptacle for bread, olives, celery, nuts, and similar foods.) At formal dinners rolls are buttered before being brought to the table so no butter spreaders are necessary.

10. *Salt and pepper.* Place individual salt and pepper dishes directly in front of each cover. They should be parallel with the edge of the table and in line with the glasses. Salt shakers are placed to the right. If individual salt and pepper sets are not available, allow, if possible, one set between each two covers. This provides salt and pepper for each guest so there is no necessity for passing them.

11. *Nut or bonbon dishes.* Place individual nut or bonbon dishes directly in front of the cover. Larger dishes for nuts or bonbons are placed symmetrically upon the table, usually allowing one dish for each four or six guests.

12. *Chairs.* Place the chairs so that the front edge of each touches or is just below the edge of the table cloth. The chair should be so placed with relation to the table that it need not be moved when the guest is seated.

13. *Decorations.* The decorations of the table should be in charge of someone not connected with the food service, although it is sometimes necessary for the food director to assume this as an added responsibility. Some attractive decoration should be provided for the center of the table. It should be low so the view across the table will not be obstructed. The decoration usually varies in elaborateness with

the formality of the meal. Cut flowers should harmonize in color with the menu, appointments of the table and the room.

The use of candles in the daytime is permissible only when the lighting is inadequate or the day is dark. When used they should be the sole source of light. Do not mix candle light and day light or candle light and electric light. At formal dinners and receptions, when the room is darkened, candles often form part of the decorations. They should always be placed symmetrically upon the table. Candles are now commonly used without shades. Tall ones in low holders are popular at present. They should be high enough that the flame is not on a level with the eyes of the guests. If the candles are thoroughly chilled in the ice box for several days before they are to be used there will be little dripping and they will burn longer. White or ivory candles are most favored for formal occasions.

Seating Arrangement. Place cards should ordinarily be put upon the napkin or above the cover. Menu cards, or booklets containing the menu and program, are commonly used at banquets. Infrequently the placing of cards is left to the food director. It is extremely difficult to lay down arbitrary rules for the seating of guests, since the matter is governed largely by the number and by the degree of formality of the meal. The guest of honor, if a woman, is usually seated at the right of the host; if a man, at the right of the hostess. The woman next in rank is seated at the left of the host. At a women's luncheon, the guest of honor sits at the right of her hostess. At banquets and public dinners a woman is seated at the right of her partner.

SERVICE

Table Service. 1. Waitresses should report to the supervisor to receive final instructions at least 15 minutes before the time set for serving the banquet.

2. If the salad is to be on the table when the guests arrive, it should be placed there by the waitresses not more than 15 minutes before serving time.

3. Place creamers at right of sugar bowls.

4. Place relishes on the table, if desired.

5. For small dinners, the first course may be placed on the table before dinner is announced. For large banquets, however, it is best

to wait until the guests are seated. Soups or hot canapés are always served after the guests are seated.

6. Place butter on the right side of the bread-and-butter plate. If no bread-and-butter plate is used and the salad is to be on the table when the guests arrive, place the butter on the side of the salad plate. This is often necessary at school banquets where dishes and table space are limited.

7. Pour water just before the meal is announced.

8. When the guests are seated, waiters or waitresses line up in the kitchen for trays containing the first course. Two persons work together, one carrying the tray and the other placing the food. Place the cocktail glasses, soup dishes, or canapé plates on the service plates, which are already on the table.

9. Place and remove all the dishes from the left with the left hand, except those containing beverages, which are placed and removed from the right with the right hand.

10. Serve the head table first, progressing from there to the right. It is preferable to have the head table the one farthest from the kitchen entrance.

11. When the guests have finished the first course, waitresses line up for removing the dishes. Follow the same order in removing dishes as in serving.

12. The waitresses line up in front of the serving table for the dinner plates, each waitress taking one plate in each hand. If the salad is to be served with the dinner plate, take a dinner plate in the left hand and a salad plate in the right hand. When each waitress has the plates in her hands the line advances as a unit to the dining room. There at a signal from the waitress at the head of the line, the waitresses simultaneously place, first, the dinner plates in front of the guests and then the salad plates. Every precaution should be taken to prevent the seemingly haphazard service that results from allowing the waitresses to serve without a line organization.

13. Finish serving one table before beginning to serve another.

14. Place the plate one inch from the edge of the table with the meat next to the guest.

15. Place the salad plate at the right of the spoons, if no beverage is served with the main course. If a beverage is served with the dinner course, place the salad at the left just above the napkin.

16. As soon as a table has been served with dinner plates and salad, specially appointed waitresses should follow immediately with the ice, rolls, and coffee.

17. At a large banquet, when serving an ice with the dinner course, carry it in on trays and place directly above the plate. Two waitresses work together as for first course.

18. Serve rolls at least twice. Offer them at the left at a convenient height and distance.

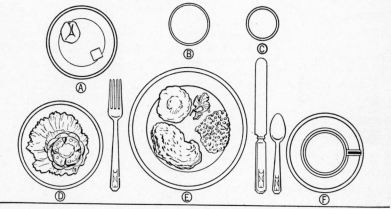

Fig. XIII.—The salad is placed at the left of the fork when salad and beverage are both served with the main course.

    a. bread and butter plate
    b. sherbet dish
    c. water glass
    d. salad plate
    e. dinner plate
    f. cup and saucer

19. Place the coffee at the right of the spoons with the handles of the cups toward the right. The coffee may be served from trays when a large number is to be served. One waitress carries the tray and the other sets the filled coffee cups on saucers and places them on the table.

20. Refill water glasses as often as necessary. If the tables are crowded, it may be necessary to remove the glasses from the table to fill them. Handle the glass near the base.

21. At the end of the course, remove all the dishes belonging to that course. Stack dishes on right hand, back of the guest.

22. The silver for the dessert may or may not be placed on the

table when the table is set. If passed later, take in on a tray and place at the right of the plate.

23. Serve desserts two at a time and in the same order that the plates were served.

24. Coffee is served by waitresses who served the ice with the dinner course.

25. If possible, the table should be cleared except for decorations before the program begins.

26. The handling of dishes should cease before the program begins. The rattling of dishes has ruined many banquets, and is an unnecessary offense to the guest.

Servers. Waitresses may wear black or dark dresses with dainty white aprons or light wash dresses; however, uniforms are in most cases preferable. Shoes with low, or medium-low, rubber heels should be worn. Waiters should wear dark trousers, white shirts, dark ties, and white coats. Waiters or waitresses serving should observe the following points:

1. Be immaculately clean in person and dress.
2. Report promptly on duty at scheduled time.
3. Be quick to see errors in table setting or service and to give help in case of accidents.
4. Appear pleasant and courteous at all times.
5. Step lightly, move quickly, but do not show a flurried manner.
6. Close doors without noise. Handle dishes and silver quietly.
7. Do not converse unless it is absolutely necessary.
8. Be as inconspicuous as possible.

Kitchen Organization. Food should be served from steam tables, if these are available. If there are no steam tables, the utensils containing food should be placed in hot water in order that food may be served hot. Some provision must also be made for keeping plates and cups hot. For serving 50 plates or less, the plan should provide that one person serve meat; one, vegetables; one, potatoes; and so on. Such an arrangement for serving may be termed a "set-up." For 60 to 100, two set-ups should be provided in order to hasten service. For more than 100, additional set-ups should be provided.

It is usually convenient to have the food placed on the steam table in the following order: meat, potatoes, vegetables, and sauces. On

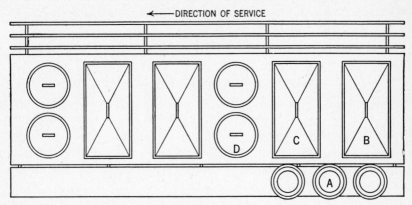

FIG. XIV.—Food arranged on a steam table in the order it is to be placed on the plate facilitates service.

    a. plates
    b. meat
    c. potatoes
    d. vegetable

FIG. XV.—The uniform arrangement of each food on the plate adds to the attractiveness of the plate when served.

    a. bread and butter plate
    b. sherbet dish
    c. water glass
    d. salad
    e. dinner plate

        1. meat
        2. potatoes
        3. garnish
        4. vegetable

an adjoining table, butter, garnish, or relish is placed. The food porter is responsible for the placing of food and for the service equipment.

The supervisor should demonstrate the size of portions to be given and their arrangement on the plate by serving the first plate and calling attention to the points to be considered.

There should be a checker at the end of the line whose responsibility it is to remove with a damp cloth any food spots from the plate, to check the plate for completeness, arrangement, and uniformity of servings.

Portions. The importance of standardized serving can hardly be overestimated, for on this may depend the financial success or failure of a meal and the enjoyment of the guests. In this matter, the old adage of the pat of butter is pertinent—if the pat is too large the management loses money; if it is too small the management loses patrons. It is also true that variations in the portions from day to day must be avoided. The pieces of pie or cake as served must be so nearly equivalent to those served on similar occasions as to cause no comment on the part of the patrons.

There are various ways in which standard portions may be secured. Perhaps the first way is by specifying the size or weight of units comprising the purchase if these are to serve as individual portions. For example, a purchase of oranges, size 150, affords assurance of standardized serving. Meat such as veal cutlets, chops, or steaks may be ordered 3, 4, or 5 to the pound, as desired, thus providing for standardized service.

Many foods cannot be brought under this category because they are mixtures or combinations of various foods, or are served in a form quite different from that in which they are purchased. Meat balls, croquettes, mashed potatoes, pudding, cakes, and pies all illustrate this point. Several different provisions are made to secure standardized portions in the foods of this group. The individual portions may be determined by weight during the process of preparation as is sometimes done in the making of meat balls and croquettes. The individual portions may be determined by the use of dippers of standardized size. This method is commonly used for such foods as are conveniently handled by a dipper as mashed potatoes, creamed and buttered vegetables, and puddings.

Another means of securing standardized portions, applicable to foods that take the form of the container in which they are prepared, as gelatin salads or desserts, cakes, pies, and meat loaf, is that of using pans of uniform size and controlling the cutting of the prepared product so that the yield is uniform. In the last three provisions cited, the use of a standardized recipe is basic to other efforts to secure standardized portions.

The exact size of a serving of food not cooked in individual portions may be determined by this method:

1. Weigh pan in which food is placed.

2. Weigh finished product and subtract weight of pan to determine weight of food.

3. Reduce weight of food to ounces.

4. Divide the weight of food by the number to be served to determine weight of a serving. (Make a small allowance for waste.)

5. Weigh out an individual serving and measure with a dipper or other serving utensil to determine the volume of food.

This method requires some time but eliminates the possibility of discovering, after half the guests are served, that there is not enough food for those not yet served.

COMMUNITY MEALS

The plans for organization that have been presented have presupposed some one person to be in charge with others working under her direction, either as students or employees. Such is not the case with many special meals that are prepared and served by community and church organizations. These meals are a responsibility which many women, active in the church and community life, are asked to assume. Often these women, who are efficient organizers in their own homes, are at a loss to know how best to proceed in the preparation and planning of food for a large group. Detailed plans previously presented as necessary for the efficient working of inexperienced class girls may be modified to fit the needs of a group of adult women who are familiar with time requirements for food preparation but who have had little experience in the managerial aspects of institutional meal preparation, including the division of labor and the delegation of various responsibilities. A necessary initial step in such planning is the assignment of definite tasks to committees. A suggested plan for such a group follows.

Planning Committee.
Duties and procedure:
Plan menu.
Plan amounts of food to be purchased.
Select and assemble recipes.
Appoint following committees:
Preparation
Serving
Cleaning
Furnish copies of menu and amounts to above named committees.

Preparation Committee. (Number determined by menu.)
Duties and procedure:
Study menu and recipes.
Prepare food according to work plan.

Serving Committee.
Duties and procedure:
Provide serving equipment and table appointments.
Arrange tables.
Lay covers and decorate tables.
Serve food in kitchen.
Serve food in dining room.

Clean-up Committee.
Duties and procedure:
Provide space for soiled dishes.
Scrape and stack soiled dishes and cooking utensils.
Wash, dry, put away dishes and cooking utensils.
Clean kitchen and dining room.

The suggestions for the preparation of the dining room, the decorations, organization of food service in the kitchen, and serving the food, given in the preceding pages, may be followed, with desirable variations, in the serving of community meals.

FORMAL MEALS[2]

Dinners. A formal dinner formerly consisted of at least ten courses. The tendency at the present time is toward a smaller dinner with greater simplicity and perfection of detail. Often only four or

---

[2] Adapted from Department of Food Economics and Nutrition: "Practical Cookery and the Etiquette and Service of the Table." Kansas State College, Department of Printing, 1939.

five courses are served. There should never be more than eight courses. More than this is now considered bad form. The order of the courses is:

1. Hors d'oeuvre.
2. Soup.
3. Fish.
4. Entrée.
5. Roast and vegetables.
6. Salad.
7. Dessert.
8. Coffee, alone, or with cheese service.

The hors d'oeuvre or appetizer may consist of oysters or clams on the half shell, fruit or oyster cocktail, canapé, or fruit. The entrée may be a timbale, a creamed dish, or any of the dishes described as entrées in cook books. A game course may be used as an entrée. A frozen punch or sherbet now often accompanies the roast where formerly it was generally served as a separate course. The meat for the main course is usually roasted or baked but may be prepared in any of a variety of ways.

The courses for a formal dinner may, when it is advisable, be diminished by omitting either the hors d'oeuvre or the soup as well as the fish and entrée. The menu then becomes:

1. Hors d'oeuvre or soup.
2. Roast and vegetables.
3. Salad.
4. Dessert.
5. Coffee.

A three-course menu includes the same foods but the salad, or an ice, is served with the meat course and the coffee is served either with the dessert or with the meat course and dessert as preferred.

Luncheons. The menu and service for formal luncheons resemble those for formal dinners so closely that it is unnecessary to give any detailed description. As a rule, the menu is simpler and is usually somewhat as follows:

1. Fruit, fruit or fish cocktail, or other suitable first course.
2. Soup. May be omitted or used as the first course.
3. Fish, poultry, or meat with vegetables.

4. Salad.
5. Dessert.
6. Coffee.

The foods chosen for a luncheon are not so heavy and rich as those used in a dinner menu and special effort is made to have the food attractively arranged. A bare table with doilies is generally preferred. The soup is served in bouillon cups; the meat is not in the form of a roast; lobster, crab, fish-fillets, chicken in patties, and similar dishes are commonly used instead. Black coffee is served, as a rule, in after-dinner coffee cups at the table. The dessert plates may be exchanged for the finger bowl service and the coffee is placed at the right of the plate. The guest removes the finger bowl with the doily and uses the plate for bonbons. The order of service is the same as for the formal dinner.

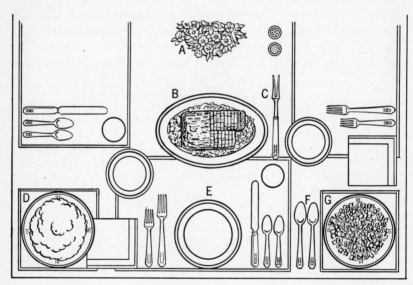

FIG. XVI.—A section of a table set for family service in a residence hall.

 a. decoration
 b. meat
 c. serving fork
 d. potatoes
 e. stack of plates
 f. serving spoons
 g. vegetable

PART V

TEAS AND BUFFET MEALS

TEAS

A table set for a tea depends upon its attractive appointments for its charm. The table covering, the tea service, silver, and serving

Courtesy, General Mills, Inc.

FIG. XVII.—The success of the tea depends largely upon the charm of a well appointed tea table.

dishes should be the best available and the foods colorful, dainty, and interestingly arranged.

Types of Teas. Tea service may be of two types, that used if tea is served in hotels or tea rooms in which the guests are seated at small tables and food is served by a waiter or waitress; that used if tea is served in a home or public building in which a large number of guests pass by a table and serve themselves to food and silver; or it may be a combination of these two in which guests may sit or stand in the serving room and are served by waitresses or friends of the hostess.

Commercial Teas. Tea served in a commercial food unit is similar in service to that of any other type of meal. The guests are seated at tables which have previously been set with linen and silver. A menu card usually containing several tea combinations is presented by the waitress and the order is placed by the guest. A more inclusive list of food may be served for such a tea, as food for only a few guests has to be prepared at one time and there is no problem involved in keeping toasted muffins hot or serving tiny baking powder biscuits as soon as baked. Foods for this type of service are hot breads, including cinnamon rolls, nut rolls, small muffins, biscuits, various types of waffles, plain waffles with sirup or chocolate waffles with ice cream. Toasted breads as raisin, nut, cheese, orange, or date, English muffins, cinnamon toast; marmalades, jellies, jams; assorted sandwiches, small cookies, cakes, ice cream and sundaes, and French pastries. Added to this type of tea menu may be simple salads, usually of fruit, fish, or chicken. Beverages include hot tea with various accompaniments, chocolate, coffee, or iced drinks.

Typical menus from commercial food services follow:

HOTEL FENETTE—AFTERNOON TEA À LA CARTE

Beverages

Java, Ceylon, Green, or Orange Pekoe Tea
Coffee, Cocoa, or Chocolate

Breads

Dry or Buttered Toast   Toasted English Muffins
Tea Biscuits   Brioche
Strawberry or Raspberry Jam
or
Orange Marmalade
or

Sandwiches

Foie Gras   Chicken
Ham or Tongue
Nut-Olive   Lettuce

Desserts

French and Vienna Pastry
Fruit Cake   Assorted Cakes
Vanilla, Strawberry, Chocolate, or Coffee Ice Cream
Tutti Frutti   Meringue Glacé   Parfait
Orange, Raspberry, Pineapple, Lemon Ice
Fruit Lemonade

JAMES-CARLTON—SPECIAL AFTERNOON TEA

Attractive Salad Plate with Finger Sandwiches
Ice Cream   Dainty Cakes   Ice or Orange Punch
Tea with Orange, Lemon, and Ginger or Coffee or Cocoa
Candies   Salted Nuts

THE VOGUE TEA ROOM—AFTERNOON TEA À LA CARTE

Beverages

Tea—Orange Pekoe, English Breakfast, Oolong, Coffee
Chocolate with Whipped Cream

Sandwiches

Honey Pecan   Toasted Cheese
Nut-Mayonnaise   Cinnamon Toast
Pineapple Wheel   Buttered Toast
              Waffles

Salads

Pear with Cheese
Marshmallow Fruit   Stuffed Tomato

Cakes

Chocolate Tea Cakes   Banana Cream Layer

Informal Tea. If tea is to be served to a large number of guests the tea table usually contains a complete service of food, china and silver. In this informal service the guests file around the tea table and help themselves. Tea and coffee may both be served. They are placed on either end of the table and served by friends of the hostess, the guest helping herself to the accompaniments. In warm weather an iced beverage may be served to replace one or both of the hot drinks. The types of food usually served at a large informal tea include:

Beverages:

Hot: Coffee, Russian tea, chocolate, French chocolate, spiced grape juice, spiced cider, or spiced tea.

Iced: Tea, fruit punch (plain or with sherbet).

Courtesy, General Mills, Inc.

FIG. XVIII.—There is infinite variety in the open faced sandwiches that may be prepared for the tea table.

Bread and Miscellaneous:

Sandwiches, open: Assorted fancy shapes spread with desired filling and decorated.

Sandwiches, closed: Assorted breads as nut, orange, banana, date, cheese, or plain with suitable filling. Rolled, ribbon, checkerboard, pinwheel, or two-tone sandwiches.

Miscellaneous: Cheese wafers, cheese straws, or miniature cream puffs filled with cream cheese or chicken salad.

Cakes and Cookies:

Petits Fours, small cup cakes, macaroons, kisses, shortbread, chocolate or date bars, tiny cookies—rolled or dropped.

Ice Creams, Sherbets, or Ices:

Any desired flavor—served in individual cups in which frozen or in sherbet glasses.

Nuts and Candies:

Nuts—salted, toasted, spiced, or crystallized. Preserved ginger, candied orange or grapefruit peel, mints in various pastel colors, and flavors; chocolate mint patties, small hard candies, opera sticks, crystallized mint leaves. Turkish paste in various flavors, colors, and shapes, and stuffed or candied fruits.

Courtesy, Kraft-Phenix Cheese

FIG. XIX.—Dainty Tea Cookies or Sprits, even though characterized by ease of preparation, add to the attractiveness of the tea table.

Miscellaneous Accompaniments:

Cube or loaf sugar—plain or decorated.

Orange—cut into thin slices or sections.

Lemon—cut into fancy shapes, sections or slices—often garnished with whole cloves.

INFORMAL TEA MENUS

(1)

Tiny Doughnuts
Salted Cashews   Assorted Hard Candies
Hot Spiced Cider

(2)

Nut Bread Sandwiches   Spiced Cheese Sandwiches
Dainty Tea Cookies
Mixed Nuts   Peppermint Patties
Tea

(3)

Assorted Sandwiches: Ribbon, Rolled, Banana Bread,
and Ginger-Nut Crescents
Tiny Chocolate Cup Cakes—Fluffy Icing   Ice Cream Wafers
Candied Orange Peel   Salted Pecans
Spiced Tea

(4)

Swedish Tea[1]

Jul Bröd Smörgåsar   Ost-Knäck Brod
(Christmas Bread Sandwiches)   Cheese—Rye Krisp

Assorted Cookies[2]:

Bordstabbel Bakels   Svenska Kringlor
Smorbakelser   Svenska Peppar Nötter
Sandbakelse   Fattigman Bakelser
Sprut Kakor[3]   Svenska Peppar Kakor[3]
Krokoner   Karameller
                           (Peppermint Sugar Candy)
Fyld Dadel
(Dates filled with nuts)
           Kaffe

Formal Tea. The formal type of tea service is similar to the informal except that in the formal service the guests are seated and the food is brought to them by waitresses or assistants to the hostess. For a formal tea at a sorority house, members of the organization

---

[1] This tea menu probably provides a greater variety of cookies than would be necessary for an informal tea.
[2] See index for recipes.
[3] The Sprut Kakor is the same as the recipe given for Butter Tea Cookies and the Peppar Kakors may be made from the Crisp Ginger Cookie recipe.

FIG. XX.—Variety in the cookies served may add interest to the formal tea table.

FIG. XXI.—Simple cheese garnishes raise crackers and jam above the commonplace level and make them worthy of a place at the tea table.

serve their guests. The foods for a formal tea or reception would be of the same type as that for an informal tea except that they are often more elaborate both in the preparation necessary and in the number of foods served.

FORMAL TEA MENUS

(1)

Bread Sticks   Two-Tone Sandwiches
Little Cream Puffs   Cream Cheese Filling
Green Gage Plum Ice
Trubičky[1] (Bohemian Pastry)   Scotch Short Bread[2]
Peanut Crescents   Cocoanut Cookies
Candied Orange Peel   Spiced Almonds
Tea

(2)

Reception
Cucumber Sandwiches   Orange Bread Sandwiches
Rolled Cracked Wheat Sandwiches
Chicken Salad in Cream Puff Shells   Carrot and Celery Curls
Rose Tea Cakes   Assorted Nuts and Mints
Fruit Punch

(3)

German Christmas Tea[3]
Klaben Brot   Pumpernickel Cheese Sandwich
Frozen Fruit
Blitzkuchen   Pfeffernuesse
Lebkuchen   Sternlein
Springerle   Macaroons
Chocolade mit Schlog Sahne
(Chocolate with whipped cream)
Marzipan

BUFFET SERVICE

Use. Buffet suppers and luncheons are increasing in popularity as a means of serving relatively large groups of people. They are characterized by an atmosphere of informality and friendliness, which extends their appeal to people in every age and occupation

---

[1] See index for recipe.
[2] Use Swedish recipe for Smörbakelser to make Scotch Short Bread.
[3] See index for recipes.

group. Some commercial food directors regard buffet service as ideal for the food service to which the family may bring the children. Others stress its suitability for festive occasions in residence halls and clubs, and still others find it advantageous for hospitality tendered groups including strangers who find a pleasant sense of inclusion attendant upon this type of service. The menu may be simple or elaborate. In general the buffet meal is limited to two courses, but a tomato juice cocktail or fruit drink may be served the guests before they are brought to the buffet.

Requisites. A large part of the success of the buffet service depends upon the attractiveness of the buffet table. It is not easy to arrange the variety and diversity of foods sometimes included in a buffet menu together with the necessary china and silver on the table in such a manner as to convey a sense of order that will heighten the interest in the food. The cloth for the buffet service may be either damask or lace. Gay colors may be introduced in the cloth, the serving dishes, the food, or the decorations. Not infrequently a bowl of fruit, gourds, and nuts replaces the more usual floral decorations in the buffet service.

If the general effect is to be good, consideration must be given contrasts in colors, shapes, and sizes in the food and agreement between the floral or other decorations and the colors presented in the menu. Another important factor in the satisfaction afforded by the meal is the delicious flavor of the food and the success attained in the menu in the combining of food flavors and the palatability of the food as served. It is much better to limit the kinds of hot foods served to those that can be prepared and served nicely and surely enjoyed rather than risk an over-crowded table and the over-cooked food sometimes resulting from attempting too much.

Arrangement. Food in a buffet service is arranged in the order in which it is usually served: Meat or meats, potatoes, vegetables or salads, and relishes. If more than one kind of cold meat or cheese is included in the menu, a pleasing grouping of the various kinds of food of this type is usually made on one platter.

Service. The type of service depends largely upon the equipment available. If ample table space is provided places may be set with covers, rolls, and water, and provision may be made for the beverage to be served by a waiter. In this case, the guests need only to pass before a buffet table and select the foods desired. Hot foods at the buffet may be served by a hostess, by a waiter or waitress, or the guest may serve himself. When his plate is filled to his liking he takes his place at one of the covers prepared. If table room for all is not available, each guest may be given an individual tray on which to place silver, napkin, water, glass, and the plate containing the

FIG. XXII.—A decorated casserole dish adds to the attractiveness of the buffet table.

assembled food. Hot beverages and rolls are then commonly served by a waitress.

Food for Buffet. In planning a menu for a buffet, certain precautions must be observed:

1. Care must be taken to keep the service as simple as possible, i.e., to avoid foods difficult to serve; or those which are soft or "soupy" on the plate; or extra utensils as bread-and-butter spreader, salad, or cocktail forks.

2. Hot dishes should include only food easily kept hot. Essential equipment for this may be large or individual casseroles, or perhaps shells for deviled fish and similar food.

3. Attractive garnishing is important. The menu should include a few attractively decorated foods, assorted salads, and an assortment of relishes.

4. A larger variety of food should be included than can be offered at table d'hôte meals.

Courtesy, John Morrell and Co.

FIG. XXIII.—Individual salads arranged on a salad platter introduce a pleasing color note to the buffet table.

5. The menu may be planned for men, women, or a mixed group, depending on the group to be served.

6. A salad bowl may be used for interest.

7. Jelly or jam facilitates the introduction of a color note and makes a pleasing accompaniment.

8. Dessert for a buffet service has no limitation except that it fit into the meal as planned.

A FEW SUGGESTIONS FROM WHICH BUFFET MENUS MAY BE BUILT

Main Dishes

Shrimp Creole
Scalloped Chicken
Creamed Ham and Mushrooms
Deviled Crab
Creamed Sweetbreads and Mush-
rooms
Sweetbread Cutlets
Welsh Rarebit—Rice Croquettes
Chicken à la King—Rosettes
Chicken Pie

Baked Ham and Spoon Bread
Scalloped Oysters
Curried Veal—Rice
Veal Birds en Casserole
Ham and Egg Scallop
Chicken Salad
Tomato Stuffed with Crab
Casserole of Corn
Hot Stuffed Eggs
Chicken-Rice-Almond Casserole

Vegetables

Latticed Potatoes
Shoestring Potatoes
Sweet Potato Croquettes
Scalloped Sweet Potatoes and Apples
Scalloped Cucumber and Pimientos
Buttered Peas—Rosettes

Cut Green Beans—Hot Vegetable
Sauce
Baby Limas in Butter
Shredded New Harvard Beets
Shredded Buttered Cabbage
French Fried Onions

Salads

Stuffed Tomato
Frozen Fruit
Spiced Pear and Orange
Orange and Grapefruit Sections
Stuffed Cinnamon Apple

Peach with Cheese
Pineapple—Tomato
Fruit Combinations
Fruit Gelatin
Lettuce Hearts—Roquefort Cheese

Salad Bowls

Julienne Vegetables
Cabbage and Caraway Seed
Watercress or Endive, Tiny Cheese
Balls

Shredded Lettuce or other Greens
Raw Cauliflower and Carrots
Celery Curls and Carrots

Desserts

Orange Cup Cakes
Meringue Shells
Lemon Chiffon Pie—Whipped
Cream
Hot Chocolate Sundae
Raspberry Ice and Ice Cream with
Marshmallow Sauce

Citrus Fruit Salad—Wafers
Date Pudding
Pecan Pie
Brownies
Assorted Cheese and Crackers
Fresh Fruit and Nut Bowl

BUFFET MENUS

(1)

Chicken Pie in Casseroles
Glazed Sweet Potatoes   Buttered Peas—Rosettes
Grapefruit-Orange Salad   Caraway Cole Slaw Salad Bowl
Spiced Peach   Apple Jelly
Cloverleaf Rolls

Steamed Pudding   Hard Sauce
Coffee

(2)

Anchovy Canapés
Steaks with Mushroom Sauce en Casserole
Buttered Cauliflower   Toasted Baked Potatoes
Tomato Stuffed with Avocado   Frozen Fruit Salad
Endive Salad Bowl   French Dressing
Celery Curls, Olives, Green Tomato Relish
Baking Powder Biscuits   Blackberry Jelly

Date Pudding   Whipped Cream
Coffee

(3)

Chicken à la King in Patty Shells
French Fried Potatoes   Julienne Beans in Drawn Butter
Banana Ice   Celery Curls and Carrot Ring Salad Bowl
Twin Half and Half Rolls   Gooseberry Conserve

Citrus Fruit Salad   Cheese Straws
Coffee

(4)

Scalloped Chicken   Buttered Brussel Sprouts
Rice in Broth with Celery, Pimiento and Green Pepper
Grapefruit, Orange and Avocado Salad   Spiced Pear and Cheese Salad
Cranberry Relish   Raw Carrot and Cauliflower Salad Bowl
Poppyseed Rolls   Jelly

Meringue Shells   Ice Cream
Coffee

BUFFET MENUS (*continued*)

(5)

Ham Timbales in Individual Molds   Egg and Parsley Garnish
Béchamel Sauce
French Fried Potatoes   Cauliflower in Cheese Sauce
Frozen Fruit Salad   Julienne Vegetable Salad Bowl
All Bran Twin Rolls   Apple Jelly

Individual Chocolate Chiffon Pies
Coffee

(6)

Creamed Sweetbreads with Whole Buttered Mushrooms
Shoestring Potatoes   Creole Tomato Slices
Pear Salad with Stuffed Prune Garnish   Pineapple Cones
Carrot Strips, Radishes, Olives, and Pickles
Hot Bowknot Rolls   Melba Toast   Cherry Conserve

Fresh Strawberry Tarts
Coffee

(7)

Fried Chicken
Stuffed Tomato Salad   Celery Curls   Olives
Hot Cinnamon Twists

Peppermint Ice Cream   Hot Chocolate Sauce
Iced Tea

FOREIGN BUFFETS

The increased interest shown by the average American in foreign foods is indicated by recent books dealing with food habits and choice recipes of various countries, by frequent magazine articles treating various aspects of the subject, and also by the inclusion, in the bill of fare, of foreign dishes as staple offerings, in many American food services. One has only to observe the frequent appearance of chow mein and hot tamale pie or chile con carne on lunch room menu cards to realize that the American taste is becoming cosmopolitan. This interest may be effectively capitalized by the presentation of the delectable dishes of a given foreign land at a buffet luncheon or supper, with due consideration concerning suitable table appointments, table setting, and costumes of the waiters or waitresses serving. Plans for foreign buffets for such countries as Germany, Sweden, and Hungary lead to the recognition that many foods are typical of more than one country. For example, spritz, a delicious cookie, is claimed by both German and Swedish people and a recipe almost identical with that given for spritz by chefs of these nations is a favorite among the Danes. A herring salad, likewise claimed by the Germans as a national dish, is found to be truly international in its interest and history. The maker or adapter of foreign menus need not be disturbed if a dish sponsored by a Russian or Hungarian friend proves also to be a popular and historic dish in Scandinavian countries, or if the reverse be true. The possible point to be made from such an instance is the wide appeal the dish has made to varied appetites. The foreign buffet affords a ready means of introducing variety and interest into meals that might tend to become routine. In general, plans for the use of foreign recipes are such that they need not be translated into formulae for quantity food preparation. Usually, even though many people are served, there is such a wide variety of food presented that each recipe need be prepared only in the small quantity characteristic of home preparation.

In the following pages there are given some discussions of the food habits of the country and buffet menus typical of certain countries, together with the recipes necessary for the successful preparation of the meal. Recipes are not given for foods often used on American menus, as cream puffs, or for foods ordinarily purchased ready to serve.

Chinese Buffet Suppers

Americans find Chinese dishes enjoyable and unlike those of any other nation except possibly Japan. Some of their dishes are difficult to adapt to American taste, because of the fact that the food items necessary in their preparation are unusual; others are difficult to secure and are expensive. Food items desired by a Chinese cook might include: Litchi nuts, mushrooms, dry lotus seeds, bamboo shoots, lotus roots, bean sprouts, shark fins, very fine noodles, rice, millet, rice flour, ginger root, bean meal, shell fish and other fish, chicken, pork, chestnuts, almonds, and walnuts. Preserved eggs, condiments and preserved fruits and ginger are frequently used. Chinese sauce or soyu sometimes takes the place of salt in Chinese cookery. Peanut oil is used for frying.

Tea is the popular beverage and is served without cream or sugar in small covered cups without handles. A party menu usually contains several meat dishes—including chicken, fish, goose, pork, lobster, crab, or shrimp. Each dish is said to be one course. Tea may be served with each course. Almond meal cookies and fruits are common desserts.

The following menu is suggested for

CHINESE CHOW

Boo Loo Gai (Pineapple Chicken)	Celery Hearts
Hop Too Guy Ding (Almond Chicken)	Kumquat and Ginger Preserves
Egg Foo Yung (Omelet)	Plain Boiled Rice
Chow Lon Fon (Fried Rice)	Soyu Sauce
Fried Shrimp	Litchi Nuts

Almond Cakes (Gum Loo)
Fruit: Fresh and Candied
Jasmine Tea

Recipes for the dishes included follow:

PINEAPPLE CHICKEN (Boo Loo Gai)

Cut a young chicken as for fried chicken, season with Soyu Sauce, salt and sugar and let stand one hour. Drain, dredge with flour and brown in hot fat. Add a little hot water and simmer until tender. Add 1 small can of diced pineapple and 1 t. Soyu Sauce. Thicken liquid with flour and serve as soon as flour is cooked. Garnish with parsley.

ALMOND CHICKEN (Hop Too Guy Ding)

Fry 2 c. shredded onions, 2 c. shredded water chestnuts and 2 c. shredded celery until slightly browned, then add chicken broth or white stock to cover, and cook until vegetables are tender. Add one young chicken that has been cut into cubes and cooked in peanut oil (or vegetable oil). Thicken liquid with a little cornstarch and water mixed. Add 1 T. Soyu Sauce and place in a hot casserole. Add 1 c. toasted almonds just before serving.

OMELET (Foo Yung)

Beat 12 eggs and add 1 c. bamboo shoots, ½ c. shredded water chestnuts, 2 T. chopped green onions, 1 c. cooked pork or chicken cut into fine strips, and 1 T. Soyu Sauce. Mix all together lightly and fry as an omelet in hot peanut oil or ham fat. When omelets are cooked pour off fat. Add ½ c. broth, 1 T. cornstarch, and 1 T. Soyu Sauce mixed and cooked 2 minutes. Serve as soon as the omelets have absorbed a little of the gravy.

CHOW LON FON (Fried Rice)

2 c. cooked rice
12 oz. ham, finely cubed
3 eggs
½ green pepper, shredded

1 onion, shredded
½ c. cooked mushrooms
1 c. chicken stock

Fry the rice in peanut oil until it is evenly browned. Fry the ham, onion, mushrooms, and green pepper for a few minutes. Add a little cold water and cook slowly 15 minutes. Season with salt and Soyu Sauce. Add rice which has been mixed with beaten eggs. Add hot chicken stock and cook a few minutes. Garnish with chopped parsley.

FRIED SHRIMP

Fry shrimp in hot peanut oil until brown. Place shrimp and shredded green pepper in a flat pan; add hot chicken broth and cook a few minutes. Season with Soyu Sauce and serve.

ALMOND CAKES (Gum Loo)

1 c. flour
¾ c. powdered sugar
¼ c. almonds, chopped

1 egg, beaten
3 T. vegetable oil

Mix dry ingredients. Add oil and then the beaten egg. Mold into small balls, brush with egg, garnish with a whole almond, and bake in a moderate oven.

LITCHI NUTS have a characteristic flavor and may be purchased dried or canned.

Hungarian Buffet Suppers

Knowledge of Hungarian cookery is for many people restricted to the more or less enthusiastic acceptance of Hungarian goulash, a dish said to be "the savory ancestor of all stews." Historically goulash has an honorable record in that for more than 1000 years it has brought gastronomic delight to the peoples now called Hungarian. It exemplifies a common practice in Hungarian cookery, that of cooking meats such as pork and beef with vegetables.

The vegetables in common use are similar to those in the American dietary and include beets, red and white cabbage, sauerkraut, carrots, cauliflower, kale, kohlrabi, peppers, and lettuce. The popular fruits include apples, apricots, cherries, melons, peaches, pears, and bananas. The large rôle of cereals in the diet is shown by the appearance of noodles and bread dumplings in many menus along with rye breads and fancy rolls.

Cheese is used freely in cooked dishes and in its natural state, and on the other hand butter is used sparingly and then unsalted. Sour cream is widely used both as a garnish and as an ingredient in cooking. Its use with paprika is regarded by many as the characterizing feature of a Hungarian dish, so popular are both with these people. Paprika, although popular, is only one of the numerous condiments used, as the Hungarians are fond of spicy foods.

HUNGARIAN BUFFET

Paprika Chicken

Stuffed Hubbard Squash   Asparagus in Sour Cream

Poppyseed Horseshoes   Sweet Butter

Cheese Cake   Fresh Fruit

Tea with Lemon

Recipes for the dishes included follow:

PAPRIKA CHICKEN

Cut chicken as for frying, salt, and let stand 2 hours. Slice 2 large onions and fry in hot fat until light brown. Dredge each piece of chicken in flour and brown in the fat. When brown add the yolks of 2 eggs mixed with 1 c. of sour cream, sprinkle with 1 T. of paprika, a little salt and pepper, and let simmer until the chicken is tender.

STUFFED SQUASH

Select 12 uniform acorn squashes and cut each into halves and remove seeds. Steam until almost tender, then place in a flat pan. Place a No. 12 dipper of the following mixture in each half: 2½ qt. steamed rice, 2 lb. chopped cooked veal, 1 small onion minced and fried in ¼ c. of butter. Pour around the squash the following liquid: 1½ qt. stock, 2 oz. of flour and 4 oz. butter made into a sauce. Sprinkle with chopped parsley. Baste and bake for half an hour. Add sour cream before serving if desired.

BAKED ASPARAGUS

Partially cook asparagus tips and pour over them a sauce made of butter, water, flour, and salt in the same proportions as White Sauce No. 1. Add thick sour cream and sprinkle with bread crumbs. Bake approximately 25 minutes in a moderate oven.

FILLED POPPYSEED ROLLS

Use the recipe for Kolaches and follow the general directions for making crescents. Spread dough with the following mixture before rolling: 2 c. water and 2 c. of sugar cooked to a thick sirup and 1 c. of finely ground poppyseed and 1 grated lemon rind added. Brush the horseshoes with beaten egg yolks.

Swedish Buffet Suppers

Sweden is famous for its Smörgåsbord, or hors d'oeuvres, which is an ancient tradition and an important accompaniment to all Swedish dinners. The hors d'oeuvres for a family of moderate means are grouped in the center of a long table laid with a spotless white linen

Courtesy, General Mills, Inc.

FIG. XXIV.—Swedish Smörgåsbord. The buffet table may have added interest because it presents interesting dishes and table arrangements characteristic of other lands.

table cloth, plates, and silver. The guests are seated at the table and the hors d'oeuvres are passed and eaten just before a regular meal of two or more courses is served. A maid removes the dishes from the first course. Typical food for the family hors d'oeuvres might include: Meats—cold spiced tongue, smoked venison, smoked salmon (sliced), fish in aspic jelly, anchovies, herring served in 2 ways, large shrimps with Thousand Island dressing, parsley, and dried beef. Vegetables—radishes, sliced tomatoes, salads (2 or more kinds), and a scalloped dish. Bread—rye bread, white bread baked in ornamental shapes. Cheese—served in a big piece on a cheese plate with a cheese knife.

Hors d'oeuvres for a family of more wealth, or for a hotel, would be arranged on a separate table as for a buffet supper. Each guest would help himself and then take his place at the dining table. The service by waitresses or waiters would be much the same as for the less elaborate meal described above. The food would be of greater variety, including 20 to 125 articles—rye krisp, butter curls, 6 to 7 kinds of cheese, very small Swedish meat balls fried in deep fat, a hot scalloped dish of fish or vegetable, pickled onions, pickled beets or cucumbers; vegetable salads—similar to our own, a bowl of mayonnaise; jellies and marmalades. A regular 3- or 4-course dinner is served after the hors d'oeuvres are eaten.

The use of colorful foods or decorations is an outstanding feature of the Swedish table. Candles are not used for decorations except for banquets. Flowers are always used and often two or more bouquets are placed on the table, if long.

A Swedish buffet supper suitable for service in this country is planned to include only the Smörgåsbord and the dessert, omitting what the Swedish diner would regard as the main part of the meal. A typical menu for such a buffet supper follows:

SMÖRGÅSBORD

Köttbullar
(Meat Balls)

Skalaperad Potatis	Gröna Bönor Mäd Champinjoner	
(Scalloped Potatoes)	(Green Beans and Mushrooms)	
Sil Salat	Canapés	Svenska Salat
(Herring Salad)	(Canapés)	(Swedish Salad)
Sur Ost		Ost
(Cottage Cheese)		(Assorted Cheese)
Fyldaägg Mäd Pärsilja		Inlagd Sill
(Stuffed Egg—Parsley Garnish)		(Pickled Herring)

Skuren Kall Tyngs
(Sliced Cold Spiced Tongue)

Rödbettor	Sliced Tomatoes	Rättikor
(Pickled Beets)		(Radishes)

Knäcke Bröd
(Rye Krisp)
Ost Kaka Mäd Vin Saft Sås
(Cheese Pudding with Thickened Grape Juice)

Karameller	Kaffee
(Sugar Candy)	(Coffee)

BORDSTABBEL BAKELS (Lumberpile Cookies)

½ c. butter	1¼ c. flour
1 c. light brown sugar	½ t. soda
1 egg	¼ t. salt
½ t. vanilla	½ c. chopped nutmeats

Cream butter and sugar. Add well beaten egg and vanilla. Add flour sifted with soda and salt, then nutmeats dredged in portion of flour. Mold dough. Let stand in refrigerator over night. Cut into strips, 3 inches by 1 inch. When done cover with White Mountain frosting and sprinkle with chopped almonds, caraway seed, or candies. Pile like lumber on serving plates. Bake in a moderate oven.

SANDBAKELSE (Sand Tarts)

1 lb. butter	1 c. white sugar
pinch of salt	1 T. cream or milk
⅓ t. baking powder	2 eggs
5 c. flour (about)	3 T. almond extract

Cream butter and sugar. Add eggs. Blend well, add extract, then flour. Press into small "picture" tins or put through cooky press. Chopped almonds may be added to dough if "picture" tins are used. Turn out of tins at once after baking or they will stick.

JUL-BRÖD (Yule Bread)

1 qt. milk	1 t. salt
2 T. flour	1 c. sugar
1 cake of yeast	2 T. butter

Add flour to make a soft dough.
Roll out round and add filling:

8 bitter almonds	1 c. raisins
15 cardamon seeds (ground)	½ c. citron (fine)
2 T. butter	¼ c. orange peel
½ c. sugar	

Mix and add to dough. Fold, let rise, and bake.

SMÖRBAKELSER (Butter Cookies)

1 c. butter (sweet)
1 c. powdered sugar
2 c. flour

Mix and pat out in 2 10-inch baking tins. Bake in a moderate oven approximately 20 to 30 min. Cut as soon as removed from oven.

SVENSKA KRINGLOR (Swedish Kringle)

1 c. butter   3½ c. flour or enough to make soft
                                   dough
1¼ c. brown sugar   2 T. baking powder
½ c. milk   1 T. cinnamon
2 eggs

Sift dry ingredients. Cream butter and sugar. Add egg yolks and flour and milk alternately. Fold in beaten whites. Bake as drop cookies.

SVENSKA PEPPAR NÖTTER (Swedish Peppernuts)

The oldest of all the cakes we know today are the peppernuts. They were in popular use long before the 11th century.

4 eggs   1 t. cardamon (ground)
2 c. sugar   ½ c. nuts
1 c. butter   ½ c. raisins
1 t. cinnamon   4 c. flour (bread)
1 t. cloves   1 t. soda
1 t. pepper   2 T. hot water

Drop on cookie sheet and bake in a hot oven.

FATTIGMAN BAKELS (Poorman's Crullers)

2 eggs   f.g. cardamon
2 T. sugar   3 T. heavy sweet cream
⅛ t. salt   1¾ c. flour (or less)

Beat eggs until light, add sugar, salt, spice, and continue beating. Add cream and enough flour to make a soft dough. Turn out on floured board, roll very thin. Cut into diamond shapes. Slash opposite ends. Pull end through slit, or cut in star shapes. Fry in deep fat. Drain on heavy paper. Dust with sugar.

CANAPÉS

Place lettuce cups filled with salad on thin slices of bread spread with butter. Salad: 1 diced boiled potato, 2 diced apples, ½ c. green peas, 1 stalk celery, diced, 1 T. chopped pickle, ½ c. each of cucumber and chicken, cut into strips, and mixed carefully with mayonnaise. Garnish with a small tomato section.

SWEDISH SALAD BOWL

1 can of pineapple (size 2½)	1 stalk celery
1 tart apple	5 tomatoes
lettuce	½ cucumber

Cut the pineapple and tomato into wedges, dice the apple and celery, cut the cucumber en julienne. Mix with pineapple dressing just before serving and add shredded lettuce leaves.

Pineapple Dressing:

Mix 2 raw egg yolks with the juice drained from the can of pineapple, stir constantly, and cook over a low heat until thick. Cool, then add 1 mashed cold hard-cooked egg yolk that has been mixed with ¼ t. mustard and 3 T. of vinegar. Fold in 2 c. whipped cream.

Serve salad in a salad bowl. Yield approx. 10 servings.

OST KAKA (Cheese Pudding)

2 gal. milk	6 eggs
2 c. flour	1½ qt. cream, coffee
½ cake of cheese rennet	½ c. sugar
(purchased from drug store)	

Heat the milk until lukewarm and stir into it the flour that has been smoothed to a paste. Add the cheese rennet that has been dissolved in 2 T. of water. Stir well and let stand. As soon as the milk has set, stir gently to separate the curds and whey. Let stand a few minutes then pour off whey or use a strainer to remove curds. (The curds should be quite moist.) Place curds in two medium-sized casseroles and pour over them a custard mixture made from the eggs, cream, and sugar. Sprinkle nutmeg over the top. Bake and test as a plain custard. Serve warm with strawberry jam or grape juice thickened to the consistency of thick cream.

KÖTTBULLAR (Meat Balls)

1 lb. beef loin	3-4 egg yolks
8 oz. veal	3 T. onion chopped
8 oz. pork	2 T. salt
½ c. bread crumbs, dry, ground	½ t. pepper
1 c. cream	⅛ t. allspice
½ c. soda water, dilute	1 c. butter

Pass the meat through a meat grinder 3 times or more if a coarse grinder is used. Add the bread crumbs, which have been soaked in the cream. Add soda water and egg yolks, mix well, and shape into small balls. Fry the onion in butter but do not brown; add the meat balls and fry using a low heat. Fry in deep fat. Shake the pan occasionally to keep the balls in shape. Place balls in casserole and pour over them the fat in which they were cooked. Garnish with a border of fried onions.

KROKONER

¼ c. sugar	1 egg
1 c. butter	1 c. milk
4 t. baking powder	f.g. salt
flour to make a roll dough	1 t. vanilla (or ½ t. vanilla and ½ t. almond)

Roll dough and cut into strips 5 inches long and 1½ inches wide. Bake over semicircular tins 12 inches long, so that cookies form a semicircle when baked. Ice with orange icing and decorate with tiny colored candies.

German Buffet Supper

German people show a decided preference for heavy food, that is, food containing much fat and starch. They also use many sauces and gravies. Many foods are seasoned with vinegar and often sugar is added. With the exception of some typical dishes, German food is very similar to our own. Many kinds of sausages, sauerkraut with dumplings and spareribs, beef with sour sauce, noodles, and rye bread with caraway seed are typical German foods. The following menu is characteristic of the "feast food" popular with the German people for New Year's parties and similar festive occasions.

NEUJAHRS ABEND SCHENKTISCH

or

(A German New Year's Eve Buffet)

Hasenpfeffer mit Spaetzle
(Sour Rabbit with Noodles)

Kartoffel Puffe   Linsens
(Potato Pancakes)   (Lentils)

Sauerkraut mit Apfeln
(Sauerkraut with Apples)

Häring Salat   Green Bean and Onion Salad Bowl
(Herring Salad)

Cucumber and Peach Pickles

Platter: Pickled Herring, Cold Tongue,
Ham, Goose Liver, Smoked Salmon
and Cervelat (Sausage)

Caraway Rye Bread   Vienna Rolls   Milchbrötchen
(Milk rolls with
caraway seeds)

Crullers   Zwieback Kaese Kuchen
(Cheese Cake)

farina, spaghetti and macaroni in long slithery coils, dry-beans, peas
and lentils are more widely used than in the cookery of many other
lands. White bread, hard and crusty, is well liked. Meat is used
sparingly. Its chief purpose, it seems, is to enhance the flavor and
give character to a dish rather than to be the main ingredient. Fish
and the cheeses characteristic of the land, Parmesan, Gorgonzola, and
Bel Paese, play a major part in supplying the protein necessary for
adequate nutrition. Both the menus and the cookery processes employed in Italy are more simple than those in France. Fruit, or cheese,
appears as the dessert more frequently than does any made dessert
or pastry. There seems little interest in dishes that present a wide
variety of diversified ingredients, or in the embellishment of dishes
with elaborate sauces or whipped creams. Seasonings finding almost
daily use in Italian food preparation include mushrooms, tomato
sauce, garlic, onions, peppers, olive oil, used for deep fat frying, and
nuts, especially chestnuts, hazel nuts, pistachio nuts, and walnuts.

The term "buffé" in Italy is used only for cold foods. A service
not unlike the buffet of other lands is called Pranzo-Italiano, hence
this term is used to designate the Italian meal which follows.

PRANZO-ITALIANO
Antipasto

Ravioli   Gnocchi

Pomodori con Rimpieno   Zucchini Imburrati
(Stuffed Baked Tomato)   (Buttered Squash)

Insalatiera di Cicorea
(Chicory Salad Bowl)

Condimento di olio con aglio e menta
(Oil Dressing with Garlic and Mint Sprigs)

Insalata di Cavolfiore
(Cauliflower Salad)

Gressini
(Bread Sticks)

Formaggio Permigiano e Gorgonzola
(Parmesan and Gorgonzola Cheese)

Uve e Banano
(Grapes and Bananas)

Caffè   Chianti

RAVIOLI

Dough:

4 c. flour	2 T. oil
2 whole eggs	Salt
1 egg yolk	Water to make a stiff dough

Roll out ½ of dough thin, as for noodles. Brush over with beaten egg. Place portions of meat filling on the dough 1½ inches apart. Cover with the remaining portion of the dough that has been rolled thin. Cut dough into squares with meat in the middle of each square; press down the dough at the edges with a fork. Drop into hot stock or salted water and cook approximately 20 minutes, or until dough becomes transparent. Remove to hot casserole, add sauce, and sprinkle with grated Parmesan cheese. Place in oven a few minutes.

Filling:

3 c. veal, cooked, ground	¾ c. cheese
1 c. chicken or pork, cooked and ground	2 eggs
½ c. spinach, cooked, drained	Salt, pepper
Mix well.	

Sauce: Stock is thickened to use for sauce or tomato sauce may be used.

GNOCCHI

1 qt. milk	2 eggs
1 c. farina	1 t. salt
	2 T. butter

Cook in double boiler, as farina for cereal, until well cooked and thick. Remove from stove and add well-beaten eggs. Pour into a flat pan to a depth of ½ inch. When cold cut into small squares and place in an oiled baking dish. Cover tops of squares with cream and sprinkle with Gruyère cheese. Place another layer on top and repeat until the dish is full. Place in oven until thoroughly heated and browned.

STUFFED BAKED TOMATOES

Remove the centers from 12 large tomatoes. Mince 4 chicken livers, ¾ c. mushrooms, and 1 onion and fry in ¼ c. butter. Add 4 egg yolks and 2 c. of bread crumbs, mixed, and use to stuff the tomatoes. Bake about 30 min. in a moderate oven.

ANTIPASTO

Arrange in the center of a large tray tiny anchovy canapés, garnished with green pepper. In a circle around the canapés arrange overlapping thin slices of salami. Arrange stuffed eggs around the salami, and stuffed olives around the eggs. Garnish with tiny celery hearts.

INSALATA DI CAVOLFIORE (Cauliflower Salad)

Cook the cauliflower and separate into flowerets. Marinate and arrange on a salad platter garnished with endive. Place a green pepper ring over each floweret and ripe olives between each floweret.

A Suggested Menu for a Feast of the Nations Buffet

Caviar Canapés (Norwegian)
Singapore Curry (Malayan)
Rusks (Danish) Kolaches (Bohemian)
Spiced Peaches and Watermelon Pickle (German)
Tomato Preserves (Spanish) Orange Marmalade (English)
Edam Cheese (Dutch)
Assorted Fresh Fruit (Italian)
Petite Choux à la Crême[1] (French)
Coffee (Swedish)
Russian Tea[1]
Punch aux Fruits (West Indies)

SINGAPORE CURRY (Malayan)

Wash and cook rice. When tender wash with hot water, add a little cocoanut, and place in a casserole. Prepare French fried onions and highly curried veal. Slice tomatoes. Cut bananas and sliced pineapple into wedges. Serve the rice in the center of each plate, curried veal on top of the rice, French fried onions on top of veal, and continue the mound, adding in turn the tomatoes, bananas, pineapple, shredded cocoanut, roasted peanuts and pepper relish. A well-served plate will be nicely rounded and self-garnished.

A fruit cup or a piece of melon is suitable to serve as a dessert with Singapore Curry.

[1] See index for recipe.

KOLACHES (Kolace-Bohemian)

Scald one pint of milk, let cool until lukewarm. Dissolve 1½ cakes compressed yeast in ¼ c. lukewarm water to which has been added 1 t. sugar. Let stand while the milk cools. Add dissolved yeast to the cooled milk and make a sponge. Let rise until light.

Cream together 1 c. sugar and 1 c. butter. Add 3 egg yolks and 2 whole eggs, well beaten, 2 t. salt. Put in the sponge and mix well. Add flour enough to handle well. Let dough rise until light and roll out to ½-inch thickness. Cut with biscuit cutter. Make a depression in the center and fill. Let rise and bake in a quick oven. Yield about 4 dozen.

Fillings: (1) Stewed prunes mixed with sugar and cinnamon and sprinkled with cocoanut or chopped nuts.

(2) ½ stewed apricot with sugar and nutmeg for each roll.

(3) Poppyseed mixed with sugar and milk.

Variations

Poppyseed Doughnuts: Roll dough, cut with a doughnut cutter, and place two together with Kolach filling. Fry in deep fat and roll in powdered sugar.

Crescent Rolls: Roll dough and cut with a crescent cutter, brush with beaten egg, and sprinkle with poppyseed.

INDEX